Truth and Compassion

Essays on Judaism and Religion in Memory of Rabbi Dr. Solomon Frank

edited by Howard Joseph, Jack N. Lightstone, and Michael D. Oppenheim

Published for the Canadian Corporation for Studies in Religion / Corporation Canadienne des Sciences Religieuses by Wilfrid Laurier University Press

The publication of this book was supported by a grant from the Spanish and Portuguese Synagogue of Montreal.

BM
42
,T78
1983

Canadian Cataloguing in Publication Data

Main entry under title:
Truth and compassion : essays on Judaism and religion
in memory of Rabbi Dr. Solomon Frank

(SR supplements ; 12)
ISBN 0-88920-143-9

1. Judaism – Addresses, essays, lectures.   2. Religion –
Addresses, essays, lectures.   3. Frank, Solomon.
I. Frank, Solomon.   II. Joseph, Howard, 1940-
III. Lightstone, Jack N.   IV. Oppenheim, Michael D.,
1946-   V. Series.

BM42.T7   296   C83-098424-0

Cover design by Michael Baldwin, MSIAD

Order from:
Wilfrid Laurier University Press
Wilfrid Laurier University
Waterloo, Ontario, Canada   N2L 3C5

Contents

Dedicatory Preface

The editors had intended to present this volume of essays to Rabbi Solomon Frank upon the occasion of his reaching his eightieth birthday. For many of us Rabbi Frank exemplified the highest virtues of our faith. He combined "Hesed and Emet," compassion and concern for his fellow human beings as well as the search for knowledge and truth. In each he excelled. His celebrated pastoral care for the ill, bereaved, imprisoned, and distressed made even the mention of his name a source of comfort to others. Equally striking was his continuous study of the complexity of human affairs from the diverse perspectives of philosophy, history, and psychology. He integrated them into a modern appreciation of the life of faith and tradition.

On behalf of the clergy, officers, and trustees, and members of the Spanish and Portuguese Synagogue of Montreal, as well as many others from numerous walks of life, we dedicate this volume as a sign of love and respect to Rabbi Solomon Frank. We hope that all those who will read it will be inspired by the outstanding characteristics of Rabbi Frank's life and career of service.

THE EDITORS

Introduction

The essays included in this volume focus on a number of diverse topics in the areas of the history of Judaism, religion, and the philosophy of religion. They deepen our knowledge of these areas by presenting novel methodological insights into the material or by beginning to treat seriously data hitherto ignored. If there is any advantage accruing to the wide diversity of this collection it is to show the benefit of a multi-disciplinary approach to the study of religion in general and to the analysis of Judaism in particular. The concerns and methods of each discipline shed a distinctive light upon religious phenomena, the one elucidating the results of the other.

In his comparative study of charity in Judaism and Christianity, Frederick Bird aims to lay bare the principal structures of the charity-ethic in these two religious traditions. That is to say, his concern is less the specific prescriptions for giving to others or the analysis of the complex of such rules in various Christian and Judaic documents than the overall patterns of social organization and institutions which directly pertain to the disposition of gifts. Bird finds the ethic of gifts in Ancient Israel to be embodied in a number of norms addressed not to the ruler, as in other Ancient Near Eastern societies, but to heads of households. No explicit measures for public enforcement seem apparent. With post-exilic religion and early Rabbinism these norms, preserved in codes, with other injunctions, become elements of a distinctively religious ethos in which ritual observances and moral practices were not distinguished. Ethical principles did not generate these norms (either in the historical or phenomenological sense); rather, such principles, in so far as they were articulated at all, seem induced from the ritual observances themselves.

Early Christianity, by contrast, propounded principles of a charitable ethic from which specific norms only later emerge. Primitive Christians advocated a communal ethic of mutual assistance governed by the commandment to love the brethren. In addition, there developed an ideal of the self-sacrificing dispossession of worldly riches. The latter focusses not on the needs of one's neighbour but upon the positive effect upon the giver. Here Bird finds one of the origins of the monastic movement in the Church.

Jack Lighstone's essay on second-temple Judaism calls for a radical revision of accepted portrayals of the period. Much of what is said about second-commonwealth, Judaic culture, claims Lightstone, stands upon a precarious inverted pyramid of "evidence" and on overly deductive speculation. By way of example, the essay reviews the generally accepted views regarding the Scribes and Hasidim in light of the state of the data. Historical claims about these groups either appear to rest upon relatively late (and tendentious) sources taken at face value, or fall prey to the "fallacy of misplaced concreteness." In short, not all references to "the pious" (hasidim) count as evidence for a group of "Pietists." Assuming the propriety of Lightstone's critique, the history of second-temple Judaism merits considerable rethinking.

Ira Robinson, in his account of a tenth-century Karaite's treatment of magic and miracle, sheds light upon the recurring issue of various religious cultures in close contact. Put succinctly, we enter the realm of "What my Holy Man does is miracle, what yours does is magic (or mere illusion)." This classical problem of intergroup polemicizing becomes more complex when all religious groups fall prey to the objections of the rationalist's critique that neither magic nor miracle exists as such. In Kirkisani, as Robinson shows, we find a typical attempt of the medieval philosopher-religionist to meet both his parochial and rationalist interests. Kirkisani must, on the one hand, differentiate magic and miracle (or prophecy), while, on the other, demonstrate the rationality of belief in miracles. Robinson sets before the reader Kirkisani's tactics and locates his thought within the context of antecedent and contemporary treatments of the same problem among Rabbinic and Muslim sages.

Shimon Levy's analysis of Numbers 11 stands within the recent application of the "synchronic" and "structura" agenda to biblical exegesis. Here Levy leaves behind the concerns of classical biblical criticism for sources, on the one hand, and the interests of the *Wissenschaft des Judenthums* in the history of interpretation, on the other. Accepting the text as a unity (at least at some literary level), Levy attempts to make sense of its apparent (and undoubtedly real) diversity. His point is that the diverse elements brought together by the redactor have been forged into a unitary piece with an idiomatic conception transcending the content of the constituent elements.

In "A Key to Nineteenth-Century Critical Attitudes Toward Religion?" Michel Despland argues that the major themes in the writings of

Jean Jacques Rousseau, the themes of culture and imagination, present the foundation for the new understandings of man and society that arose in the nineteenth century. While historians of modern Judaism have acknowledged the great impact of the philosophers Kant and Hegel both on Jewish thought and on the general intellectual climate of modern times, the influence of Rousseau has been largely overlooked. Yet, as Despland indicates, Rousseau's views about the nature of man, the history of culture, and the nature of true religion were the indispensable inheritance of later critical theories about society and religion. Rousseau's great contribution was to treat society and religion as products of man's history and thus to clear the way for man-made changes in social and religious life.

Charles Davis seeks to unravel Walter Benjamin's highly complex and original philosophy of history in his essay, "Walter Benjamin, The Mystical Materialist." Benjamin was a German-Jewish literary critic and philosopher whose death in 1940 at the age of forty-eight is part of the tremendous tragedy of the Nazi horror. In examining Benjamin's enigmatic understanding of history, Davis focusses on the *Theses on the Philosophy of History*, written in 1940, and on Benjamin's earlier reflections on this topic. The *Theses*, short aphoristic statements that total only a few pages, reveal Benjamin's attempt to achieve a secular redemption of man's history by combining elements that he gathered from Kabbalistic thought and from Marxism. While Benjamin refused to step beyond the secular world, he believed that theological language was necessary in order to speak of the meaning of history. Davis calls this Benjamin's "mystical materialism."

In "Some Underlying Issues of Modern Jewish Philosophy," Michael Oppenheim argues that the common core of questions that modern Jewish philosophers address provides the thread that binds together the diverse thinkers included in this area. Oppenheim believes that the particular issues that reappear in the works of modern Jewish philosophy arise out of the philosophers' struggle with modernity, their identification with Jewish ideas, values, and ways of life of the past, and their deep commitment to the Jewish community of their own day. Although the field of modern Jewish philosophy is often ignored by scholars of modern Judaism and of modern philosophy, modern Jewish philosophers have addressed questions and offered solutions of importance for all who are interested in the confrontation between modernity and religious tradition.

Gershon Hundert's insights into some features of contemporary Jewish historiography are presented in "Reflections on the 'Whig' Interpretation of Jewish History." The essay focusses on the Jerusalem school of Zionist historians and their interpretation of past Jewish experience in terms of a particular event in the present, the regaining of sovereignty by the Jewish nation. Hundert argues that the examination of Jewish history with one eye trained on the present distorts and limits our understanding of even those phenomena that are of particular importance for this group of historians. He concludes his reflections by affirming that the responsibility of the national historian to his community can only be fulfilled by repudiating any ideology that stands in the way of the search for truth.

The last decade has witnessed an explosion of Holocaust-related works onto the literary scene. After years of numbed silence, Jews and non-Jews as well have begun to examine this catastrophe from numerous perspectives. Theologians, too, have begun to tackle this subject, continuing the issue of theodicy in modern garb. Will the Holocaust arouse some new insights into this traditionally thorny issue? Will older approaches be reworked? Or must the Holocaust shatter any semblance of traditional faith? Howard Joseph surveys a sampling of the literature indicating the options the thinkers under review see as most worthy of continued focus.

Modern Orthodoxy considers Rabbi Dr. Joseph B. Soloveitchik to be its most outstanding representative. Soloveitchik combines the Talmudic genius of the Lithuanian Yeshiva world as well as a thorough mastery of the Western intellectual tradition. Although Soloveitchik has usually shied away from written publication in favour of the classroom and public lecture format, certain key articles have appeared in recent years. The most widely discussed piece, entitled "The Lonely Man of Faith," appeared in 1965. Jerome Eckstein examines the categories of thought suggested by Soloveitchik, testing their descriptive adequacy. In so doing, Eckstein presents some corrections and his own alternative categories of thought.

B. Barry Levy enters the fray of intra-Orthodox debate with an exhaustive examination of the Artscroll series of translations of biblical literature and commentaries thereon, and now extended to Mishna and other works. The series has been presented with unusual claims of definitiveness and authenticity. Levy examines the major assumptions and methodology of the series as well as the hidden agenda that emerges from a careful survey of the extensive material. He writes with a combination of polemical style and scholarly care that is obviously designed to arouse a response from the authors, a group usually reluctant to enter into dialogue on their views.

A Comparative Study of Charity in Christianity and Judaism

FREDERICK B. BIRD

INTRODUCTION

Over the past three millennia and more, Jewish and Christian charity ethics have assumed a variety of forms. In this essay I will describe and analyze the characteristic approaches to the practice of charity by Jews and Christians during three periods which have been subsequently regarded as normative. I will focus on the charity ethics of Ancient Israel, especially in the pre-exilic period; the charity ethics of early Christianity; and the charity ethics of Early Rabbinic Judaism, noting briefly in the process subsequent developments.

At the outset we must define what we mean by the practice of charity. Too narrow definitions of charity must be avoided. Charitable practices cannot be restricted only to acts of voluntary, unreciprocated generosity. Charity programs often involve involuntary as well as voluntary elements, unreciprocated as well as reciprocal activities, generous as well as begrudging contributions. Charity programs have been undertaken as public welfare policies and as private benevolence; they have involved self-sacrificing altruism as well as quite self-serving philanthropy.[1] For the purpose of this essay I will define charity as a gift and not as an exchange of goods and services given to benefit persons outside one's own family.

---

1 Richard Titmuss, *The Gift Relationship* (London: Allen and Unwin Limited, 1968), 73. An earlier version of this chapter appeared in *The Journal of Religious Ethics* (Spring, 1982).

There are several characteristic features of charity. It is not an exchange like wages, rent, or sales, where goods and services of equivalent economic value are transferred in a single transaction. Recipients are indeed expected to make appropriate responses to the gifts received. Minimally, they are expected to recognize their debt and demonstrate their gratitude by accepting and honouring as given the relationship they have with their donors and by being willing to serve as donors to others. The giving of charity and the response to the gift involve two distinct transactions different in timing, in kind, and in economic value. Considerations about ability to give and about neediness inherently influence charitable transactions. Charity takes place when gifts are given beyond family groupings. The most primitive expressions of charity were gifts to persons who fell outside normal family networks and the mutual assistance expected within such groupings. They were extended to orphans, widows, strangers, and ascetics. In principle charity is voluntary. Potential donors are assumed to be free to give or not give, and to determine the extent of their contributions. In practice, the distinction between voluntary and coerced contributions often becomes blurred as communal groups institute systems of tithing or taxing to support their charitable projects. Charity may assume varied forms as in-kind benefits, money, privileges, licenses, credit, fee waivers, debt cancellations, and case-work services. It may be financed by offerings, tithes, taxes, and/or endowments. Charity ethics refer to the normative standards which identify to whom gifts should be given, what kinds of grants should be made, how contributions should be solicited, for what reasons gifts should be made, what particular rights are enjoyed by recipients, and what kinds of specific responses recipients are expected to make.

As we begin this study of Jewish and Christian charity norms, it is well to recognize that neither religion ever developed an explicit, distinct charity ethic as such. The attitudes and standards relevant to charity have been imbedded within and communicated by a wide range of legends, laws, letters, meditations, philosophies, gospels, and histories which make up the normative scriptures of these religions. I have attempted to focus on the charity ethic of these religions as reflected in their general ethos rather than in particular documents, such as Deuteronomy contrasted to Leviticus.

This paper focusses on norms of charity and not on the much larger question of the relation of charity to norms regarding distributive justice. The paper does observe how concerns about justice, about the fair arrangement of social institutions, influenced attitudes toward charity in both religious traditions. However, I do not analyze in detail specific norms regarding wages, loans, property, power relations, and social reform integral to these religions' theories of justice.

A. CHARITY ETHICS OF ANCIENT ISRAEL

The first thing to be said about the charity ethic of Ancient Israel (1200-300 B.C.E.) is that it comprised a set of moral standards and not a state policy instituted by a patrimonial government. Elsewhere in the ancient world, Greek city states, the Roman Republic, the Egyptian monarchy, and the Persian empire established programs of public philanthropy by which surplus foods were periodically distributed to the poor, especially those conscripted by forced labour, both in order to curry their allegiance and in order to enhance the status of the state and of the ruling families.[2] In contrast, the Israelite charity ethic was embodied in a number of norms addressed not to ruler but to heads of households who were held responsible for their enactment. There were no explicit measures for the public enforcement of these norms. These norms were enunciated, initially at least, by priestly families called Levites, who were themselves in part dependent upon others for their own material well being. The charity ethic called upon the Israelite landowning families to provide hospitality, food, loans, and material goods to other persons within the Israelite community who were landless and, at least in part, economically dependent. Recipients included orphans, widows, Levites, guest-workers, and indentured servants. Equally important to this charity ethic were other norms which called upon the landed households not only to make assistance available to those in need but also to treat fairly and honorably these materially-less-privileged classes. Overall, the Israelite charity ethic comprised a fairly broad spectrum of norms which specified a range of institutionalized practices.

These norms were carried out not in order to gain public renown, or heavenly rewards, or personal merit, but in order to enhance the chances of good harvests, interpreted as God's reward, and to protect the Israelite people as a whole from certain feared disasters, interpreted as the judgment of God, which would cause them to lose their claim to their lands and be annihilated as a people (Deut. 11:18-32; Deut. 30). This charity ethic was commanded by God. Failure to honour God's commands would result in "curse, confusion, and frustration until you are destroyed and perish quickly. . ." (Deut. 28:28).

In the pre-exilic era (before 587 B.C.E.) the Israelite charity ethic incorporated norms with regard to hospitality, public offerings, private assistance, interest-free loans, and fair treatment. In general, Israelites were counselled to "open wide your hand to your brother, to the needy and to the poor, in the land" (Deut. 15:11). They were also

---

2 Max Weber, *Ancient Judaism*, trans. by H. H. Gerth and Don Martindale (New York: The Free Press, 1952), 255-63; A. R. Hands, *Charities and Social Aid in Greece and Rome* (London: Thomas and Hudson, 1968), chaps. 2, 3, 4, 7.

directed, much more specifically, how they ought to respond to the
needy and the poor.

First, they were counselled to be hospitable to guest workers and
Levites (Ex. 22:21, 24; 23:9). Hospitality probably meant providing
temporary shelter and food for transients, sometimes for several days
and even longer for some indentured servants (cf. Judg. 19:8). Frequently this counsel was stated in words to the effect that the Israelite
should be hospitable to strangers since the Israelites had been strangers
in Egypt. The word *gerim* within the Hebrew Bible seems to refer to a
particular class of propertyless people who worked for or served as
tradesmen within the families of particular tribes with whom they had
no kin relations. Hence I have used the word guest workers to refer to
the *gerim*. The Israelites possessed exactly that status in Egypt where
they were treated like a special caste under the protection of the
Pharoah. After the confederation of Israelite tribes was established in
Palestine, the word *gerim* might have been used to refer to Israelites
who had been indentured to or who were conducting trade among
families of a tribe to which they did not belong, or to landless Levite
priests, or to Canaanite families who had allied themselves with the
Israelites but had not yet been fully integrated within the kinship
structures through intermarriage (cf. Gen. 19; 24:16-20), or to all of
these.[3] That the Levites were clearly intended as possible objects of
hospitality is illustrated by the story in Judges 19-21, in which a war
breaks out between the tribe of Benjamin and the other tribes because
of the failure of the former to treat hospitably a particular Levite and
his wife.

Second, the Israelites were instructed by their ancient codes to
make public offerings at annual festivals held at particular sites
(Ex. 23:14-17). Householders were directed to set apart a portion of
their harvests and every third year to make a formal contribution which
would be given over to the Levites at these festival centers in order to
be distributed to them, to widows, orphans, and guest-workers
(Deut. 14:22-28). Offerings were also to be made more often at the
three annual festivals when all the male heads of households were to
gather to celebrate the festivals of unleavened bread, weeks, and
booths (Deut. 16:16-17). Although references were made to economically dependent persons (Deut. 26:12-15), it seems likely that the primary recipients of these offerings of grains and wines and other foods
were the priestly families, who otherwise had no other sources of
sustenance and income (Numbers 18). As with many other peoples,
among the Israelites the religious officials were among the first objects
of public charity programs.

---

3   Weber, *Judaism*, 32-36, 46, 47; Roland deVaux, *Ancient Israel* (New York:
    McGraw-Hill Book Company, 1965), part 1, chap. 2.

Third, the ancient codes directed the Israelite householders to help their needy neighbours through a series of private assistance programs. For example, when harvesting their fields they were counselled to leave the corners of their fields and not to go back to collect grain or fruit which might have been missed during the initial harvesting (Lev. 19:9-10; 24:19-22). Needy, landless neighbours would in theory then be free to gather these foods. In practice, as the story of Ruth suggests, this privilege was extended only at the discretion of the proprietors and probably to particular persons known to them (Ruth 2:7).

Fourth, Israelites were also counselled to help their needy neighbours by providing them with interest-free loans (Deut. 15:7-11; Ex. 22:25-27). These loans probably assumed a number of forms: food was loaned in the lean season before harvest; wool was loaned for clothing; and perhaps even property was loaned until the time when the new tenant could make the borrowed land productive enough to buy it outright. As a form of charity, these loans were not extended without an expectation of return. Creditors were permitted to take some form of pledge from their debtors, as long as the rights and needs of the latter were still protected and the creditors expected an equivalent return in time (Ex. 22:14-15). There seems to have been considerable tension between the idealism of this loan assistance and practical realities. The ideal was permissive: no one was required to extend loans, and many seemed disinclined, particularly because at the end of seven years debtors were released from their debts (Deut. 15:1-6). More seriously, some of those willing to become creditors seemed to have demanded excessive pledges from debtors. Some required that the latter provide their children as indentured servants or slaves (1 Kgs. 4:1-7); others charged interest (Neh. 5:1-7); and others seized the land of those unable to repay their loans (Amos 5:11; 1 Kgs. 21:1-3). In spite of these inevitable difficulties, the free loan system was especially characteristic of Israelite charity. Its aim was to reinforce communal solidarity by aiding those economically marginal through provisions which were reciprocally beneficial.

Fifth, these various programs for extending material assistance were complemented by a series of norms designed to protect the economically needy and dependent neighbours from unfair treatment. These were not norms for charity strictly defined but were inter-related with and influenced by charity practices. These norms identified certain minimal rights which all Israelites, especially the needy, were supposed to enjoy. These rights were guaranteed not by certain governmental action, but unevenly, by social convention. Included were the right to a fair hearing of economic disputes (Ex. 23:1-8), the right to maintain one's claim to property even if indebted (Mic. 5:2-3), the right not to be sold into slavery, and the right of indentured servants to some material provisions at the termination of

their servitude (Gen. 20:25-43; Ex. 21:1-4). Similarly to the provisions
for interest-free loans and private assistance, these norms of fair treatment regulated the relationship between the prosperous households
and those which were economically deprived. These rights were
viewed as means of protecting the needy from extreme poverty just as
were the measures providing for assistance and hospitality. That these
rights were held to be normative is evident from the numerous com-
plaints made by prophets about instances when they were violated
(Isa. 5:8, 11:4; Jer. 5:27; 22:13; Amos 5:12).

Only with caution is it possible to summarize this fairly complex
system of social norms by referring to two typical expressions used to
define charity, namely, *zedakkah* and *hesed*. These terms, which referred to attributes of God as well as to human virtues, meant "righteousness" and "graciousness." God required *zedakkah* of his people,
namely, rightly ordered human relations that did not neglect those
who were disadvantaged. God also commanded *hesed*, graciousness
and loving-kindness, of his people as they extended hospitality and
assistance to their needy neighbours. It would be inaccurate to argue
that the charity ethic of Ancient Israel devolved from these values;
rather, these values expressed characteristic features of a much more
complex system of customary social norms.

In the post-exilic era there were several modifications of the inherited Israelite charity ethic, occasioned largely by historical developments. The Israelites lost their status as an independent nation, and,
while still in large a self-governing ethnically distinct people, they
became vassals of the Babylonian, Persian, Hellenic, and Roman em-
pires. Over the same period and even previously, the Levite priests lost
status as the northern kingdom was conquered and as the cult was
centralized in Jerusalem and the priests associated with the temple
there gained ascendancy.[4] As the Levites became greatly reduced in
numbers (Neh. 7:43; Ezra 2:40), they no longer retained their status as
special objects of charitable assistances (Ezra 7:21-24). The Holiness
Code, for example, calls attention to the plight of the guest workers, old
persons, needy neighbours, and indentured servants but makes no
mention of the Levites (Lev. 19:1-37). Most importantly, the economic
position of the poorer households seemed to deteriorate: the lands of
many families were expropriated probably because of defaulted debts
(Ezra 18:12; Prov. 22:22; Job 22:5-9; 30:14); many families neglected
to bring offerings to the annual festivals (Ezra 16:49); and some creditors openly defied the ancient customs (Psalms 10) by over-charging
the poor (Lev. 25:35-38).

---

4 It is worth noting that in neither Amos, First Isaiah nor Micah are the Levites and
   gerim made the objects of special charity considerations. Deuteronomy gives great
   attention to the problems of the Levites (and *gerim*), no doubt, because with the
   centralization of the cult at Jerusalem the Levites lost status as administrators of
   de-centralized shrines.

There were several responses to these developments. The first and major response was to re-affirm the ancient norms by collecting them in distinct written codes which were to be learned by all male adults. In the process, in a subtle but profound way, these norms changed their social status: rather than being aspects of the customary social policies of various tribal groupings, they became elements within a distinctly religious ethic in which ritual observances and moral practices were not distinguished. This religious ethic was addressed to all individuals and not just to the heads of households and family groupings. It was a system of ideals and obligations which were to be frequently called to mind, studied, and revered. Within this ethic charity became more of an individual responsibility.

A second response was to reassert the ancient collective charity ethic but in a utopian form. This response is well-exemplified by the priestly rulings about a Jubilee year at the end of the Holiness Code (Leviticus 25). At the heart of this chapter, which was preceded by other rulings regarding sacrifices, purity laws, and transgressors (Leviticus 22-24), is an expression of moral and religious outrage at the disordered conditions of the land of Israel, where many families had become separated from the land given them in ancient times by decrees of their tribes. The chapter argues that people should not be free to buy and sell land as they see fit, independent of God's will for the people as a whole (Lev. 25:23). The passage proposes a scheme whereby the original owners were to be allowed to claim or buy back their former properties at the end of fifty years (Lev. 25:10, 13-19, 25-28). It is not clear that these rulings were ever literally followed or enforced by governing authorities. Rather they served as a moral ideal, an ideological program, in relation to which present abuses were criticized and current property claims were justified.

A third and comparatively pervasive response was to alter the soteriological and sociological context of the ancient charity norms by interpreting them far more as a matter of individual virtue or vice rather than as a concern of communal conventions and obligations. As Job himself recounted, aiding the poor was supposed to be a sign of virtue and a means of gaining civic reputation (Job 29:12-16, 21-25). Those individuals who assisted the poor were promised good fortune by both Psalms and Proverbs (Ps. 41:1-3, 11-13; Prov. 14:21, 31-32). Aiding the poor, either by private means or public offerings, was viewed as a meritorious action. The charity ethic was here set within expectations about personal not communal fortune and merit. Furthermore, as being charitable was interpreted at times as an individual virtue, being poor itself was correspondingly viewed as an indication of vice or wrong doing. In Proverbs we read: "A rich man's wealth is his strong city; the poverty of the poor is their ruin. . . . The poor is disliked by even his neighbours but the rich has many friends" (Prov. 10:15; 14:21). No wonder Job, whose former fortunes were lost, protested at great lengths that his present impoverishment was no sign of moral failing on his part.[5]

At the outset it is best to acknowledge that there are some difficulties in identifying the charity ethics of early Rabbinic Judaism (200 B.C.E.-200 C.E.). The rabbis produced no one explicit tractate or discussion of charity; rather, discussions of topics related to charity are found interspersed through a wide range of materials, dealing with concerns such as the preparation of produce for market, the status of widows, the sayings of the fathers, the role of the courts, as well as collections for the poor.

In the period after the destruction of the temple at Jerusalem (70 C.E.), early Rabbinic Judaism can be identified as an ethnically distinct, stateless, geographically dispersed, religiously defined people which lived in a number of culturally interconnected self-governing communities. The Jewish people at this time comprised neither a nation state or empire like the Romans or Persians, nor a voluntary religious association or sect, like the Christians. They were a religiously defined, ethnic collectivity. Most Jews could identify themselves as the heirs of families who had made up the distinct people and nations of Israel and Judah. Moreover, even those who had become part of this people through intermarriage or religious conversion (prior to 130 C.E.) identified themselves in relation to this idealized biblical history of the people.[6] As a people they identified themselves primarily in religious terms, in relation to shared beliefs, and to a wide range of shared, ritualized practices. To be a Jew meant not only to believe certain things about God and about the Jews as a special people of God but also to adhere to and participate in a number of public and private ceremonies, observances, and ritual activities, including weekly and yearly festivals and fasts, dietary rules, and other ordinances related to tithing and cleanliness.[7] Even though they were stateless, the Jews lived in self-governing communities. The primary institutions for self-governance were local synagogues where public religious services were held and religious ordinances were affirmed and guarded, communal councils of elders, and periodically established courts to adjudicate disputes.[8] Education and learning had a determinative influence on

---

5   An additional response, not discussed in the body of the paper, was that taken by the Essenes who founded a utopian community which practiced austerity, self-support, and mutual assistance.
6   George Foot Moore, *Judaism*, vol. 1 (New York: Schocken Books, 1958), 233.
7   Weber, *Judaism*, 385-404; Jacob Neusner, *From Politics to Piety: The Emergence of Pharasaic Judaism* (Englewood Cliffs, N.J.: Prentice-Hall, 1970).
8   Ephraim Frisch, *An Historical Survey of Jewish Philanthropy* (New York: The Macmillan Company, 1924), 33.

the governance of these communities, for councils, judges, and synagogues were not free to operate at their own discretion but governed in keeping with the Torah, the revealed word of God in its written (biblical) and oral (Mishnaic) forms. These texts were read and discussed in weekly religious services and at home. Some form of elementary schooling in many communities helped many young men commit to memory much of these works.[9] More able students furthered their learning in advanced schools with revered rabbis. Finally, those who were most learned in the Torah often assumed leadership in the synagogues, councils, and courts, not like priests who had not other occupation, but as laymen who usually had other occupations as well (cf. *Aboth* 2.2; 3.21).

The charity ethic of early Rabbinic Judaism represents an expansion, specification, and idealization of the charity ethic of post-exilic Israel. This ethic was spelled out by an articulate, well-educated elite, the Tannaiam, who both insisted on faithful attention to traditional moral ideals and sought to render these standards practical by examining at length and in detail their possible meanings. The people were commanded to adhere to these high standards in hopes that God would send his Messiah and the glories of ancient Israel would be restored. This was a rigorous but not an heroic ethic, an ethic that called for attention to the details of religious and moral practices but not for self-abasing or ascetic practices.

The charity ethic of early Rabbinic Judaism was intertwined with ritual observances; administered locally by these councils, synagogues, and judges; and communicated and defended by these schools and elders. These factors affected the character of early Rabbinic charity ethics in three ways. First, Rabbinic thought made no clear distinction between what we today might refer to as communal ritual observances, moral practices, economic regulations, and some aspects of personal piety.[10] For example, as I shall demonstrate further below, stipulations with regard to tithing were set forth largely in material concerning the ritually appropriate ways of preparing produce for market.

Second, provisions for charity were spelled out simply and in great detail in ways that would have made it possible for persons in quite dispersed communities to administer these practices in strikingly parallel ways. The specificity of these standards is noteworthy. Welfare assistance, for instance, was to be distributed discriminately to certain

---

9 Shmuel Safrai, ("Elementary Education: Its Religious and Social Significance in the Talmudic Period," in H. H. Ben Sasson and S. Ettinger, eds., *Jewish Society Through the Ages* [New York: Schocken Books, 1969]), argues that most communities had established some form of elementary education between the years 70-135. Of course, such education may not have been universal, may have occupied only a few hours a week, and like subsequent Sunday Schools focussed primarily on religious topics.

10 Moore, *Judaism*, vol. 2: 5-8.

categories of persons who met quite specific standards of eligibility.[11] Particular kinds of foods were called for (cf. *M. Kethboth* 5.8). Stipulations were set forth about when particular categories of people might glean fields for unharvested crops (*Pe'ah* 1.2). Detailed rulings were made regarding loans. The specificity of these standards reflect concerns with the practical exigencies faced by those responsible for administering self-governing communities. The specificity of these standards also reflected the authors' beliefs that the written Torah provided a necessary guide for communal practices. Where the Torah was vague, as regards amounts to be tithed or the length of hospitality to be extended, the rabbis were wont to add specific stipulations.[12] The rabbis, unlike the early Christians, articulated no over-arching principles of charity from which diverse norms and practices could be deduced. Epigrammatic statements such as those of Simeon the Righteous—"The world is sustained by three things, by Torah, by worship, and by charity" (*Aboth* 1.2)—were set forth not as deductive principles but as wise sayings for personal reflection.[13] *Zedakkah* was associated specifically with alms-giving and *hesed* with non-material assistance.

Third, the communal character of the early Rabbinic charity ethic is evident as well in the absence of any appeals for heroic efforts by individuals. To be sure, numerous appeals were made to the generosity and sympathy of individuals and to the worldly advantages that benefitted those who were charitable. Legends were repeated about how the charitable lived longer, enjoyed material comfort, and became renowned, and how tragedies occured to particular stingy persons (*B. T. Kethuboth* 66b; *Aboth*, 3.8; 4.2; 4.17). However, charity was not primarily defended in individualistic terms. Self-sacrificing practices, such as those associated with voluntary poverty, were shunned.[14] From the Rabbinic perspective it was, in any case, more desirable to be rich than poor, and riches themselves were not criticized as a force that might entice individuals away from communal commitments and moral standards (Hengel, 1974, ch. 3). Rabbinic documents appealed prima-

---

11   Weber, *Judaism*, chap. 15; Moore, *Judaism*, vol. 2: 168.
12   Whether these documents reflect the practical concerns of communal administrators during the second commonwealth period, as Y. Baer argues, or perhaps at a later time is difficult to determine. (Yitshak Baer, "Social Ideals of the Second Jewish Commonwealth," in Ben Sasson and Ettinger, eds., *Jewish Society*, 69-91.) In some cases, to be sure, the specific concerns focussed on matters which would have been of greater concern to agricultural communities than the largely urban and commercial communities which existed in the period after the destruction of the temple. The setting of these stipulations no doubt also reflected the quite different milieu of the master and his pupils where the attempt to fix the meaning of the inherited law was more of an intellectual discipline than practice concern.
13   Moore, *Judaism*, vol. 2: 29-88.
14   *Ibid.*, vol. 2: 177; Martin Hengel, *Property and Riches in the Early Church* (London: SCM Press, 1974), chap. 2.

rily not for individual acts of exceptional philanthropy, but for all individuals, regardless of their position, to uphold charitable obligations shared by all. All Jews were promised a part in the world to come (*Aboth*, introduction). The ultimate justification for honouring these obligations was expressed in communal and eschatological terms.[15] Again and again Jews were warned to maintain and protect their communal existence: "Let the property of thine associate be as dear to thee as thine own" (*Aboth* 2.17). "Let the honor of thine associate be as dear to thee as thine own" (2.15)."sever not thyself from the congregation" (2.5; 4.7). "Let thy house be opened wide and the poor by thy household" (1.5). Ultimately, charity was justified as a means of seeking God's good favour and avoiding his judgment, both of which were defined largely but not exclusively in communal and worldly terms. Judgment was often associated with political subjugation and oppression, and God's favour with political independence and economic prosperity.[16]

Substantively, the charity ethic of early Rabbinic Judaism was articulated in a number of different communal norms which spelled out the benefits which the needy might receive, the appropriate manner for administering these gifts, the expected procedures for gathering contributions, and the fitting attitude of communal members towards these practices.

Depending upon their particular circumstances, needy Jews might expect to receive specified amounts of food or money as gifts, tax rebates, interest-free loans, and/or special assistance for certain extraordinary circumstances. Missing from the list of possible beneficiaries of charity were priests and guest workers. After the destruction of the second temple, priests had been replaced as pre-eminent religious officials by rabbis, who were largely self-sufficient. The strangers in their midst were no longer Israelites from other tribes or Canaanite guest workers with whom they might intermarry, but quite powerful foreigners with whom they lived in tension in Palestine, Babylon, Egypt, and elsewhere. Widows, orphans, impoverished travellers, temporarily needy families, and aspiring scholars all qualified for assistance. The rights of widows and orphans were spelled out much more clearly than in the Hebrew Bible. For example, widows were given the right of inheritance to their husband's property instead of his relatives and the guarantee of remaining in their husband's house even if it meant having to sell some of his belongings (*M. Kethuboth* 12.3). Other categories of temporarily needy persons were defined quite specifically in relation to minimal levels of income or minimal levels of available food (for example, less than two meals per day for a week, *M. Pe'ah* 8.8). These temporarily needy persons along

---

15 Moore, *Judaism*, vol. 2: 173; Neusner, *Politics to Piety*, 13.
16 In some cases judgment was defined in individualistic terms. See the following sayings in the *Pirke Aboth*: 2.1; 3.1; 3.16 (cf. Moore, *Judaism*, vol. 2: 169-70).

with more permanently impoverished widows and orphans could qualify for assistance from a weekly distribution of money and supplies called the Kuppah. Other transients, which might have included otherwise economically self-sufficient traders, scholars, and immigrants, were assisted from a daily dispersement of food called Tamhui. All were allowed to gather specified amounts of crops intentionally left unharvested by farmers.[17] Scholars and teachers may have benefitted from several additional measures. They were exempted from some taxes, allowed at times to sell their produce in market before others, sometimes given the interest earnings on what would otherwise be usurious loans, and probably in some case remunerated in part for teaching young people.[18] Special funds were established for helping needy Jews in extraordinary circumstances, for example, so that female orphans might have dowries and therefore be eligible for marriage, and that the impoverished dead might receive decent burials.

The relationship between charity and the practice of providing interest-free loans had become complex and confused over time. This practice, which had originally been designed as a means of offering temporary relief to needy neighbours, had been modified over the centuries in several ways largely to the benefit of creditors. In most cases loans were utilized with no relation to charity primarily in commercial activities where the charging of interest worked no significant hardships. Overall, the early rabbis sought to allow for the development of legitimate commercial loans, but also to discourage both lenders and borrowers from initiating loans as a form of temporary relief for the poor, and to insist on specific traditional restrictions on such loans. Thus, the early rabbis allowed for ways of obviating the traditional seventh-year cancellation of debts, and they also found ways of allowing for interest payments by referring to these payments as gifts or service charges. The rabbis also maintained that the prohibitions against usury fell on both lender and borrower. Furthermore, they sought through specific stipulations to protect debtors' interests, restricting creditors, for example, from using what debtors had given them as pledges.[19]

Local communities supervised these charity programs by appointing two men as trustees to make weekly collections and three men to make weekly allocations (M. Pe'ah 7.1). When disputes arose regarding loans, regarding the rights of widows, or the rights of poor persons to gleanings, communal councils arranged for special courts to be estab-

---

17 In an increasingly urban milieu, these provisions which were articulated in great detail may have been largely theoretical.

18 Weber, *Judaism*, chap. 15; Avinoam Cohen, "The Development of the Prohibition Against Usury in the Jewish Law During the Mishnaic and Palmudic Periods" (M.A. thesis, Concordia University, Montreal, 1975), 97.

19 *Ibid.*, 92; Boaz Cohen, *Jewish and Roman Law: A Comparative Study*, vol. 2 (New York: Jewish Theological Seminary of America, 1960), 434.

lished to settle disputes (cf. *Sanhedrin* 3.1; *Pe'ah* 1.6; 4.11; 6.5-6). Since these *ad hoc* tribunals had little power of enforcement, they probably largely served as vehicles for mutual compromise.

Contributions for these charity programs were collected probably through weekly offerings, solicited by the trustees of charity funds, and by some forms of communal taxation or tithing. The Mishnah does not present an entirely clear picture regarding this matter. Several tractates consider at great length and in much detail what produce should be tithed, in what manner the tithes should be prepared, and what produce was exempt from tithing.[20] The early rabbis and the pharisees before them evidently considered that tithing in the appropriate manner was a sign of true piety (*Aboth* 1.16; 3.17). But they also, equally evidently, assumed that there were many Jews who slighted or wholly ignored these revered procedures. What is most striking is that these tractates contain no discussion of what uses will be made of the tithed produce. It is possible to make several conjectures: one, local communities used some forms of offerings, tithes, and pledges to support local synagogues, educational programs, and charity; two, there was some latitude in the manner and frequency of making contributions; and three, some of the more pious communal members probably prepared their contributions according to the traditional and now even more detailed stipulations regarding tithing.

<hr>

C. THE ETHIC OF CHARITY IN EARLY CHRISTIANITY

<hr>

The early Christian churches were voluntary associations or sects constituted largely by persons without much material wealth. The apostle Paul made explicit references to communities in Macedonia and Jerusalem that were extremely impoverished (2 Cor. 8:2; Rom. 15:26-27). The New Testament as a whole contains countless implicit references to the marginal economic status of the disciples (Gal. 1:53; 2:10; 4:18; 6:20).[21] Some of Jesus' sayings suggest that becoming a disciple might have involved economic risks (Luke 18:18-24); however, the early disciples in general do not appear to have been scourged by constant material deprivation. In a few cases, in fact, communities may have benefitted from the largess of well-to-do benefactors who had become disciples, like Joseph of Arimathea, for example, and Philemon (John 19:38-42; cf. Matt. 27:55-56; Phil.).[22]

The early Christians were awaiting and preparing for an imminent future, variously referred to as the Day of Judgment or the Coming

<hr>

20   Necha Laks, "Biblical and Mishnaic Teachings Regarding the Poor and Needy" (M.A. thesis, Concordia University, Montreal, 1976), chap. 3; Moore, *Judaism*, vol. 2: 55-78.
21   Hengel, *Property*, chap. 4; Ernst Troeltsch, *The Social Teaching of the Christian Churches*, vol. 1 (New York: Harper Torchbooks, 1960), 45.
22   Hengel, *Property*, 69-73.

of the Kingdom of God, when they expected a dramatic change in their own fortunes and life conditions (Matt. 19:30).[23] Many disciples felt that at this time the mighty and wealthy would lose their power and riches, and the poor and oppressed would be liberated, honoured, and provided for (Luke 1:47-55; 4:18-19). The disciples felt that this sacred future was foreordained and certain. It was envisioned in both trans-historical images as a time of eternal life or eternal damnation as well as in historical images as a day of resurrection and judgment (Mark 1:15; Matthew 24; 1 Clement 24).

The aim of the Christian life was to prepare for this future. The disciples correspondingly assumed that how they lived their lives would have an impact on how they would experience this future. Hence, Christian moral standards necessarily assumed a teleological character, because they were viewed as a means to help foster this predestined, desired, and anticipated end. In no case do teleological ethics judge the rightness or wrongness of behaviour relatively, as do consequential or utilitarian ethics, in relation to the degree of benefits realized. Rather, basic norms are authoritatively announced as foreordained means integrally bound to the desired ends.[24] To be sure, early Christians viewed this sacred future as a time of rewards and punishment (cf. Matt. 8:2; 13:50; 22:13; Romans 5), but the disciples assumed that how persons would fare at this time of judgment could not be predetermined by strict observance of either ritual or moral codes but rather by unswerving devotion to the community and God's purposes (cf. Luke 10:38-42). However, acts of hospitality and charity, especially when they included some element of self-sacrifice, were viewed as indications of such devotion (Matt. 25:31-46; Luke 18:18-30; John 13:34-35).[25]

Unlike the contemporary Jewish charity ethic which was embodied in a whole fabric of specific norms and institutional practices, the early Christian charity ethic largely was expressed and communicated in relation to two or three fundamental principles. Briefly, primitive Christians adhered to a communal ethic of mutual assistance summarized by the second great commandment about loving one's neighbour. They also held up a more radical ideal of self-sacrificing

---

23   Richard Batey, *Jesus and the Poor* (New York: Harper and Row, 1972), 42-44; Oscar Cullman, *Jesus and the Revolutionaries* (New York: Harper and Row, 1970), chap. 5.

24   I am here arguing against the framework used by David Little and Sumner Twiss who fail to distinguish between teleological and consequential forms of moral reasoning. David Little and Sumner Twiss, *Comparative Religious Ethics* (New York: Harper & Row, 1978). The distinction between teleological and consequential ethics parallels Weber's distinction between value rational action and purposeful rational action. Gustafson notes this distinction and its importance in his study of Catholic and Protestant ethics. James Gustafson, *Protestant and Catholic Ethics* (Chicago: University of Chicago Press, 1977).

25   Little and Twiss, *Ethics*, 177, 204; Rudolf Schnackenburg, *The Moral Teaching of the New Testament* (New York: Herder and Herder, 1971), 151-61.

devotion, summarized by the first great commandment, about love for God, which tended at times to render the ethic of mutual assistance as relative and of lesser import. Finally, the early Christians reiterated a norm, which was at times assimilated to either of these previous standards, that evil lay in a too great attachment to material goods and wealth. Primitive Christians made little direct mention of the ancient Israelite social norms regarding charity. They continued to adhere to many of these standards regarding hospitality, private assistance, and interest-free loans. However, they considered that Christ's commandments, which called for a more active, intentional practice of charity, had assumed pre-eminence (cf. Matt. 5:17-34; John 12:1-8).

At one level the early Christians embraced a charity ethic which assumed the form of a communal ethic of mutual assistance. The disciples were counselled to share their goods, extend their hospitality, and look after the needs of their fellow disciples. Specifically, they were urged to feed those who were hungry, visit those who were imprisoned, care for those who were sick, and welcome those who were strangers (Rom. 8:35; James 1:27; Matt. 20:42; Rom. 12:20; 1 Thess. 5:4). In 1 Clement hospitality and charity are linked with faith as cardinal Christian values (1 Clement 10:7; 11:1; 12:1). Frequently the disciples met the needs of their fellow disciples through special collections raised within one congregation either for persons in that congregation or for a more distant congregation in special need. The apostle Paul, for example, helped to raise a collection for the churches in Jerusalem and Macedonia (Acts 4:38; Gal. 2:10; 1 Cor. 16:1-4; 2 Cor. 9:1-5). In some cases, in the primitive church in Jerusalem, for example, the disciples pooled all their belongings together out of a combination of spontaneous enthusiasm and perhaps need (Acts 2:44-47;5:1-16), but these cases seem to be exceptional.[26] Everywhere the early churches relied upon freewill offerings to address their on-going needs. A formal system of tithing was not established until third or fourth century.[27]

There is little evidence that non-Christians were in fact viewed as primary objects of this hospitality, solicitousness, and beneficence. In the Didache and 1 Clement it is the brethren who are viewed as objects of charity (Didache 4:78; 1 Clem. 10-12). A close analysis of the parable of the last judgment, in which humankind is judged on the basis of charitableness, results in the same conclusion. Persons are judged to enter eternal life or eternal damnation depending on whether they helped "one of the least" or "one of the least of these my brethren" (Matt. 25:40, 45). In parallel passages these phrases are consistently used to identify fellow disciples (Matt. 10:42; 12:49-50; 18:6; 11:1;

---

26 Hengel, *Property*, chap. 4.
27 Gerhard Ulhorn, *Christian Charity in the Ancient Church* (New York: Charles Scribner's Sons, 1883), 142, 257.

18:4-5; 23:8; 28:10).[28] To be sure, the disciples were also counselled to act like good Samaritans, stopping momentarily to help persons in distress even if they were not co-religionists (Luke 10:29-37).

If any group of persons was identified as the special object of charity, it was probably the apostles, preachers, and travelling missionaries. Both Paul and the Didache counselled the disciples to esteem and to honour as their Lord those who spoke to them the Word of God (Didache 4:1; 1 Thess. 5:12). 1 Clement counsels disciples to provide hospitality for these preachers and apostles in particular (1 Clem. 10:7; 11:1; 12:1). As Paul could testify from his own experience, these preachers and travelling apostles in particular often had to rely upon the munificence of others to receive food and drink, to be welcomed when strangers, to be cared for when sick, and to be visited when in prison.

This ethic of mutual assistance was not spelled out in a series of norms detailing specific actions either in relation to particular categories of needy persons or in relation to institutionalized means for collecting donations. Rather than attempting to make the Deuteronomic codes more specific, early Christians tended either to assume these codes or translate them into a more abstract and general commandment. Repeatedly, the disciples were counselled to love their neighbours as themselves. As Paul wrote the Galatians, "the whole law is fulfilled in one word, Love your neighbour as yourself" (Gal. 5:14). In relation to the ethic of mutual assistance, this love commandment served both as a universal normative standard, like the natural-law principle which might inspire and be used to criticize particular efforts, as well as a contextual guide which counselled disciples to look with fresh eyes at each situation, attentive to the changing needs of others. Jesus' story of the Good Samaritan was used to illustrate precisely this last point. For the early Christians, the commandment of neighbour love was not a summary of the essence of a much broader system of rules, precepts, and practices—as were similar Rabbinic statements— but rather a first principle from which other, relative, situational norms might be derived. As a result, subsequent generations of Christians were easily able to assimilate this norm to the abstract principles of the Stoic philosophy.[29]

At another level, the early Christians embraced a more demanding and radical charity ethic which called for individuals to live with a self-sacrificing devotion to Christ and his purposes. Disciples were counselled to be perfect like God, to follow Jesus' example, to be willing to forsake their own lives and interests for the sake of others. In Mark, Jesus speaks to his disciples and to a large crowd, saying, "If any man

---

28   Troeltsch, *Social Teaching*, vol. 1: 56; Ramsey Michael, "The Church Vigilant" (Ph.D. dissertation, Harvard Divinity School, 1962), 109-33.
29   Troeltsch, *Social Teaching*, vol. 1: 62-69.

would come after me, let him deny himself and take up his cross and follow me" (Mark 8:34). In Luke's gospel, Jesus argues that even sinners extend mutual care and assistance; rather, he proclaims: "Love your enemies, and do good, and lend expecting nothing in return. . . . Be merciful, even as your Father is merciful . . . for he is kind to the ungrateful and selfish" (Luke 35:6). By this ethic disciples were called to be unconditionally generous. Unlike the ethic of mutual assistance, which was a norm for congregational behaviour, this ethic of self-sacrificing devotion was addressed to disciples as individuals. There were varied means by which disciples might give evidence of their self-denying generosity: one might sell all his goods and give the proceeds to the poor (Luke 18:18-25); another might face imprisonment; while still others might voluntarily forsake their families (Luke 18:28-30). Rather than a standard of minimal obligation required of all disciples, this was a standard of excellence to which many disciples aspired.[30] The virtue of this ethic of self-sacrificing devotion primarily lay not in the benefits which would accrue to others as recipients of such self-denying generosity, but in the single-minded, unself-serving devotion to Christ and his gospel. In Luke's account, the reason the rich young man is counselled to sell all his goods, and the reason why Peter exclaims that he and others have left their homes and families to be with Jesus, was in hope of earning eternal life.

Because few disciples had surplus wealth, the early Christian charity ethic did not assume a philanthropic form; that is, a form in which those living in comfort were praised and honoured for contributing from their superfluous goods and wealth donations to benefit those of a lower economic class. Philanthropic forms of charity had been widely practised in the Roman and Greek city states by patrician families who donated food and festivals as a means of gaining the loyal allegiance of the lower classes. The early Christians seemed to scorn such forms of charity, because they felt that philanthropic altruism was largely motivated by a desire for prestige and involved no genuine concern for others, nor any real sacrifice on the part of the donors (Luke 21:1-4).

The charity ethic of primitive Christians was also expressed and embodied in their attitudes towards material possessions. The early Christian writings contain a number of statements critical of wealth and the wealthy. In the gospel of Luke, Jesus preached, "Woe to you that are rich. . . . Woe to you that are full. . ." (Luke 6:24-25). He warned that it is easier for a camel to pass through the eye of a needle than for a rich man to enter the Kingdom of God (Mark 10:25). In several other, complementary passages, the disciples were counselled to give away their money and goods indiscriminately to any who begged of them (Luke 5:30-31; Didache 1:5). What kind of practical norm is implied by these statements? Some have argued that these sayings suggest an

---

30 *Ibid.*, 55, 59, 174; Ulhorn, Charity, 345.

initial statement of an ethic of voluntary poverty according to which disciples were counselled to renounce claims to property. This argument is reinforced by citing examples of the way in which the disciples in Jerusalem pooled their resources, the way in which Jesus himself urged his disciples to have little care for property and housing (Matt. 6:25-33), and by the ways in which some of the apostles obviously renounced their occupations and claims to inheritance by joining with Jesus. However, there is also considerable contrary evidence that no rigorous ascetic ethic of voluntary poverty was advocated.[31] After all, Jesus is depicted as banquetting with the rich, much to the displeasure of the followers of John the Baptist who adopted an ascetic ethic like the Essenes. Wealthy followers like Joseph of Arimathea were not counselled to give away all their goods. Moreover, in a number of places, disciples were commanded not to make themselves economically dependent upon others (2 Thess. 3:10-11; 1 Tim. 5:9-16; 2 Tim. 6:16-19). Rather, the concern in these passages was not with wealth and property as such, but with a too-great attachment to these things, because such attachments often stood in the way of genuine concern for others and devotion to Jesus and his mission. Jesus summarizes this message by saying, "You cannot serve two masters . . . you cannot serve God and mammon" (Matt. 6:24).

But as a correlate to an ethic of charity, these sayings about wealth and material possessions are not wholly clear and self-evident. At one level they might be interpreted as austerity standards reinforcing the ethic of mutual assistance by counselling disciples to be ready and willing to share their superfluous belongings with their brethren in need (2 Cor. 8:3-4). At another level and more generally, these sayings seem to be more closely related to the heroic ethic of self-sacrificing devotion. For example, in those places where disciples were urged to practise a kind of indiscriminate generosity, it was to demonstrate their devotion and virtue. Persons who received their wealth by suspect means were urged to divest themselves of their riches in order to demonstrate their changed characters.

There is considerable difference between a charity ethic of mutual assistance, which serves as a congregational norm, and a charity ethic of self-sacrifice, which serves as an heroic standard for individual excellence. But early Christians drew no sharp line between these principles. For example, while appealing to the Corinthians out of their abundance to offer brotherly assistance to the Macedonian Church, Paul proceeded to invoke the more radical standard of self-denial by referring to Jesus, who, "though he was rich, yet for your sake He became poor" (2 Cor. 8:9; cf. Phil. 2:4-11). As we shall see below, over the centuries Christians found a number of ways of resolving the tension between these two somewhat different standards for charity.

---

31   Hengel, *Property*, 27; Troeltsch, *Social Teaching*, vol. 1: 59.

D. FURTHER DEVELOPMENTS IN JEWISH AND CHRISTIAN CHARITY

It would be impossible to summarize briefly the manifold developments among Jewish communities and among Christian churches in the centuries following. However, we can note some of the more significant developments in charity ethics during the Middle Ages, leaving for subsequent studies more detailed analyses.

Jewish Charity Ethics

During most of the period from the Tannaiam to emancipation, the charity ethic of the early rabbis remained normative. However, this ethic was modified in several ways, reflecting largely later sociological changes in the settings of Jewish communities.

There was a further institutionalization of charitable practices. In larger communities, organized associations were formed which undertook, in addition to whatever fraternal purposes they served, to provide assistance for particular categories of needy persons: some provided shelter for travellers, and others sought to make ransoms available for captives; some provided dowries for female orphans, and others visited the sick; some established funds for the burial of the poor, and others looked after the aged. In some communities, particular associations were formed for provide loans to the poor. Some of these societies may well have been instituted during Talmudic times. They attained standardized form in European Jewish communities in the late Middle Ages and Renaissance.[32] During this period there was a decline in the practice of daily distributing food randomly to needy transients. However, the practice of collecting subscriptions from all for the weekly poor-box fund was reinforced.[33] The rules regarding borrowers and lenders were further refined, particularly in the Babylonian Talmud, in ways that fostered commercial loans.

Scholars and students continued to be viewed as special objects of charity, in a large part because the study of the Torah was viewed as a supreme obligation and virtue. From ancient times teachers, students, and scholars may well have been subsidized in part by their families and local communities.[34] However, the scholars were urged not to become wholly dependent upon others but to support themselves in part through their own occupations (cf. *Aboth* 1.10; 2.2, 20; 2.2). Still, scholars and rabbis received benevolent assistance not only from their families but also from others, partly because of the difficulties of pursuing Torah study assiduously while undertaking other occupa-

---

32   Frisch, *Jewish Philanthropy*, chap. 10.
33   Israel Abrahams, *Jewish Life in the Middle Ages* (Philadelphia: The Jewish Publication Society, 1896), chap. 17.
34   *Ibid.*, chap. 14; Frisch, *Jewish Philanthropy*, 115.

tions, partly because of the increasing demands for rabbis' attention, and partly because of the associated merit derived from assisting such revered figures. By the thirteenth century, rabbis and scholars were regularly supported by their communities.[35]

Beginning in the late Middle Ages and increasing in the subsequent centuries, Jewish communities expressed considerable concern about the problem of begging.[36] Permanent economic dependency of able-bodied males was scorned as unnecessary and as a sign of disrepute. Alarm over the problem of begging was expressed as well by Christian communities in Italy, France, and England during the same period.[37] Sociological factors occasioned by the crusades, the beginnings of urbanization and commerce, the end of barbarians' raids, and the long periods of war and plagues upset traditional social arrangements in ways that left many able-bodied men without regular employment. In fear lest economic dependency be encouraged, Maimonides calls for charity programs that would not only support the needy in their dependency but would root out the problem of dependency and need altogether. He argued that the aim of charity should be to put the poor person "where he can dispense with other people's aid . . . strengthen him in such a manner that his falling into want is prevented."[38] The goal of creating a world without economic need was a new one, not found in either biblical or Mishnaic materials, occasioned in part by the optimism of the new urbanized European world as well as by the new dilemma posed by the existence of increasing numbers of able-bodied men without regular sources of employment.

Subtly but increasingly, Jewish communities identified charity in ways that pictured it more as an individual and meritorious activity than as a whole series of communal obligations and norms. These shifts were never complete; charity continued to be understood primarily in relation to a broad spectrum of communal observances and rules related, for example, to tithing and the status of widows, and defended as collective obligations. But at the same time there was an increasing appeal to individuals, particularly to those who were economically successful, to seek personal merit and honour. There was a tendency to associate being charitable with being righteous and to focus more on the motives and virtues of the donor than on charitable institutions and their effects.[39]

---

35 Abrahams, *Jewish Life*, chap. 3.
36 *Ibid.*, 308-11.
37 Lester K. Little, *Religious Poverty and the Profit Economy in Medieval Europe* (Ithaca: Cornell University Press, 1978); Brian Pullan, *Rich and Poor in Renaissance Venice* (Oxford: Basil Blackwell, 1971).
38 Moses Maimonides, *A Maimonides Reader*, ed. by Isadore Twersky (New York: Behrman House, Inc., 1972), 137.
39 Maimonides, *Reader*, 51, 135, 138, 332; Abraham Cronbach, "The Me'il Zedakkah," *Hebrew Union College Annual* 11: 503-67; 12-13; 635-96; 14: 479-557 (1936-1939).

Christian Charity Ethics

By the third century of the common era the heroic ethic of self-sacrificing charity had assumed a definitely ascetic, world-denying form. Literally following the example of the rich young man, some disciples forsook families and possessions to practice a celibate, property-free existence dedicated to their own spiritual development.[40] Monastic life itself was an expression of charity both because upon entering the monastic orders persons gave away their worldly possessions to the poor and because they were able to develop more fully within their hearts compassion and charity for others.

Monastic orders and the celibate clergy also became increasingly the objects of lay charity.[41] They depended upon lay support for their initial properties, for contributions of food and clothing, and for financial assistance. To be sure, many monasteries became self-sufficient, as the land over which they had jurisdiction became productive through their own efforts and the labour of lay serfs and tenants. The benevolence they received grew in size as monastic orders developed, and as they in turn, like the Levites of old, served as the primary dispensers of charitable assistance for transients, temporarily impoverished peasants, widows, and orphans.[42]

As Christian churches spread through the ancient world and multiplied in numbers and size through new converts, Christian congregations began to change their characteristic structure from small, voluntary associations of active converts to larger, more diffuse assemblies of persons, many of whom had been born and raised as Christians and were led by a well-organized, distinct clergy, headed in turn by regional bishops. These shifts in congregational patterns modified the primitive egalitarian ethic of mutual assistance in a more philanthropic, hierarchical direction. Parishes developed varieties of charitable programs, institutions and hospices to care for travellers, the sick, the aged, the handicapped, and the abandoned. Often bishops assumed responsibility for developing these programs. With these developments the churches became more concerned with reliable sources of contributions. Hence, churches instituted programs to solicit regular tithes from their members, not only to support these philanthropies, but to support the clergy and church programs as well. The churches and monasteries also encouraged members to donate their properties to the church at their deaths, with the consequence that by the end of the fifth century the churches together constituted the largest landowner in the Roman empire.[43]

---

40 Troeltsch, *Social Teaching*, vol. 1: 104-11; Demetrios Constantelos, *Byzantine Philanthropy and Social Welfare* (New Brunswick, N.J.: Rutgers University Press, 1968), 93.
41 Constantelos, *Byzantine Philanthropy*, chap. 1; Troletsch, *Social Teachings*, vol. 1: 137.
42 Constantelos, *Byzantine Philanthropy*, chap. 2.
43 *Ibid.*, chap. 6; Ulhorn, *Charity*, 250-66.

With the rise in philanthropic forms of benevolence, Christian preachers increasingly described charity as a meritorious act. As a virtue, charity was an expression of love and dedication to Christ's gospel. To be charitable was to show mercy like God himself. Christians were both coaxed to contribute and threatened if they did not. Disciples were promised that God would reward their gifts by forgiving their sins after death and that he would punish them by denying eternal life if they refused. In relation to the ultimate end or *telos* of the Christian life, namely, seeking God's good favour, whether or not one was charitable was a matter of great import.[44] In making their donations, Christians often were encouraged not to make themselves poor but to contribute their superfluous wealth. Augustine implored his parishioners: "All that God has given us beyond what is necessary, He has not properly speaking given to us. He has entrusted it to us, that it may be our means come into the hands of the poor."[45] Augustine thereby left Christians free to determine in good conscience what was and was not a necessity. Since goods and properties were no longer necessities at death and the state of one's own soul was of paramount importance, the churches remained relatively successful in securing bequests.

With the development of territorial churches in the east beginning in the fourth century and in the west a century or more later, public state welfare programs were often integrated with church philanthropies. From the perspective of governing authorities, the churches provided well-organized means for the distribution of public largess directed especially at pacifying the otherwise discontented lower classes. For example, Constantine donated state funds to the churches to distribute to the poor. Government rulers sought to legitimize their authority through these practices much as the ancient city states of Rome and Greece had also periodically distributed food and staged spectacles in order to maintain their favour with the landless classes. In practice, the charity programs of the churches became increasingly like the classical state welfare programs.[46]

Beginning in the eleventh and twelfth centuries with the papal attacks upon political influence in the churches, a number of different reform movements attempted to institute changes which would modify existing ecclesiastic practices, including charitable activities, so that they were more in keeping with their own particular interpretations of New Testament norms. The Franciscan and Dominican movements were especially influential. They reaffirmed the vow to live in volun-

---

44   Troeltsch, *Social Teaching*, vol. 1: 114-36; Hengel, *Property*, 82; Constantelos, *Byzantine Philanthropy*, 23.
45   Ulhorn, *Charity*, 301.
46   Constantelos, *Byzantine Philanthropy*, chaps. 5, 8, 10; Troeltsch, *Social Teaching*, vol. 1: 213-23.

tary poverty, to offer charity to those who were really impoverished and suffering, to live exemplary lives of self-sacrificing ascetic devotion, and to preach penitence and reform publicly in order to overcome abuses of the larger society.[47]

<hr>

E. CONCLUSIONS

This brief survey of Jewish and Christian ethics of charity yields several conclusions. We can note that what people mean by the word charity is not obvious and simple. Charity has assumed quite diverse forms even within these religious traditions.

We can observe as well that charitable activities are usually intertwined with other practices and institutions and that the relationship between givers and receivers usually involves some reciprocity. In sectarian voluntary associations, charity may indeed assume the form of mutual assistance. In small, self-governing communities, charity may be integrated with communal norms related to the support and cohesion of the community as such. Where charity takes philanthropic form, the givers are often honoured with prestige and promised religious merit, and the recipients are expected to demonstrate their gratitude through subservience, loyalty, and/or the performance of otherwise difficult and disreputable tasks. In some cases, philanthropic forms of charity seem to focus greater attention on the virtue of charity than on the practical steps by which benevolence can be of the greatest benefit to those in need. These religious traditions have both succeeded in encouraging the generosity and fraternal concern of many of their adherents. They have set forth lofty ideals. But they have also solicited actual charitable actions by appealing to a person's sense of advantage, self-respect, honour, and religious status.

Charity practices have tended to exert conserving rather than revolutionary influence; they have reinforced social solidarity by linking communal members together. The practices of charity within these religious traditions have reinforced social cohesion by offering assistance to economically marginal members and by supporting and honouring those persons valued as moral and religious leaders and emblematic of their communal existence. Typically, the recipients of charity have included not only impoverished persons (orphans, widows, guest workers, and transients), but also highly revered officials and workers (Levites, priests, apostles, monks, rabbis, scholars) who have forsaken ordinary economic pursuits in order to devote themselves full-time to administering and preserving the rites and teachings integral to their communal existence.

In both religious traditions, religious officials have from time to time become the major beneficiaries of charitable assistance. These

<hr>

47 Little, *Religious Poverty, passim.*

religious professionals, as both the recipients of assistance and the primary advocates of charity, have markedly influenced the character of charity ethics. The focus on ritual observance reflected the Levites' concerns as a priestly caste just as the focus of self-sacrificing devotion reflected the ardour of early Christian apostles, who in many cases renounced their families and possessions to share in the ministry of the early church. Similarly, the importance of Torah study reflected the early rabbis own preoccupation with scholarship and learning. We could say that in each case the charity ethic served in part an ideological function, reinforcing the authority and prestige of the most articulate spokesmen of these moral ideals.

More importantly, we can conclude that Jewish and Christian charity ethics bear the unmistakable imprint of their formative periods. Though modified, at times markedly in subsequent generations, the focus of charitable concern, the typical forms of these norms, and characteristic reasons for adhering to these norms were all determined during particular historical periods. Ancient Israelite charity ethics reflect the milieu of pre-monarchic, inter-tribal confederacy in which tribal elders rather than public officials assumed responsibility for administering collective norms. The sectarian and heroic character of the early Christian communities deeply influenced Christian attitudes towards charity. In contrast, the charity ethics of Judaism reflect the concerns of self-governing communities responsible for perpetuating given forms of social existence and culture. If the charity ethics of Christians have in subsequent centuries assumed more diverse forms, it has been partly because the sociological patterns of Christian communities have changed dramatically since New Testament times.

The charity ethics of early Rabbinic Judaism and primitive Christianity differed in similar ways from the standards of Ancient Israel. Rather than being woven into a fabric of social policies of a traditional political society, norms regarding charity were stipulated within religious ethics, centrally concerned with the pursuit of a dramatic religious transformation, and identified with the coming or return of the Messiah.

Early Rabbinic Judaism and primitive Christianity differed regarding their own standards for charity. For the Tannaiam, charity norms were imbedded within a wide range of religious and moral standards normative for their own communal life. They were at once a series of obligations and institutionalized standards regarding widows, orphans, tithes, loans, and scholars, and standards of personal virtue. Charity, or *Zedakkah*, which might be translated as either justice or righteousness, was both: both institutional arrangements that sought to order society fairly with due respect for all in light of God's word and an expression of personal valour of those who faithfully preserved these institutions and responded graciously to their neighbour's needs. For primitive Christians, charity first and foremost referred to heroic norms of self-sacrifice supplemented by other standards of mutual assistance. Ascetic values influenced Christian ideas of charity which in time became associated with monasticism, vows of poverty, and philanthropic giving to support religious institutions. In its varied forms charity was an expression of *agape*, self-giving love, which within the history of Christianity has been variously viewed as self-sacrificing devotion, mutual care, and philanthropic assistance.

Judaism of the Second Commonwealth: Toward a Reform of the Scholarly Tradition

JACK N. LIGHTSTONE

There has existed for many decades a firm scholarly consensus regarding the character of Palestinian Judaism from roughly the middle of the fourth century B.C.E. to about 70 C.E. Any student of the period can rattle off a litany of such religious institutions as the Men of the Great Assembly, founded (of course) by Ezra; the era of the Scribes (and "Scribism"); Hellenizers, Ḥasidism, from whom sprang the Pharisees and Essenes; Sadducees; and so forth. To be sure, we have always disagreed about particulars. Some, for example, claim that Ḥasidism gave rise to Pharisaism, which in turn produced the Essenes. Others vehemently protest this configuration, preferring to see the Essenes and Pharisees emerging independently from their pietistic predecessors.[1] In spite of many a scholarly row, however, the basic characters and the plot of the drama remain constant, and have been so for about

---

1　With regard to the relations between Hasideans, Pharisees and Essenes see G. F. Moore, *Judaism in the First Centuries of the Christian Era*, vol. 1 (New York: Schocken, 1971, reprint of the 1930 edition), 59; E. Schürer, *A History of the Jewish People in the Time of Jesus*, ed. by N. N. Glatzer (New York: Schocken, 1961, based on the first English edition of 1886-1890), 17, 21, 29, 39-40, 75-76; M. Hengel, *Judaism and Hellenism*, vol. 1 (London: SCM, 1974, based on the second German edition of 1973), 176, 227, 229, 251, 253-54, 305, 311. Particularly interesting is the fact that the literature spans a seventy-year-plus period.

a century. Even the discovery of the Qumran documents has not
seriously impinged upon this academic orthodoxy, the valuable insights gained from these documents notwithstanding.

I should like to contend, by contrast, that the time has come not
only to question the details of the scenario, but also in significant
instances to reconsider what have too long stood as irrefutable certitudes. One cannot, of course, in the confines of a short paper rewrite
the history of second-temple Judaism. Indeed, I have no alternative
construct to offer, all limitations of time and space aside. Nor, for
reasons which will be clearer by the end of this paper, may we expect
ever to have a detailed picture of matters in which we might have the
most assured confidence. For the basic problem in the end lies not
merely in the interpretation of the evidence, but in what is to count as
evidence in the first place. Where we have facts we may always hope
better to understand them and their significance. If, on the other hand,
we erode the data base, then nothing (or little) remains to be interpreted, and consequently the only fact seems that, barring discovery of
new evidence, we cannot know many things regarding the second
temple period. To be sure, scholars and students might wish to specu-
late and extrapolate—with the proviso, however, that they continually
remind themselves and others that that is indeed what they are doing.

To illustrate the cogency of these contentions the remainder of the
paper will consider two cases, the Men of the Great Assembly and early
Ḥasidism. The choice is not meant to indicate that these two groups
have constituted the linchpins of accepted conceptions of second-
commonwealth Judaism—although they have not proven unimportant
either. Rather, they highlight in a straightforward manner some of the
basic methodological problems at hand. The former case, the Men of
the Great Assembly, raises the issue of which documents we may turn to
in expectation of reliable evidence. For example, one must ask whether
stories about the Men of the Great Assembly in a fifth or sixth century
compilation (such as the Babylonian Talmud) deserve *prima facie* the
same credence that narratives in literature from the second commonwealth itself would command. These and other related matters we shall
discuss in the second part.

Our discussion of the Ḥasidim involves us, by contrast, in issues of
textual exegesis. Here our concern will be not whether what is stated is
reliable, but, rather, determining precisely about what a passage or
document speaks. In particular, this second case raises the spectre of
what Arthur Darby Nock and Whitehead called the fallacy of misplaced concreteness.[2] Nock meant by this the tendency among scholars
of early Christianity to see in passages from early Christian and related
literature which evinced a preoccupation with "true knowledge"

---

2   A. D. Nock, "Gnosticism," in Nock, *Essays on Religion and the Ancient World*, ed. by
    Z. Stewart (Cambridge: Harvard, 1972), 944-45.

(*gnosis*) the literary remains of a Gnosticism. Certainly, held Nock, not every document or person seeking *gnosis*, knowledge, does so because of having come from an institutionalized, religious movement which we might call Gnosticism. Similarly, one must consider whether all pericope which value "the pious" (*heḥasid*) have in mind members of a Ḥasidism. These issues, then, will occupy us in the third section.

II

One would be hard pressed to find a modern history of the second commonwealth in which the Men of the Great Assembly—or the Great Synagogue—do not enjoy a principal place. Generally speaking, the Great Assembly, according to such works,[3] was establishing contemporaneous with or soon after Ezra's reformation in the fifth century B.C.E., constituting the major legislative body within the commonwealth until just prior to the Maccabean revolt in the former part of the second century B.C.E. This group, it is said, arose in response to the need to ramify the Torah-law. Ezra established the "Torah of Moses" as the constitution of the people. But the injunctions of the Torah could not, even in Ezra's time, provide an adequately specific political, social, and religious system. Hence, the Great Assembly, among others, worked to bridge that gap through exegesis of the Torah and promulgation of various edicts (*gezerot* and *taqanot*). Thus far the scholarly orthodoxy. To be sure, modern historians have disagreed about the details of this scenario. For example, the precise composition of the Great Assembly remained an ongoing issue of debate. Some, moreover, have doubted whether the Assembly constituted a standing body or one convened only at moments dictated by the necessity for some major legislative decision.[4] In all, however, the basic elements of the picture remain inviolate.

Admittedly, there exists no evidence, to my knowledge, which mitigates against presenting matters as we have just done. The role of the Great Assembly as normally portrayed, furthermore, fits neatly into the historical puzzle of emergent post-biblical Judaism. Among the perennial problems of some one hundred forty years of Judaic scholarship has been filling the gap between biblical law and religion on the one side and a rather different and considerably more developed Mishnaic and Talmudic law on the other. It is generally considered unreasonable to suppose that Mishnaic religion arose without antece-

---

3   See, e.g., J. Lauterbach, "Sanhedrin," *Jewish Encyclopedia*, vol. 11 (New York: KTAV, 1901), 41-44; J. Klausner, *Historiah Shel Bayit Sheni*, 5 vols. (Jerusalem: Ahiasat Press, 1951), see especially vol. 2: 35-40; G. Allon, *Mehqarim Betoldot Yisrael*, vol. 2 (Tel Aviv: Haqibuz Hameuhad, 1958), 155-56; S. Zeitlin, *The Rise and Fall of the Judean State*, vol. 1 (2nd ed.; Philadelphia: Jewish Publication Society, 1968), 24-25; M. Stern, "Yemai Habayit Hasheni," in H. H. Ben Sasson, ed., *Toldot Am Yisrael Bimai Qedem* (Tel Aviv: Devir, 1969), 184.

4   See especially the works of Lauterbach, Klausner, Allon and Stern cited in note 3.

dents (other than biblical literature) in the late first and second centuries C.E., especially since so much of Mishnah and other rabbinic documents contain legal materials of no practical value in the post-70 C.E. situation. I do not intend to debate here the merits of such suppositions about early rabbinism. That lies beyond the scope of this discussion. But given an entire scholarly field which consistently defined its problem to be the fleshing out of proto-rabbinic law, one may little wonder that the existence and role of the Great Assembly as outlined above should meet with ongoing acceptance.

Whatever the plausibility, which I do not question, of the scenario, the actual, relevant evidence remains, as we shall see, shockingly thin. What data we do have, furthermore, have been used in overly positivistic fashion. First, there exist no references to the "Great Assembly" in any documents dating from the fifth to second centuries B.C.E. Nor does the literature describe any institutionalized body remotely resembling the usual descriptions given of the Great Assembly. Second, no works from the Maccabean period to the approximate date of Mishnah's final redaction (circa 200 C.E.) refer to the "Great Assembly" (*pace* Allon),[5] although, by contrast, for this period there exists evidence from a variety of sources concerning the Sanhedrin (of which the Great Assembly was supposedly the antecedent).[6] One has, in fact, to wait until Mishnah (*Avot* 1:1-2) for any mention of the "Great Assembly." And the standard depictions of the institution's character and role find their basis in still-later rabbinic compilations. That is to say, the first references to this council come from documents some four hundred and more years removed from the supposed demise of the phenomenon about which these compilations speak. What is the historian to do with this type of evidence?

In this regard I think it instructive first to see how scholars have treated the data up until now. Here J. Klausner's writings may serve us well—particularly because his work represents *Wissenschaftliche* scholarship in its better modes, rather than in its excesses. Klausner states,[7]

There is no basis for concluding that the Men of the Great Assembly constituted a permanently standing institution [*mosad qavu'ah*] of 120 or 85 members. . . . But in spite of this there is, moreover, no reason to deny the existence of the Great Assembly altogether . . . or to view it as a single and unique gathering in the Hasmonean era [see n. 5 above]. The Mishnah [*Avot* 1:1-2] unambiguously states [*mishnah meforeshet*], "Moses received torah from Sinai and committed it to Joshua, and Joshua to the elders, and the elders to the

---

5   Allon, in *Mehqarim Betoldot Yisrael*, sees in the terms ἐκκλησία μεγάλη and συναγωγή μεγάλη (1 Macc. 5:16) references to the Great Assembly. I take Allon here to have committed the "fallacy of misplaced concreteness." The case in question appears parallel to that of the Hasideans (discussed at length in the third section).
6   See Lauterbach, "Sanhedrin."
7   Klausner, *Historiah Shel Bayit Sheni*, vol. 2: 36-37.

prophets, and the prophets committed it to the Men of the Great Assembly. They used to say three things: Be deliberate in judgement, and raise up many disciples, and make a fence around the Torah. Simeon the Righteous was among the last of the Great Assembly. . . ." These two Mishnaic passages alone are sufficient evidence to assuage any doubt concerning the existence of the Great Assembly. That the latter, furthermore, existed from the time of Ezra and Nehemiah and that the great gathering for the purpose of ratifying the covenant which took place at the time of these two figures is related to the Men of the Great Assembly is borne out by three biblical passages which the Talmud associates with the Men of the Great Assembly.

I cannot present and analyze all of the rabbinic sources to which Klausner refers or alludes in his work. I. Schiffer,[8] in any case, has done just this. More germane to our purpose, rather, is some critique of the contours of Klausner's argument as representative of a certain genre of historiography. Klausner seems not to be bothered by the fact that his conclusions about the Men of the Great Assembly stem solely from Mishnah and later rabbinic documents, even in the face of the seeming ignorance on the part of earlier literature concerning the Assembly. The scholars of whom Klausner is exemplary will indeed point to inner contradictions within the rabbinic literature and qualify accordingly their conclusions—but the principal epistemological assumption remains that rabbinic literature preserves accurate historical information.[9]

Given the present state of the art in the study of Late-Antique Judaism, these types of premises have become untenable. Such changes, I might add, are not the result simply of "healthy" scepticism replacing naïve credulity—as much as that might seem to be the case to the educated outsider watching historians of ancient Judaism "slug it out" anew. The *Wissenschaft* had reasons for its seemingly credulous stance, reasons grounded in notions about the origins, transmission, and redaction of rabbinic materials. Klausner and others generally accepted Sherira Gaon's claim that an ideology of meticulous preservation of traditions (*ipsissima verba*) governed the development of rabbinic literature.[10] They failed, however, to appreciate the apologetic

8 I. Schiffer, "The Men of the Great Assembly," in W. S. Green, ed., *Persons and Institutions in Early Rabbinic Judaism* (Missoula, Montana: Scholars Press, 1977).

9 To be entirely fair to antecedent scholarship, a few dissenting voices were raised among the scholars, most notably G. F. Moore in the 1920s and A. Kuenan in the 1870s. Their enlightened scepticism regarding the Great Assembly is not as surprising as the lack of impact their ideas had on the mainstream of historical scholarship through to the present day. See G. F. Moore, *Judaism in the First Centuries of the Christian Era*, vol. 1: 34; A. Kuenen, "Vebur die Männer der grossen Synagoge," in K. Budde, ed. and trans., *Gesammelte Abhandlungen zur biblischen Wissenschaft von Dr. Abraham Kuenen* (1894), 125-60.

10 For analyses of the methodologies of various *Wissenschaft* figures see J. Neusner, ed., *The Formation of the Babylonian Talmud* (Leiden: E. J. Brill, 1970); J. Neusner, ed., *The Modern Study of the Mishnah* (Leiden: E. J. Brill, 1973); J. Neusner, *The Talmud as History* (Montreal, 1978); J. Neusner, "Bibliographical Reflections," in J. Neusner

character of Sherira's own "historical" statements and of his sources. Systematic analysis of Mishnah, moreover, has substantially revised earlier conceptions of Mishnaic literature and of the origins of its present content and literary formulations.[11] We have just begun to appreciate the truly radical roles played by Mishnah's final redactors. Only in light of these recent insights do the once-reasonable assumptions of *Wissenschaftliche* scholars seem naïve.

To return to the issue at hand, it follows from our general remarks that a more appropriate stance to Mishnah *Avot* and later rabbinic materials about the Men of the Great Assembly ought to be one of extreme caution rather than confidence. That caution, or scepticism if you will, entails, and is reinforced by, close analyses of the sources. One will want to consider their literary character and provenance, their interests and *Tendenzen*, etc. *Avot* 1:1, for example, is integral both in form and content to the larger structure which it serves to introduce. That is to say, among other things, that we have not before us in 1:1-2 language which may be shown to be earlier than its greater literary context. The chain of tradition at 1:1-2, furthermore, constitutes part of *Avot*'s theological apologetic for the authority of rabbinic teachings and for Torah-study.[12]

None of these particular observations inspires confidence in *Avot* 1:1-2 as a reliable source for the history of Judaism in the early centuries of the second commonwealth or for the Great Assembly. And analyses of other relevant rabbinic sources would only reinforce our impressions. Are we to say, therefore, that we have proven the Great Assembly not to have existed? Of course not. The question itself betrays a misconception of the historian's task as, in part, distinguishing what certainly happened from what certainly did not. One can and must, however, formulate historical claims as probability statements with the appropriate qualifiers.[13] And the warrant, in our instance, for talking confidently about the existence, character, and role of an institution called the Great Assembly seems weak indeed.

III

The Ḥasidim or Hasideans have figured less importantly in the standard handbooks than the Men of the Great Assembly, although they remain far from insignificant in the histories of Late-Antique Judaism.[14]

(ed.), *The Rabbinic Traditions about the Pharisees before 70*, vol. 3 (Leiden: E. J. Brill, 1971).

11 See J. Neusner, *A History of the Mishnaic Law of Purities*, vol. 21 (Leiden: E. J. Brill, 1977). See also my introduction to J. Lightstone, *Yose the Galilean: I. Traditions in Mishnah-Tosefta* (Leiden: E. J. Brill, 1979).

12 See also Schiffer, "The Men of the Great Assembly."

13 Van A. Harvey, *The Historian and the Believer* (New York: Macmillan, 1966), 38-64.

14 Moore, *Judaism in the First Centuries of the Christian Era*; Schürer, *A History of the Jewish*

Most scholars have seen this pietistic movement as the immediate predecessor of Pharisaic Judaism and, therefore, by second remove of early Rabbinism as well. That the Dead Sea community and the Essenes too sprang from Hasidean ranks also finds not a few supporters. The group supposedly came into existence with the beginning of the Maccabean revolt, providing the initial popular support for the Hasmonean war against the Seleucid Empire and the Jewish Hellenizers. In short, they appear a major generative factor of important religious groups in Palestinian Judaism as well as of the "highpoint" of Judea's political history, the Hasmonean "State."

Again, however, it is surprising how thin the evidence for the existence of the Hasideans seems to be, depending, in this case, upon how one understands the texts and passages usually adduced as relevant data. To be sure, the Hebrew *hasid* and its other forms riddle the Hebrew Bible and rabbinic literature. These substantives no doubt appeared liberally in the original Hebrew and some of the Apocryphal and Pseudepigraphal literature as well. Matters, therefore, are completely unlike that state of affairs as regards the Great Assembly, in which case total silence was the problem—until Mishnah *Avot*. Our present difficulty seems a more subtle issue of hermeneutics. Ought we to render every instance of the word *hasid* with the simple noun, pious, or transliterate the Hebrew and turn the word into a proper noun, that is Hasid or Hasidean? Obviously, there is a world of difference. The latter implies the existence of an institutionalized movement or party which self-consciously sees itself as such; the former does not.

Of course, no scholars have wished to argue that every instance of *hasid* in the literature of the second commonwealth and the rabbinic period refers to a Hasidean movement. But not a few passages have generally been taken to provide evidence about just such a group—in almost every case with insufficient justification, to my mind.[15]

To clarify the issue an exemplary passage will serve us well. Mishnah Berakhot 5:1, one of the most commonly adduced (rabbinic) sources for the Hasideans, reads as follows:

1. They stand to pray only in a sober mood.
2. The pious of old (*hsdym hr'snym*) used to tarry for a time and [then] prayed, so that they might direct their minds (*lbm*) to Heaven.

People in the Time of Jesus; and Hengel, *Judaism and Hellenism*. See also E. Bickerman, *From Ezra to the Last of the Maccabees* (New YorkG Schocken, 1962), 128; Zeitlin, *The Rise and Fall of the Judean State*, 94ff.

15   A dissenting voice to the scholarly tradition about the Hasideans has, of late, been raised by P. Davies in his article, "Hasidism in the Maccabean Period," *Journal of Jewish Studies* 28 (1977), 127-40. His treatment is, in the main, exemplary, and I refer the reader to his rather more comprehensive discussion of the "Hasidic hypothesis." In addition, I leave the reader entirely in Davies' hands as regards 2 Macc. 14:6, with which I shall not deal explicitly. With regard to 1 Macc. 2:29 and 7:12-13, however, Davies in the end waffles; my own discussion below takes his treatment of these sources one step further.

Section one of the text provides a general rule. The second part relates, by way of precedent and example, how some particularly devout persons (*hasidim harishonim*) ensured their sobriety during prayer. While many have seen in the second section a reminiscence of the ritual of a Hasidic Judaism, few have seriously considered what indicators would warrant such an exegesis. Certainly, the words *hasid* or *hasidim* (in the absolute form) are in themselves of no help. For that matter, even the use of the *emphaticus* (*hehasid/or hahasidim*), which roughly corresponds in English to the use of a noun and definite article, cannot bear the burden of the existence of the Hasidean movement. Surely only the context in which the terms are used can help us distinguish between *hasid* as a simple noun and its use as a title for an institutionalized religious group. But not one of the commonly adduced sources, including the pericope we have cited, offers this type of clear contextual signpost.

In spite of this state of affairs, there are several sources which, nevertheless, unambiguously indicate that some persons in the ancient world believed there to be a Hasidean movement. The Greek text of 1 Maccabees (and parallel passages in 2 Maccabees) twice refers to a group of *'Asidaioi*. By transliterating what appears to be the Hebrew *hasidim* as opposed to translating it, there can be no doubt about at least this recension's intent. Indeed all of the other supposed sources for the Hasideans have, I suspect, been drawn in the wake of the passage from Maccabees. That is to say, scholars in all probability would never even have adduced pericope like Mishnah *Berakhot* 5:1 as evidence for the Hasideans were 1 (and 2) Maccabees not known to them. Still, the pericopae from Maccabees hardly are probative, as a closer examination of the sources will indicate.

1 Maccabees 2 tells of the massacre of a number of Jews who refused to bear arms on the Sabbath in their own defense, the Seleucid army having taken strategic advantage of the Jews' loyalty to Sabbath-law. Verses 2:39-44 continue:[16]

And when Mattathias and his friends knew of it they mourned greatly for them. And one said to another, "If we all do as our brethren have done, and do not fight against the Gentiles for our lives and our ordinances, they will soon destroy us from off the earth." And they took counsel on that day, saying, "Whosoever attacketh us on the Sabbath day, let us fight against him, that we may not in any case all die, as our brethren died in their hiding-places." Then were there gathered unto them a company of Chasidim ['Ασιδαίων][17] mighty

---

16   The translations of 1 Maccabees cited below are from R. H. Charles, ed., *The Apocrypha and Pseudepigrapha of the Old Testament* (Oxford: Clarendon Press, reprinted 1971).

17   *Cod. Sinaiticus* and *Cod. Alexandrinus* read, "The whole company of Jews." If, of course, the latter is the "original" Greek reading, then 1 Macc. 2:39ff. falls to the ground as a source for the Hasideans. Indeed, *Alexandrinus* and *Sinaiticus* are often considered the better texts (see Oesterly's introduction to 1 Maccabees in R. H.

men of Israel who willingly offered themselves for the Law, every one of them
And all they that fled from the evils were added unto them, and reinforced
them. And they mustered a host and smote sinners in their anger, and lawless
men in their wrath; and the rest fled to the Gentiles to save themselves.

Again at 1 Maccabees 7:12ff. one finds:

The Chasidim ['Aσιδαῖοι] were the first among the children of Israel that
sought peace from them [i.e., the pro-Seleucid party of Alcimus and Bac-
chides]; for they said, "One that is a priest of the seed of Aaron is come with the
[Seleucid] forces, and he will do us no wrong."

To be sure, the texts as we have them in Greek cannot but be taken
as referring to a Hasidean movement; but it is inaccurate to suppose
ipso facto that the author of 1 Maccabees held the same view of matters.
Scholars generally agree that the Greek recensions ultimately depend
upon Hebrew versions. Hence, in all likelihood, some form of the
Hebrew *hasidim* lies behind the translator's 'Asidaioi. This being the
case, the author's intentions appear ambiguous, even if those of the
translator do not—for versions in Hebrew, whatever their precise wording, of 1 Maccabees 2:39-44 and 7:12-14 would present the exegete
with much the same problem as passages like Mishnah *Berakhot* 5:1.
That is to say, only the context in which *hasidim* appears will warrant
talking about a Hasidean movement. The same canons adduced in our
discussion of the mishnaic pericope, therefore, must come into play in
the present circumstances—in spite of the Greek text's 'Asidaioi.

Assessed in such terms, the use of the word *hasidim* in 1 Macc.
2:29-44 looks very much part and parcel of 1 Maccabees' general
religious apologetic for the Hasmonean revolt and subsequent assumption of power, even when *hasidim* is taken as a simple noun. Those who
fought with Maccabees did so in defense of Torah and thereby evince
their piety as well as confirm the pious motives of the Hasmoneans
themselves. Their enemies, whether Jew or Gentile, are vilified as
Godless. So too, in 1 Macc. 7:12-14. The treachery and consequent im-
piety of the Jewish opponents of the Maccabees is contrasted with
the devout longing for peace and goodwill among the anti-Seleucid
faction. In sum, the larger context of the *hasidim*-passages of 1 Maccabees seems not to demand that we understand the term as anything
other than "the pious." With the exception of what subsequent Greek
translators thought, we seem, therefore, bereft of unambiguous evidence for the existence of a Hasidean movement—a shaky basis indeed

---

Charles, ed., *The Apochrypha*). I would, in any case, be prepared to give those who cite
1 Macc. 2:39ff. as evidence for the Hasideans the benefit of the doubt in this regard,
for the sake of argument. In this instance, however, I do not believe "the whole
company of Jews" to be the better reading, since it seems reasonable that some Greek
copyist of the verse, unable to make any sense of *Asidaioi* and doubting whether his
readers would find it any more comprehensible, would substitute "the whole company of Jews" for the foreign term.

upon which to build a history of Judaic sects in the second commonwealth.

<hr>
IV
<hr>

Just as our analyses of the evidence pertaining to the Men of the Great
Assembly and the Hasideans represent a prolegomenon only to a
general reassessment of Judaism in the second commonwealth, so too
our discussion of methodological pitfalls of previous scholarship in no
way constitutes a comprehensive critique of antecedent historiography. The wholesale acceptance of rabbinic materials about early
figures and institutions—whether originating in Sherira or not—and
the tendency to what Nock called the fallacy of misplaced concreteness
seem only symptomatic of the character of nineteenth and most
twentieth-century scholarship of ancient Judaism. It appears facile to
say, as I have too often, that our predecessors were "uncritical" in
contrast to ourselves. That ignores their own statements to the contrary
and their own struggle against tradition. In rallying under the banner
of the *Wissenschaft des Judentums* these historians clearly meant to place
themselves within the camp of "scientific historicism." If today myself
and others find their renditions inadequate, it is because the
methodology of criticism and interpretation moves forward, making
previous critical insights appear naïve fallacies. To paraphrase Collingwood,[18] there is a history of history.

The scholars of the *Wissenschaft*, corporately and as individuals,
established for themselves a body of historical facts which in accordance with contemporary historical sensitivities and hermeneutics they
laid out in a coherent pattern. These points of reference "pegged
down," again to borrow Collingwood's imagery,[19] their inferred historical reconstructions. In theory I do nothing different. Rather my and
others' sensitivities, culled from recent philosophy, anthropology,
psychology, and other disciplines, force us to reopen questions about
which pegs belong, how they are to be laid out, and what queries ought
to be asked of them. Admittedly, it seems simplistic to describe all such
shifts in analytic agenda as advances; to some extent our interests have
changed, as dictated by the forum in which the work proceeds. The
task of rewriting the history of Judaism in the second commonwealth in
particular and of Judaism in Late Antiquity in general ultimately must
become part of the history of history. But it must be done.

<hr>

18   R. G. Collingwood, *The Idea of History* (Oxford and New York: Oxford University
     Press, 1946), 231-49; reprinted in H. Meyerhoff, ed., *The Philosophy of History in our
     Time* (Garden City, New York: Doubleday, 1959), 66-84.
19   *Ibid.*

Jacob al-Kirkisani on the Reality of Magic and the Nature of the Miraculous: A Study in Tenth-Century Karaite Rationalism

IRA ROBINSON

INTRODUCTION

All religions based on a divine revelation face the problem of the legitimation of that revelation. One way of legitimizing revelation is the prophetic miracle, a supernatural wonder attending the revelation. However, the miracle itself, deemed by the believer to be proof of the legitimacy of revelation, can be construed differently by non-believers. These latter may prefer other explanations for the "miraculous" event. Particularly in societies in which occult and demonic powers are presumed to co-exist with the divine, the similarity of the "miracle" and feats of magic brought about either through natural causes unknown to the majority of the people or through manipulation of supernatural powers may cause the "miracle" to be subjected to a great deal of scepticism. There is, therefore, a nexus between miracle and magic which has to be reckoned with by the proponents of revealed religion. It is a nexus which has historically been noted by two groups: rationalist critics of religion and those religious believers living in eras and areas in which the folk religion attributed powers to beings other than the deity.

Believers in divine revelation, confronted by those two types of critics, had to find a way of authenticating revelation and differentiating between the true prophet, with a valid divine message, and the false

41

prophet. Thus, the authenticity of the prophetic miracle and the miracle/magic nexus in general became an issue. On the validity of the prophetic miracle rested, in part, the validity of the prophecy. In the debate over the differentiation between miracle and magic, revelation itself was at stake.

It is no surprise, therefore, that one of the greatest and most encyclopedic Karaite scholars of the early tenth century should deal with this issue. Writing in a period in which the integrity of biblical prophecy was challenged and undermined by both rationalist scepticism and popular belief in the efficacy of the occult arts, Jacob al-Kirkisani[1] chose to devote a major excursus in his *magnum opus, Kitāb al-Anwar wal-Marākib (The Book of Lights and Watchtowers)*, to the elucidation of the problems posed by the nexus of magic and miracle.[2] This excursus will constitute our main source in investigating the early Karaite attitude toward prophecy, magic, and miracle.

Before turning to an examination of Kirkisani's excursus, however, it is necessary to place his views on the subject in the context of his age by ascertaining as far as possible the attitudes of his predecessors and contemporaries, Rabbanite, Karaite, and Muslim.

I

The attitude of Rabbanite Jews contemporary with Kirkisani toward magic and its efficacy was in large measure a continuation of attitudes expressed in both Rabbinic and Apochryphal literature. The Torah in general,[3] and the names of God in particular,[4] were felt to contain great powers which could be unleashed by the initiate and employed for good or ill. This belief found its corollary in the widespread use of amulets employing divine names by Jews, as is amply attested in both Rabbinic and Patristic literatures.[5] The influence of divine names of Jewish origin in non-Jewish magical texts is likewise well attested.[6]

---

1 On Kirkisani, *see* Leon Nemoy, *Karaite Anthology* (New Haven, 1952), 42-45. On Karaism, see Zvi Ankori, *Karaites in Byzantium* (New York, 1959), chap. 1.
2 *Kitāb al-Anwar wal-Marākib* was edited and published in five volumes by Leon Nemoy (New York, 1939-1943). Kirkisani's excursus on magic and miracle was translated into French and annotated by Georges Vajda, "Etudes sur Qirqisani," *Révue des Etudes Juives* 106 (1946), 87-123.
3 Salo Baron, *Social and Religious History of the Jews*, vol. 8 (2nd ed.; New York, 1952 *et seq.*), 20-21. In the later Middle Ages, similar views were expressed by Kabbalists such as Abraham Abulafia and Moses b. Naḥman.
4 Ephraim Urbach, *The Sages—Their Concepts and Beliefs* (Hebrew) (Jerusalem, 1971), 81-114. Ludwig Blau, *Das altjudische Zauberwesen* (Strassburg, 1898). Cf. also Samuel Cohon, "The Name of God: A Study in Rabbinic Theology," *Hebrew Union College Annual* 23, part 1 (1950-1951), 579-604.
5 Urbach, *The Sages*, 110 and the sources cited there. A. Lukyn Williams, *Adversus Judaeos* (Cambridge, England, 1935), 132.
6 Urbach, *The Sages*, 106. Cf. Gershom Scholem, *Jewish Gnosticism, Merkaba Mysticism and the Talmudic Tradition* (New York, 1965), 65ff.

Although Rabbinic literature shied away from advocating the employment of occult practices and even seemed, in certain passages, to be sensitive to the problem posed by the miracle/magic nexus,[7] the authority of the Babylonian academies which propagated the ideology of Rabbinic literature was not universal, and there are a number of instances of syncretistic and magical beliefs among Jews. These beliefs expressed themselves notably in the messianic movement of Abu Issa al-Isfahani and his disciple, Yudghan, in Iran.[8]

In this era, the sixth through the eighth centuries C.E., a Jewish magical literature flourished. Some of the works of magic of that era *Harba de-Moshe* (*The Sword of Moses*) and *Sefer ha-Razim* (*The Book of Secrets*) are still extant.[9] In these books the use of the names of God and the angels in their manifold permutations was seen as a fecund source for magical formulae designed to be used in many different situations.

Just as in classical literature Egypt was considered the main source of sorcery, so Babylonia was the home of the occult for Jews of the post-Talmudic era.[10] Moses ha-Kohen, a leading Babylonian teacher, was a reputed practitioner of the occult arts.[11] Joseph b. Judah, another Babylonian, prided himself on his visions of Elijah.[12] From Babylonia, magical practices were transferred by Jewish emissaries to Byzantium.[13] In Byzantine-controlled Sicily in the eighth century, the sorcerer Heliodorus was said to owe his occult knowledge to a Babylonian Jew. This Jew had given him an amulet with which he claimed he could master the devil himself.[14] Another such Babylonian Jewish emissary of the occult was Aaron of Baghdad, in the ninth century, whose feats of magic were recorded in the *Megillat Aḥimaaẓ*.[15]

The writings of the Babylonian *gaonim* have much to say concerning the magical beliefs and practices of contemporary Jews. In particular a responsum of Hai Gaon (939-1038 C.E.) to a question addressed to him by the leaders of the North African Jewish community of Kairouan reveals a great deal concerning the contemporary attitude toward the occult. The questioners enumerated a number of different types of magical feats about which they had heard, and they wanted Hai to tell

7   *Talmud Bavli, Berakhot*, ff. 6b, 9b. Cf. Urbach, *The Sages*, 86.
8   See Nemoy, *Karaite Anthology*, 51; Benzion Dinur, *Yisrael ba-olah*, vol. 1, part 2, 228-34. Cf. Baron, *Social and Religious History*, vol. 8: 4.
9   *Harba de-Moshe* was published and translated into English by Moses Gaster in his *Studies and Texts* (2nd ed.; New York, 1971). *Sefer ha-Razim* was edited by Mordecai Margoliot (Jerusalem, 1967).
10 The "center" of sorcery in Babylon was supposed to be the palace of Nebuchadnezzar. B. Lewin, *Oẓar ha-Geonim*, vol. 4, *Ḥagiga* (Jerusalem, 1931), 20.
11 *Ibid.* Cf. Baron, *Social and Religious History*, vol. 8: 7.
12 *Ibid.*
13 Lewin, *Oẓar*, vol. 4: 16, 20.
14 Baron, *Social and Religious History*, vol. 11: 140.
15 Adolph Neubauer, ed., *Mediaeval Jewish Chronicles*, vol. 2 (2nd ed.; Jerusalem, 1967), 112-14.

them whether such feats were possible. Was it possible to invoke the
name of God in order to perform such miraculous feats as making
oneself invisible to others, calming a raging sea, or traversing great
distances in a short time?[16] The Kairouanese leaders also reported to
Hai that there were men who claimed to be able to induce visions of the
celestial *Hekhalot*,[17] as well as people who claimed to practice a form of
divination through the interpretation of dreams.[18] What of them? The
questioners also described the occult literature available to them, a list
which Hai was able to supplement, commenting that such works were
"quite numerous" in his locality.[19]

However, of all the questions which concerned the men of
Kairouan, the one which seemed to bother them the most cut to the
heart of the miracle/magic nexus: "What is the explanation of this [feat
of magic] and how can the hand of sinners be so strengthened as to
perform those feats which appear to the beholder to be similar to the
acts of prophecy. What is the difference between the acts of prophecy
and those of sorcery?"[20] It was this question to which Hai devoted the
major part of his responsum. A moderate rationalist in matters of
halakha,[21] Hai conceded the existence of angels and demons unseen by
the human eye,[22] and admitted the magical efficacy of the name of God
when properly employed.[23] However, when it came to the question of
the similarity of miracle and magic, Hai took a strong stand in denying
the claims of the magicians.[24] He warned his readers not to believe such
claims, especially those brought forward by men claiming the prophet's
mantle.[25]

How, then, is one to differentiate between magic and miracle? In
his answer, Hai posited that feats of magic either involved no abroga-
tion of normal processes of nature, or else constituted an act within the
power of a created being, be it angel or demon. A prophetic miracle is
not so. It has to be something beyond the power of created beings to
achieve and must involve a disruption of nature (*minhag ha-'olam*).[26]

Hai's father-in-law, the Gaon Samuel b. Ḥofni, likewise denied
that a miracle would be vouchsafed to any but a prophet, thus going
beyond Hai's formulation, for Hai had asserted that it would be entirely possible for God to cause miracles for righteous people who had

---

16   Lewin, *Oẓar*, vol. 4: 16, 20.
17   *Ibid.*, 14.
18   *Ibid.*, 16-17.
19   *Ibid.*, 20-21.
20   *Ibid.*, 18.
21   Baron, *Social and Religious History*, vol. 8: 27.
22   Lewin, *Oẓar*, vol. 4: 19.
23   *Ibid.*, 22.
24   *Ibid.*, 23-25. Pages 24-25 deal specifically with the interpretation of dreams.
25   *Ibid.*, 26-27.
26   *Ibid.*, 26.

not achieved the level of prophecy.[27] Both Hai and Samuel agreed, however, that the ability to change the course of nature is a power reserved to God and employed only on behalf of his prophets. Thus a mere necromancer, like the woman of En-Dor (1 Sam. 28), would be powerless to resurrect the prophet Samuel.[28]

Saadia b. Joseph Gaon, like Hai, seems to have avoided direct disapproval of many of the magical practices current among the Rabbanite Jews of his time.[29] Like Hai, he also strongly differentiated between miracle and magic in his interpretation of the competition between Moses and the sorcerers of Egypt (Exod. 7-9).[30]

Beyond the opinion which assimilated miracle into magic, which Saadia attempted to refute, there was yet another school of thought on prophecy which Saadia felt the need to confront. Some of Saadia's rationalistic contemporaries held that men had no need of prophecy or revelation since reason alone is a sufficient guide for human actions.[31] These rationalists posed a threat different from that posed by believers in the efficacy of the occult. Believers in the occult, while they may have been hazy concerning the line of demarcation between miracle and magic, nonetheless believed in the possibility of miracles. For the rationalistic sceptics, however, there was no such thing as a miracle. All supposed miracles were open to a naturalistic explanation.[32] This sceptical tradition, which can be traced from Celsus in the second century[33] to the school of the tenth century Muslim thinker, Ibn al-Rawandi,[34] attacked revealed religion by attempting to place prophets and their alleged miracles in the same category as magicians and their feats.

Saadia's opponent in his polemic against rationalistic scepticism was a Jew named Hiwi al-Balkhi, whose views on the Bible and on the miracles recorded therein were widely discussed and refuted in the Jewish world.[35] Hiwi's work on the Bible is lost, but from what can be reconstructed of his work from Saadia's polemic, we find that he "naturalized" biblical miracles including the parting of the sea,[36] the

27   *Ibid.*, 15, 18.
28   *Ibid.*, 3. A practically identical formulation is found in a document from the Cairo Geniza edited by Louis Ginzburg, *Ginze Schechter*, vol. 1 (New York, 1928), 300.
29   Baron, *Social and Religious History*, vol. 8: 29.
30   Saadia b. Joseph Gaon, *Sefer Emunot ve-Deot* III.5. Cf. Samuel Rosenblatt, trans., *Book of Beliefs and Opinions* (New Haven, 1948), 152-53.
31   Saadia, *Emunot ve-Deot* III.4. Rosenblatt, *Book of Beliefs and Opinions*, 150.
32   Georges Vajda, "An Unknown Rationalistic Explanation of Miracles from the Middle Ages" (Hebrew), *Hagut Ivrit be-Europa* (Tel-Aviv, 1969), 72-73.
33   Lynn Thorndike, *History of Magic and Experimental Science*, vol. 1 (New York, 1923), 437-38.
34   P. Krauss, "Beitrage zur Islamischen Ketzergeschichte: Das *Kitab az-Zammurrud* des Ibn ar-Rawandi," *Revista degli Studii Orientali* 14 (1934), 124.
35   Cf. Israel Davidson, *Saadia's Polemic Against Hiwi al-Balki* (New York, 1915); Jacob Mann, *Collected Articles*, vol. 3 (Gedera, Israel, 1971), 43-44.
36   Davidson, *Saadia's Polemic*, 98-99.

manna,[37] and the "shining" of Moses' face.[38] Apparently he also saw the change in the name of the first patriarch from Abram to Abraham as a form of magical practice.[39] Clearly, in the tenth-century Jewish world, the integrity of biblical prophecy was being attacked on several fronts.

When considering the Karaite stand on the miracle/magic nexus, the first point to bear in mind is that the early tenth-century Karaite scholar was decidedly rationalistic in inclination. Thus, one Kariate biblical commentator denied entirely the existence of demons (*shedim*).[40] This rationalistic stance, however, is expressed mostly in the context of the anti-Rabbanite polemic in which the Karaite polemicists denounced what they felt to be the irrational, superstitious practices of Rabbanite Judaism.

An important element in this polemical context was the Rabbanite acquiescence in the belief in astrology, the practice of which had been forbidden by 'Anan b. David who felt that it was included in the biblical prohibition against divination and soothsaying (Lev. 19:26).[41] The differing calendrical practices of Karaites and Rabbanites must also be seen in this context since it caused Karaite scholars, like Daniel al-Kumisi[42] and Judah Hadassi[43] to link Rabbanite astronomical practices to astrology and, hence, to sorcery.

In at least one Karaite source, Rabbanite Judaism as a whole is compared to idolatry.[44] In many Karaite condemnations of Rabbanite practices, the use of amulets and magical formulae are often included, supplemented at times by lists of Rabbanite books of magic.[45] Likewise, the Rabbanite custom of visiting graves of saintly people with their petitions was roundly condemned as a magical, idolatrous practice by Sahl b. Masliah[46] and Judah Hadassi.[47]

Thus, the comparative leniency shown by the Rabbanite leadership toward popular Jewish magical beliefs and practices was grist for the Karaite propaganda mill. That does not mean, however, that the problem of the verification of prophecy was not also a bothersome issue to them. The statement of Benjamin al-Nahawandi that he was "neither a prophet nor the son of a prophet," but merely "one of the

37   *Ibid.*, 101-102.
38   *Ibid.*, 102.
39   *Ibid.*, 62, note 42.
40   Jacob Mann, *Texts and Studies*, vol. 2 (Philadelpha, 1935), 100, app. 6.
41   Simha Assaf, *Tekufat ha-Geonim ve-Sifrutah* (Jerusalem, 1967), 119-20.
42   Abraham Harkavy, *Likkutei Kadmoniot*, vol. 2 (St. Petersburg, 1903), 189. Mann, *Texts and Studies*, vol. 2: 75-76, 79, app. 1.
43   Judah Hadassi, *Eshkol ha-Kofer* (Gozlow, 1836), f. 43b (alphabet 104).
44   Mann, *Collected Articles*, vol. 3: 387.
45   Ankori, *Karaites in Byzantium*, 282-83; Mann, *Texts and Studies*, vol. 2: 75-82, app. 1; Salmon b. Yeruham, *Sefer Milhamot ha-Shem*, ed. by Israel Davidson (New York, 1914), 111, lines 45-52.
46   Mann, *Texts and Studies*, vol. 2: 387-88. Cf. Nemoy, *Karaite Anthology*, 115.
47   Hadassi, *Eshkol ha-Kofer*, f. 43a (alphabet 104).

thousands and ten thousands of Israel,"[48] seems to have been a reaction
to widespread popular beliefs, still extant in the tenth century, in the
messianic sectarian leaders Abu Issa and Yudghan, both of whom
claimed to be prophets and to have performed miracles.[49] Such beliefs
in the medieval Jewish community were invariably countered and
suppressed by the Jewish communal leadership.[50] Nonetheless, among
extant Karaite works, it is only Kirkisani who discusses the problems
inherent in the miracle/magic nexus in a full and systematic manner.
Kirkisani's excursus on magic and miracle will be discussed fully in the
second part.

In Islamic literature, the magic/miracle nexus was discussed by Ibn
Waḥshiyya, who wrote a work entitled "The Nabatean Agriculture" in
904. That work purported to give an account of the religion of ancient
Babylonia against which the patriarch Abraham rebelled. In that book
the ancient Babylonians were said to have denied the divine nature of
miracles and to have asserted that supposed miracles were in actuality
tricks based on the marvellous properties inherent in certain plants.[51]

Mostly, however, the Muslims discussed the miracle/magic nexus
in the context of the miracles recorded in the *Quran*. Thus al-Ghazzali
considered that there was no strict dichotomy between magic and
miracle. For him, the occult was a valid science, and in his classification
of the natural sciences he included judicial astrology, dream interpretation, the talismanic art, and the art of incantation.[52] He felt that the
prophet was one who, by virtue of his special qualities, is in touch with
the powers of the occult. Miracles performed by a prophet, therefore,
cannot be used to verify belief in divine revelation.[53] That miracles *per
se* cannot constitute an absolute verification of a prophetic mission was
assumed by the Mutazilite school of the Kalam.[54]

On the other hand, al-Shahrastani, while he agreed that magic had
an objective existence, argued that there was indeed a palpable difference between magic and miracle. A sorcerer, in order to perform a feat
of magic, must make elaborate preparations beforehand and exert
himself with bodily movements and incantations in order to succeed.
Therefore, according to Shahrastani, there is no possibility of an ob-

---

48 This statement is cited by Yefet b. Ali, cf. Ankori, *Karaites in Byzantium*, 214.
49 See note 8, above.
50 See especially Moses b. Maimon, *'Iggeret Teman*, for an expression of the attitude of
    the Jewish communal leadership toward messianic activism.
51 Cited in Moses b. Maimon, *Guide of the Perplexed* III.29. Cf. Schlomo Pines, introduc-
    tion to Moses Maimonides, *Guide of the Perplexed* (Chicago, 1963), cxxiii.
52 Al-Ghazzali, *Tahafut al-Tahafut*, ed. and trans. by S. Van den Bergh, vol. 1 (Oxford,
    1954), 311. Cf. al-Shahrastani, *The Summa Philosophiae of Al-Shahrastani*, ed. and
    trans. by A. Guillaume (Oxford, 1934), 134.
53 Al-Ghazzali, *Tahafut al-Tahafut*, vol. 2: 176. Cf. Moses b. Maimon, *Mishneh Torah,
    Hilkhot Yesodei ha-Torah* 8:1-3.
54 Cf. Van den Bergh, *Tahafut al-Tahafut*, vol. 2: 124, who claims that this view was held
    also by Baqullani of the Asharite school of the Kalam.

server confusing sorcery with a true miracle. A miracle makes clear to all that it must be the act of God, attesting to the truth of his prophet.[55]

It is against this background of contemporary thought on the miracle/magic nexus that we have to evaluate Jacob al-Kirkisani's discussion of the subject.

II

Kirkisani devoted chapters nine through eleven of book six of his *Kitāb al-Anwar wal-Marākib* to the discussion of magic and miracle. He began with a description of the claims put forward by the practitioners of the magical arts. These men were identified by him specifically as Rabbanite Jews, thus putting his remarks squarely within the context of the anti-Rabbanite polemic which, as we have seen, greatly influenced the Karaite discussion of the theme. These Rabbanite magicians claimed to have produced, by occult means, the transformation of elements, the inducing of love or hate between two people, and diseases or cures in people without the aid of drugs.[56] These things, the magicians claimed, were brought about through the manipulation of divine names.

Immediately, Kirkisani pointed out the danger inherent in these claims. In a statement similar to that of Hai Gaon,[57] he warned that once one believes in the reality of the occult arts, it becomes impossible to distinguish a prophet, whose mission is verified by miracles, from a sorcerer. Thus the certainty of the prophet's mission, and of revealed religion itself, would be in jeopardy.

In response to this important challenge to the integrity of Judaism, Kirkisani arose to combat those who would assimilate prophecy and miracle into the classification of magic. True to the form of medieval polemical literature, Kirkisani first set forth carefully the arguments of his opponents before proceeding to refute them.

The first argument Kirkisani attributed to his opponents was that there are certain materials in nature, like the lodestone,[58] which seem to operate contrary to the natural order of things. These materials are known to many but not to all men. Why could there not, therefore, exist other materials of an equally wonderous nature, whose properties are known only to a few men? Would not these men be able to exploit these wonderous but little known materials in order to claim leadership over their brethren under the guise of prophecy?[59] Thus Moses and Aaron, in their confrontation with the sorcerers of Pharaoh's court, were

---

55 Al-Shahrastani, *Summa Philosophiae*, 138.
56 Cf. the works cited in note 9, above.
57 Lewin, *Ozar*, vol. 4: 18.
58 For an example of the use of the lodestone in a similar context, see Solomon ibn Adret, *Responsa* a/413 (Bnei Brak, 1958).
59 Cf. Moses b. Maimon, *Guide of the Perplexed* II.36.

superior to them merely because they were better versed in the properties of various *materia occulta*.

Another argument Kirkisani's opponents were said to have brought forward was the case of the woman necromancer of En-Dor, who was supposed to have been able to bring the spirit of Samuel back from the dead by means of the occult. The final argument of these opponents derives from the description of the false prophet in Deut. 13:2ff., in which the possibility that the "sign" of the false prophet may indeed come to pass is treated seriously.

It is significant that Kirkisani began his refutation of these arguments with counter-arguments based on the dictates of reason. Proofs from scripture were dealt with afterwards *seriatim*.

According to Kirkisani, the philosophers possessed an encyclopedic knowledge of nature, which they derived from the prophets.[60] Had they known of the existence of these *materia occulta* and their special virtues, they would surely have mentioned them in their works. Furthermore, they had heard of the prophetic miracles and did not refute them. Had they been able to demonstrate that these "miracles" were in fact due to natural causes, they would have refuted these miraculous claims in their books. That they did not do so indicated that they were not able to do so.

Anticipating the logical objection that prophetic miracles have been accepted without sufficient examination of the possible natural causes of the event, Kirkisani asserted that there are some natural phenomena, like death, which must be accepted as true even by those ignorant of the totality of natural phenomena. Such a self-evident phenomenon, argued Kirkisani, is prophecy and the attendant phenomenon of the prophetic miracle. Moreover, Kirkisani asserted that the example of the lodestone is not really apposite, since divine miracles, such as the dividing of the sea, are manifestly such as could only be performed by God.[61]

Regarding the biblical accounts which seem to admit the reality of magic, Kirkisani was just as adamant in his refutation of his opponents' arguments. In the case of the confrontation of Moses and the sorcerers of Pharaoh, the Egyptian magicians indeed made it appear that, in response to the metamorphosis of Moses' staff, they were able to transform their rods into serpents. Thus, according to Kirkisani's opponents, the power of Moses and of the Egyptians was of the same type, though Moses' occult power was far superior. In his response, Kirkisani used the same basic argument as in the case of the lodestone. Pharaoh, like the philosophers, would certainly have unmasked Moses as a charlatan and a mere magician had he been able to do so. He could

---

60 Cf. Seymour Feldman, "Aristotle in Jewish Legend," *Encyclopedia Judaica*, vol. 3 (Jerusalem, 1970), col. 448-49.
61 Cf. Al Shahrastani, *Summar Philosophiae*, 138.

not do this, however. Moreover, God, in order to unmask the Egyptian sorcerers, made Moses' serpent eat theirs. Having proved his case through reason, Kirkisani then proceeded to argue the case on the basis of scriptural evidence. He thus observed that the biblical narrative distinguished between the feats of Moses and Aaron and those of the Egyptians, since the latter performed their feats "*be-lahatehem*," imply-ing artifice and illusion,[62] and their rods were transformed "*le-taninim*," which Kirkisani interpreted as merely "in the *likeness* of serpents."

The first two plagues brought upon Egypt, blood and frogs, saw an attempt by Pharaoh's sorcerers to match the feats of Moses and Aaron. These attempts demonstrated a major difference between divine and man-made wonders—the difference of scale. Moses and Aaron trans-formed all the waters of Egypt into blood. The Egyptians, on the other hand, were able to transform only minute quantities of water from cisterns and wells. The Egyptians could well have used a material which has the property of changing water to the likeness of blood. However, it would have been a physical impossibility to do something similar to all the waters of Egypt. The very scale of a miracle, therefore, is a proof of its divine origin. The same thing is true of the plague of frogs.[63]

Kirkisani offered two explanations for the incident of the necro-mancer of En-Dor. The first, essentially identical to that of Samuel b. Hofni Gaon,[64] makes her out to be a ventriloquist who merely pre-tended to make Samuel appear. The voice Saul heard was that of the woman. The "prophecy" put into "Samuel's" mouth that Saul and his sons would die in battle the next day was merely a matter of common sense prognostication on the part of the woman, based on her knowl-edge of the relative strengths of the Israelite and Philistine armies.[65] Kirkisani's second solution also denies the woman any actual occult powers. In this version, God, who had up to that moment refused to answer Saul, did so. It was he and not the woman who brought up the spirit of Samuel from the dead, and when Samuel appeared, the woman was just as amazed as Saul.

When the "sign" of the false prophet of Deuteronomy does come to pass, this does not mean, according to Kirkisani, that a true miracle has been accomplished. In a formulation once again similar to that of Hai Gaon,[66] Kirkisani asserted that the "sign" of the false prophet consists of an earthquake or some similar natural occurrence, which could be predicted by anyone with knowledge of the natural signs portending such an event. The accomplishment of such a prediction of an event belonging to the natural order of events cannot validate a

---

62   Cf. Abraham ibn Ezra, commentary on Exodus 7, 11.
63   Cf. Saadia, *Emunot ve-Deot* III.5; Rosenblatt, *Book of Beliefs and Opinions*, 152-53.
64   Cf. Lewin, *Oẓar*, vol. 4: 2-5.
65   Cf. Levi b. Gerson, commentary on 1 Sam. 28:19.
66   Cf. Lewin, *Oẓar*, vol. 4:19.

prophetic mission. Apparently not quite satisfied with this position, Kirkisani proposed an alternative explanation in which the false prophet overheard the predictions of a true prophet and passed them off as his own in order to gain a position of leadership.

In his summary of chapter nine, Kirkisani asserted that whatever scriptural difficulties were present in differentiating between miracle and magic, the essential factor was belief through rational proofs in God, creator of the universe, in the authenticity of the Torah, and in the divine mission of the prophets. Given these beliefs, scriptural difficulties become secondary. This attitude, the very paradigm of the approach of medieval Jewish rationalism, meant that scriptural problems need not be a matter of essential concern: any scriptural detail which does not seem to fit into a rationalist interpretation implies a fault in our understanding rather than in the detail itself.[67]

The remainder of Kirkisani's excursus, a condemnation of sorcery, is once again very much in the spirit of the Karaite-Rabbanite polemic.

Chapter ten deals with various forms of augury which the Gentiles and some Rabbanite Jews held to be proper, according to Kirkisani. The Rabbanite Jews argued from scripture that Eliezer, the servant of Abraham, used a form of divination in order to choose of wife for Isaac (Genesis 24). They also claimed that Jonathan had used divination in the incident recounted in 1 Sam. 14:8ff. Kirkisani countered these arguments by asserting that all forms of augury and divination are included in the biblical term *kesem*. If one form of *kesem* is prohibited, then all forms, even those not specifically enumerated in the biblical prohibition, must be forbidden. Furthermore, neither Eliezer nor Jonathan had practiced divination as far as Kirkisani was concerned. They had rather requested that God should provide them with a sign that their mission would succeed. This request was granted them by God.

Chapter eleven of the excursus deals with astrology. In the beginning of this chapter, Kirkisani divided the science of the stars into two categories—one licit, the other prohibited. The licit study of the stars, for Kirkisani, has to do with calculating the motion of the spheres, the movement of the planets and stars, etc. It is a study of objects which make no pretence to control human actions. Judicial astrology is the unlawful study of the stars, included by Kirkisani under the prohibition of *kesem*. Since judicial astrology deals with the determination of future events, it would therefore constitute a rival to prophecy, the only legitimate way men may learn of the events of the future. To the objection that astrologers often make correct predictions, which seemed to many to indicate that astrology is a valid means of predicting the future, Kirkisani replied that the fact that it is prohibited in the

---

67   Cf. Moses b. Maimon, *Guide of the Perplexed*, Introduction.

Torah should be sufficient. Moreover, the correct predictions made by astrologers are made not from astrological calculations, but from their reason and common sense, as in the case of the prediction of the woman of En-Dor. Furthermore, the correct predictions of the astrologers are more than balanced by their incorrect ones. Astrology, thus, is not a true science. The astrologers disagree among themselves and some philosophers deny outright the validity of astrology.

Even if one should assume that there was some reality behind the claims of the astrologers, Kirkisani continued, there would be no contradiction between God creating something and then forbidding its use. Furthermore, assuming that the stars have power over the fate of mankind in general, Israel, under the personal protection of God, is immune from astral influence.[68]

Kirkisani then considered the possibility of the study of magic for theoretical purposes. He condemned such study as a waste of time which could more profitably be spent in the study of the Torah. He did admit that such study could be undertaken, however, provided that it would not interfere with Torah study and provided further that the purpose of this study of magic would be to recognize its falsity and to refute its claims. Kirkisani concluded with the general statement that magic is all illusion and artifice and possesses no objective reality. Any claims for the reality of magic must be exposed and refuted.

III

In Kirkisani's excursus on magic and miracle, we have been able to observe an early tenth-century Karaite rationalist at work. Using the tools of reason and scriptural analysis, he attempted to defend divine revelation and prophecy against two sorts of critics: those who would deny their reality from the point of view of a radical rationalism and those who would assimilate the phenomenon of prophecy into the corpus of occult phenomena.

In his defense of the validity of prophecy, Kirkisani argued against the rationalist radicals that true miracles could not be reduced to natural elements. Against the opinion that magic and miracle were part of the same phenomenon, he asserted that magic was not, contrary to popular belief, a real entity. Through artifice, small scale tricks might be performed which appear miraculous. However, there is a differentiation in both scale and kind between such illusions and a true miracle.

It has been noted that much of this argumentation was paralleled in contemporary Rabbanite argumentation on the same subject. This bespeaks a Karaite-Rabbanite intellectual contact which was no less real

---

68 Cf. the Talmudic formulation, "*eyn mazal le-Yisrael*" and its interpretations, *Bavli, Shabbat*, f. 156a.

than the polemical barbs each camp hurled at the other. It also demonstrates the similar concerns of religious rationalists out to counter the arguments of the same sorts of critics of the validity of prophecy.

Nonetheless, there is a difference between Kirkisani and the Rabbanite scholars on the subject of the magic/miracle nexus which goes beyond the polemics present in the excursus. Hai and the other Rabbanites stopped short at a complete denial of the reality of magic. Whether they were afraid of alienating the broad sectors of the Rabbanite community which subscribed to magical beliefs or not, their stand was one of compromise. They did not venture to take the uncompromising stand espoused by the intellectual leaders of the Karaites, which received its most detailed exposition at the hands of Jacob al-Kirkisani.

A Key to Nineteenth-Century Critical Attitudes Toward Religion? The Work of Jean Jacques Rousseau

MICHEL DESPLAND

INTRODUCTION

The nineteenth century stands out in the religious, intellectual and social history of the West because of the spread of critical attitudes toward religion. The liberal Protestant school of theology tries to reinterpret Christian faith and secure its epistemological bases in the post-Kantian context. Numerous thinkers wrestle with loss of faith and with the problems of religious belief in a context of deep moral seriousness. Utopian reconstructions of society are proposed or experimented with, and they all include some definitive solution of the religious question. The scientific-historical-critical study of religions, their scriptures and their histories, also gets going in earnest. What are now called the classical anthropological and sociological approaches to the field have practically all their origin in the nineteenth century. Besides such developments among the learned, we should also note the broad cultural realities: European legislatures keep seeking some fresh equilibrium between the traditional expectations of the dominant religious groups and the aspirations of religious minorities and intellectual dissenters. The religious—or the a-religious—education of the masses is the object of vast strategies and earnest efforts. Religion has become a public issue in quite a new sense.

Much work has been recently done on various aspects of nineteenth-century religious life. No one, however, has been bold or foolish enough to undertake telling the whole story. One has written

55

histories of Catholic or of Protestant theology, histories of Church-
State relations, histories of secularization, or histories of religious
motifs in the romantic literary school or the nineteenth-century novel.
Can a common theme be found to organize all these histories?

The work of Jean Jacques Rousseau may well offer such a key. I
need not document how his influence spread all over Europe, as indeed it did. I rather intend to suggest that in his work some new
themes find expression, and a new manner of writing in religious
matters finds a voice that expresses deep and vastly shared tendencies
of the age. The essay has three parts: I first give an exposition of the
relevant themes in Rousseau's work; I then try to interpret the significance of this work; and in the last part I formulate a hypothesis that
might be useful for a systematic examination of the nineteenth-
century evidence.

I

"Man is born free; and everywhere he is in chains."[1] With such a
sentence Rousseau announces as obvious fact something that, in reality, is a recent discovery: Europeans have just seen—or started to
believe—that culture is an historical phenomenon. Man, they now
think, is living in and shaped by a man-made environment. A radical
question is also asked about the quality of this environment. Rousseau
undertakes to say how this came to be. His new way of looking at man,
his nature, and destiny, is articulated by means of a story. Man used to
be a certain kind of being. He then became different. Five original
themes emerge in his narration.

1. The hiatus between nature and freedom: "The principle of
any action is to be found in the will of a free being." *Emile* is categori-
cal: "one cannot go beyond that."[2] With this affirmation of human
freedom Rousseau destroyed the world in which ethics, politics, and
religion, as well as literature and philosophy, were traditionally cast.
Man is invited to become aware of his will (rather than contemplate
and submit to a necessary order). The unity and coherence of Rousseau's work hangs upon the affirmation of the freedom proper to
man. The animal is enclosed in his nature and his behaviour is dictated by instinct. Man, however, determines his behaviour as a free
agent. The ancient view of human nature as a dynamic, end-oriented
norm is replaced by an entirely new one: human nature amounts only
to a simple, animal-like functioning, which can be posited as existing
in the origins but does not hold the key to an understanding of man's
present condition. The essence of man is rather to be seen as a nega-

---

1 Jean Jacques Rousseau, *Contrat Social*, III: 351. (Roman numerals refer to the
   volumes published in the Pleiade edition, Paris: NRF.)
2 Jean Jacques Rousseau, *Emile*, bk. 4, IV: 586.

tive freedom: men differ from animals thanks to the absence of determination for their conduct. The new vision of man has something
exalting. "It is a great and beautiful sight to see man coming out of
nothingness so to speak by his own efforts, and lifting himself above
himself."[3] It is easy for us to point out that the state of nature rejected
by Rousseau is not what the ancients meant by life according to nature. The contrast made by Rousseau nevertheless takes hold upon
the mind; what men freely make of themselves and of each other
becomes the paramount question.

2. Historical becoming: Rousseau undertakes to show how
human beings broke from nature and innovated in their behaviour.
The need to work—and to organize socially—to meet difficult circumstances and defeat hunger is presented as the hinge. The use of
reason also appears in the course of that crisis. The need to work, the
birth of society, and the development of reason thus are presented as
simultaneous occurences. Rousseau never misses a chance to sharpen
the contrast. Socialization is a genuine metamorphosis of man. Social
man is denatured man. Human beings *became* rational.

One must first of all stress the convincing power of the description of this basic metamorphosis: "amour de soi," self-preserving affirmation, is being overlaid with "amour propre," that is the "fureur
de se distinguer." Man in society has an image of himself which he
compares with his view of others and which he "needs" to protect;
there is henceforth a quality of strain and competitiveness in self-love.
There is no telling what desires human beings may develop in their
competitive social situation and what they may make of themselves as
they pursue their desires. Free human beings are perfectible; they can
also deprave themselves. Rousseau offers numerous such genetic
analyses of human development. A very penetrating one is that of the
birth of language; as Starobinski puts it: "Rousseau presents as
'oeuvre humaine' what the tradition had defined as original gift of
nature or of God."[4]

3. The genesis of moral evil: The account of the birth of reason
and of the rise of society also includes an account of the genesis of
moral evil. Man in society lives "outside himself." He has lost himself.
While Rousseau still uses the word "alienation" in the meaning it had
acquired in jurisprudence, namely, the sale or surrender of a piece of
property or of a right, he nevertheless is the first to start the analyses
of social alienation that were to be such a recurrent theme of modern
intellectual life. He even launches most of the basic themes. Property
causes man to put himself in the things he appropriated. Social life
causes man to accept on himself the opinion which others have of
him. The master and the slave deprave each other. The effort to

---

3 Jean Jacques Rousseau, *Discours sur les Sciences et les Arts*, III: 6.
4 J. Starobinski, *De la Transparence à l'obstacle* (Paris: NRF, 1971), 344.

dominate over others stems from a desire to compensate for a lost happiness. Finally he also believed that his own social marginality made him a privileged observer.

Rousseau thus always held that the social condition is both a development and a maiming of the human potential: rationality itself is an ambiguous achievement. The very crises he observes in his society are symptoms of a conflict which ruins mankind; social life secretes moral evil.[5] "L'être" and "le paraître" are at odds with each other. Life in society includes dissemblances *necessarily*. Rousseau tells a story of loss of innocence, of *fall* into man-made suffering and human oppression.

Let us note here that Rousseau is making use of biblical metaphors. (There will be more of this later.) Let us also note that Rousseau is not prevented thereby from breaking from a whole tradition of Christian interpretation of the biblical account of the origin of sin: his letter to Mgr. de Beaumont makes clear that he has no use for the idea of the original sin. How then can Rousseau reconcile his belief that man is "naturally good" with his perception that "everything degenerates in the hands of man"? Starobinski offers a solution: everything degenerates in the hands of man but not in his heart.[6] The self thus suffers evil rather than commits it. Rousseau has such confidence in this permanent goodness of the heart that, commenting on the story of Genesis 3, he excuses, even commends, the spirit of revolt: the divine command is said to be "a useless and arbitrary prohibition," and to kick up against it is not vicious in itself but rather "in conformity with the order of things and the good constitution of man."[7]

There is of course no devil in Rousseau's scenarios. The fall is entirely our work. As such we can undo it. Man is captive but he can break loose. So the Rousseau who can give to social vices the appearances of inevitability can also write that "these vices do not so much belong to man as to badly governed man."[8] And Rousseau clearly distances himself from all the "déclamateurs" who repeated that society is corrupt by claiming to have unveiled the cause of this corrup-

---

5   There is here a clear break from the Enlightenment main stream. Most enlightened minds tried to reintegrate evil within a rational cosmic process. Evil was only "apparently" evil or hopefully on its way out (since men seem on their way toward becoming more rational). But to Rousseau society has created an apparent order which marks a real disorder. Evil is a moral scandal to be overcome by conversion and by social reorganization. See B. Baczko, *Rousseau: Solitude et Communauté* (Paris: Mouton, 1974), 185-89, 299.

6   Jean Jacques Rousseau, *Confessions*, bk. 1, I: 18-20. See Starobinski, *Transparence*, 18-21.

7   Jean Jacques Rousseau, *Lettre à Mgr de Beaumont*, IV: 939. Starobinski appropriately emphasizes that the famous sentence on "man who reflects" being "a depraved animal" does not mean that he is thereby morally guilty, *Transparence*, 245.

8   Jean Jacques Rousseau, *Preface to Narcisse*, II: 969.

tion. His account of a fall from a state of nature into a state of culture includes the key to the moral ascent of man. (The state of innocence is thus amoral or premoral rather than properly moral.) In social life, conscience is aroused and man begins to judge his society.[9] Moral conscience is included in the list of human capabilities acquired in the historical process of becoming.

4. Reintegration: Division, separation—the expressions establish the tone of Rousseau's account of the present condition of mankind. But the account of this development can also show the road toward reintegration. Baczko argues that Rousseau analyzes the contradictions which tear social man apart in order to overcome them.[10] Gouhier finds Rousseau asking a new question: shall we have the history we have had so far or shall we have another one? It seems somehow apparent that mankind entered into the wrong history accidentally, not unlike a traveller who takes the wrong turn.[11] There is thus a new emotional climate in Rousseau's work: man is invited to undertake afresh the realization of missed opportunities. Schiller goes clearly beyond Rousseau's explicit meaning, but he remains within the same emotional climate when he writes that mankind acts now as if it had to start its existence afresh.[12] Rousseau believes in regeneration: a currently powerful moral evil can be defeated by a moral conversion. To the destructive social denaturation must succeed a creative, moral denaturation.

The vision of Vincennes (1749) which launched Rousseau upon his authorship climaxes in a dominant passion which is enthusiasm for "truth, freedom and virtue."[13] Virtue is the key notion: freedom introduced turbulence, moral virtue will restore unity. The dynamic movement started when man broke from nature goes on: freedom is not curbed, but the movement of expansion will, when virtuous, proceed without division. The permanent goodness of man manifests itself by a requirement for unity, by a longing for reunion which never leaves man.[14] Thus Rousseau believes he can "derive from the evil itself the remedy which will cure it."[15] Moral freedom will find the art of expressing itself and limiting itself. In the age when freedom and laws cooperate, man is morally transformed so that he can be happy in society. Henceforth men make history knowingly, consciously.[16]

9   P. Burgelin, *La Philosophie de l'existence de J.J. Rousseau* (Paris: PUF, 1952).
10 Baczko, *Rousseau*, 385.
11 H. Gouhier, *Les Méditations métaphysiques de J.J. Rousseau* (Paris: Vrin, 1970), 20, 30.
12 Jean Jacques Rousseau, Letter 3 in *Aesthetic Education of Mankind*. Cited in Baczko, *Rousseau*, 77.
13 Rousseau, *Confessions*, bk. 8, I: 351.
14 Burgelin, *La Philosophie*, 260, 311. Burgelin rightly adds that for Rousseau as for Kant divided man remains entirely responsible. p. 318.
15 Rousseau, *Contrat Social*, III: 288.
16 See R. Polin, *La Politique de la Solitude* (Paris: Sirey, 1971), 70, 282.

The prodigious effort to overcome the evil suffered—and committed—by social man takes a first form in active, civic virtue. Law and education will allow man to prosper in association with his fellow man. *Emile* offers a plan for social redemption through reformed pedagogy. The *Social Contract* then offers the formula to resolve at the political level the tension between human nature and social convention.

There is, however, another side to Rousseau: deterioration is so far gone that he despairs of restoring republican virtues and republican happiness in most societies. His hopes are really robust only about Corsica, Poland, and the more remote valleys of Switzerland. And there is also in him a tendency to substitute progressively "personal apology" for "speculative thought."[17] Virtue still recaptures the lost unity, but virtue in this second form becomes withdrawn, private, even hidden. Social alienation remains entire, but the self recaptures itself wholly in confession and reverie.

5. Providence: In a famous passage Kant announces that Rousseau, along with Newton, "justified" the providence of God. "Rousseau was the first to discover in the variety of shapes that men assume the deeply concealed nature of man and to observe the hidden law that justifies Providence."[18] Rousseau himself was quite aware that his account of the genesis of evil resolved the problem of theodicy in a satisfactory manner never before approximated. God and man alike are innocent. "Providence made man free, not for him to do evil, but for him to do good by choice. Moral evil is undoubtedly our work." "Take away man's work and all is good."[19]

Evil is thus an accident of history, a social accident. It is not the fault of "essential man." It results from a passion of man for that which is exterior, but man, even social man, can always go back to himself. And, *mirabile visu*, this very phenomenon of fall and corruption initiates the re-ascent or return to innocence. Fallen man is perfectible man. Society corrupts man, but like Satan in *Job*, society never ceases to be an instrument of moral good. In society human beings are moralized, either in discovering their rational will and civil virtue or in discovering each other's genuine hearts and withdrawn virtue. Becoming is the magic key. Man who has a history is man who has lost himself—and who is in the process of finding himself again. "Let us derive from the evil itself the remedy that will cure it. . . ." Moral evil is being made into an instrument for a greater good. In this moral universe the very idea of God being morally inadequate is again preposterous as it was in the days of *Job* (more preposterous even, since now we *know* how God made Leviathan . . .).

---

17 Starobinski, *Transparence*, 47.
18 *Gesammelte Schriften* 20: 58-59, cited in E. Cassirer, *The Question of J. J. Rousseau* (Indianapolis: Indiana University Press, 1963), 72.
19 Rousseau, *Emile*, bk. 4, IV: 587-88. See also 593-94.

This new theodicy manages to proclaim the innocence of God by making history a radically contingent affair. Evil in history is a human fact which men can remedy to their advantage, and it is only that. It is not a crisis in a divine plan. Man for Rousseau has no divinely appointed destiny, only a history. No providential God watches over—and manipulates—his progress. The problem of theodicy is solved because God lets men write their own history. Social mechanisms and individual biographies are at work in history, not providence. (There is an important correlate: Rousseau has no faith in history; progress is not inevitable.)[20]

II

Once launched by Rousseau, these five themes pursue a brilliant philosophical career. The works of Kant and of Hegel are evidence enough. But what I want to stress here is that Rousseau offers a new, compelling story. Furthermore his story is a work of imagination. It does not result from a painstaking survey of all known historical facts. It results from an act of intuitive penetration: an account is given which, brilliantly, instantly, makes sense of all the facts which are known to the minds of concerned people. This work of imagination is therefore profoundly satisfying—and not just for epistemological reasons. Man was provoked (instinct, desire, opportunity); he invented a response; it was disastrous. He lost all control over the consequences of his behaviour, but he remained innocent through it all—captive, but not guilty. Society, a creature no one thought, before Rousseau, of placing in the dock, is responsible. As Rousseau accuses society, he absolves himself and vice-versa.[21]

We also find in Rousseau a new—and profound—account of *the power of the imagination*—because he is quite conscious that he lets imagination preside over the elaboration of his account of God and man.

At the outset, Rousseau is aware that the imagination has very ambiguous powers. "Such is the power of imagination and its influence that it gives rise not only to virtues and vices, but also to the goods and the woes of human life and that it is the manner in which one surrenders to it that makes men good or evil, happy or miserable down here."[22] The role of the imagination is seen to be particularly decisive in the area of theology that has so many insoluble issues.

---

20 This is Baczko's interpretation. *Rousseau*, 102, 130, 390. On this view, Kant misunderstood the matter when he claimed that Rousseau justified Providence or certainly masked the difference between this new justification and the older ones.

21 Starobinski, "La mise en accusation de la société," in Université de Neuchâtel, *J.J. Rousseau Quatre Etudes* (Neuchâtel: A la Baconnière, 1978).

22 Jean Jacques Rousseau, *2nd Dialogue*, I: 815-16.

"Impenetrable mysteries surround us everywhere ... we think we have intelligence to pierce them, but we have only imagination."[23]

Moreover, Rousseau is entirely aware of the imaginative nature of language itself. He can describe semantic transfers and analyze the role of imagination in social relations. (His favorite examples draw upon erotic love—and significantly compares its feelings to those of religion—but as we shall see, the point can be extended to cover large groups.) "Love is but an illusion; it creates for itself another world as it were; it surrounds itself with objects that do not exist, or to which it alone confers reality; and since it expresses all its sentiments with images, its language is always figurative.... Just as the enthusiasm of devotion borrows from the language of love, so the enthusiasm of love also borrows from the language of devotion."[24]

The conclusion is clear; imagination to Rousseau is no longer what it was to all rationalists, namely, a disease, a sort of pollution of the mind by the senses. It is rather a faculty that can create a world to make us happy. Civilized man is highly reflexive, self-conscious, torn. His loving aspirations find no support in the world. He experiences reality through conflicts and contradictions. But in imagination, this man can become other. In his imaginative life unity is restored.[25] We may well label this recapturing of unity to be a merely psychological magic. To the imaginative person, by opening doors beyond the real, the imagination opens doors to a "spiritual" world that is real. It lends reality to unreality. Rousseau is thus quite firm: what is imagined tends to become real; to live in the imagination is to anticipate one's own immortality. This "unreality" is reality.[26] Rousseau is also quite lucid as to his own recourse to the imagination. Such trust in the imagination is rooted in his temperament and lies at the source of his art. "My stubborn head does not want to improve; it wants to create." Nothing is beautiful except what is not."[27]

What we find in Rousseau's work is thus a uniquely self-conscious invasion of the power of an individual imagination into philosophical and theological language. Rousseau does not merely launch new themes around the notion of human freedom, he uses a new freedom in writing and writes with a new voice. (His talent, he says, lies in his heart, not in his pen. Writing cannot be a métier: with him it must be the expression of a moral passion.[28]) To understand Rousseau, there-

---

23 Rousseau, *Emile*, bk. 4, IV: 568.
24 Jean Jacques Rousseau, *2ème Préface de Julie*, II: 15-16.
25 J. Starobinski, "J.J. Rousseau et le péril de la réflexion" in *L'Oeil vivant* (Paris: NRF, 1961).
26 See Marc Eigeldinger, *J.J. Rousseau et la réalité de l'imaginaire* (Neuchâtel: la Baconnière, 1962).
27 Rousseau, *Confessions*, bk. 4, I: 171-72; *Emile*, bk. 5, IV: 821; *Nouvelle Héloise*, Part 6, Letter 8, II: 693.
28 Rousseau, *Confessions*, bk. 9, I: 402-403.

fore, one must also try to grasp the roots of his persuasive power. A very talented pen is part of it. But so is a new, vibrant appeal to his own experience. To put it in a nutshell, we hear in his work *a new voice, that of sincerity*.[29]

Numerous factors enter into the making of this new voice. Rousseau enters the fields of political theory with a lower-town Genevan background, i.e., with a republican (or plebeian) egalitarian passion. A sharp moral demand is made: the social order is to be shaped in such a manner as to allow full spiritual authenticity to all. This demand is sounded by someone who will suffer no compromise. If society cannot "provide" such authenticity for all, Rousseau wants nothing of it and will withdraw from it. Rousseau speaks of justice for all with the rigour of one who will rather have authenticity for himself alone than modest improvements for the many. Personal authenticity—and his alone, if need be—is the reality to be protected at all costs. A very significant text from a fragment on public happiness puts the matter very well; "make man one and you will make him as happy as he can be. Give him entirely to the State, or leave him entirely to himself, but if you divide his heart you tear him apart."[30] The alternative is sharp: egalitarian order or romantic isolation. "One must be absolutely like everyone else, or absolutely like oneself."[31]

Frequently Rousseau prefers what we may call the withdrawn virtue to the civic one.[32] (Ever lucid, he allows that, too lazy to be virtuous, his own wisdom lies in understanding his own self.) The sight of his own conscience, its undisturbed unity, is the sight of a world without shadows: it awards him the deepest satisfaction. His ever-renewed good faith justifies him. Writing is so soothing. His *Confessions* is an exemplary book, and he is confident that he can appear before the last judge with them in his hand.[33]

---

29 Some good work has been done lately on the history of sincerity. See Lionel Trilling, *Sincerity and Authenticity* (Cambridge, Mass.: Harvard University Press, 1971) and the Summer 1979 issue of *Daedalus* "Hypocrisy, Illusion and Evasion," especially the opening article by Judith Shklar "Let Us Not Be Hypocritical." See also my article "Can Conscience Be Hypocritical? The Contrasting Analyses of Kant and Hegel" in *Harvard Theological Review* 68/3-4 (1975).

30 *Du Bonheur Public*, III: 510.

31 Jean Jacques Rousseau, *Correspondence complète*, XXIII: 42.

32 The extraordinary power of *La Nouvelle Héloïse* comes from its hovering between the cultivation of social and of private virtues. We see at Clarens a happy little society—presumably complete, there are workers on the estate. Its leading figures are both men *and* citizens. Yet the idyll of innocence lost and innocence restored takes place far from the European society at large, and, moreover, the ladies and gentlemen who head the Alpine haven enjoy a happiness in their leisure which is different from that of its humbler denizens. The happiness of these united beautiful people is really quite free from the requirements of ordinary citizenship. The élite of Clarnes *enjoy* spiritual authenticity. All they do is show themselves as they are; the servants do the work.

33 Rousseau, *Confessions*, bk. 1, I: 5.

The sharpness of the contrast between the withdrawn and the civic virtue must not hide the dialectic relationship. For Rousseau solitude is redemptive. The solitary self is released from the world of social "appearances" and begins to find the way to man as he is in himself. When he emerges from his solitude his voice has the ring of sincerity but also the power of those who have seen through lies.[34]

In time this new voice will gain a revolutionary impact. For the time being we must stress the literary dimension of this new hunger for and achievement in authenticity. Starobinski offers here a helpful analysis which begins by citing one of Hegel's commentators: "The content of the language spoken by the good conscience is the self which knows itself as essence."[35] *Vitam impendere vero* becomes *vitam impendere sibi*. The autobiographical insight into oneself is a transposition of the divine search of the heart; through it all duality is gone and one is known (by oneself this time) better than one (ordinarily) knows oneself. The consciousness experiences, in itself, the source of its unity. Nothing manifests this "discovery" better than the literary voice of the last work, published posthumously, *Les Rêveries du Promeneur Solitaire*. Speaking, or rather writing, becomes an immediate experience as well as the means of a mediation; the writer communes with his inner source and meets his judge successfully; the singular acquires a universal significance. This language is not aimed at anything, or at any one. It *is* the authentic self authentically communing with itself and restoring its unity. "One can say that [Jean Jacques] has been the first to live in archetypal manner the dangerous pact of the I with language; the "new covenant" in which man makes himself word."[36] We have only Rousseau's word that he is innocent and we are made to feel this is all we need.

The merging of new content and of new literary voice is particularly apparent in Rousseau's handling of religious issues. First of all, we find there, not surprisingly, *a new religious feeling*. The opening page of the *Confessions* informs us of what Rousseau will say to God as he presents his book on judgment day: "I have unveiled my inmost self even as Thou has seen it."[37] An earlier age would have been horrified at the arrogance of this statement, or amused at the extent of the self-deception. But Rousseau manages to give a religious tone to this assured sincerity. Like many in his century, Rousseau repeatedly discovers an unbridgeable gap between the rational de-

34 Baczko, *Rousseau*, 166.
35 Starobinski, *Transparence*, 141.
36 *Ibid.*, 234, 239. See also 238, 246, 328. See also the comments of K. Barth, *Protestant Theology in the 19th Century* (London: SCM Press, 1972), 212 and 225-29 on the completely new discovery in the realm of anthropology: goodness is in the heart, the heart being simply the man himself, discounting everything he produces or which confronts him as alien existence or as the work of alien hands.
37 Rousseau, *Confessions*, bk. 1, I: 5.

monstrative basis that is offered to uphold religious belief and the unshakable certitude characteristic of the believer. But besides the unshakable certitudes of the theologians he also finds, entirely distinct from them, the unshakable confidence of the individual (more or less pietist) heart. And there is no doubt in the mind of this Protestant: genuine religion is to be found in what this heart feels and knows rather than in the beliefs philosophers and theologians squabble about. (The Christian religion rests on so many good and persuasive reasons, assures the Savoyard Vicar according to Gouhier, why should we excite ourselves to invent doubtful ones?)[38]

But what the heart knows is not any more what the individual appropriated of the religious tradition; it is rather what the heart comes to feel as it tries to make sense of its total life experience. (The distinction should not, of course, be absolute: there are some Christian and many Protestant precedents that root the theological enterprise in the autobiographical one. It still remains true that with Rousseau what the heart knows becomes uniquely rooted in the biography.) On her death bed, Julie makes the only confession of faith that sincere people—and God—can require: she states she may have been often wrong but "I have always believed what I said I believed."[39] No one is henceforth to blame the heart for not learning things, as long as it remained sincere.

With this command of a religious kind of sincerity Rousseau can make decisive interventions on the public religious scene. D'Alembert committed a serious breach in writing that Geneva's ministers were Socinians: nothing they wrote or said publicly warrants such label; and if the ministers have private sentiments, they should have the right to keep quiet or express them in their own words. Why should D'Alembert—or anyone—undertake to profess the faith of others?[40] The letter to Mgr. de Beaumont, archbishop of Paris, makes a powerful and systematic demonstration of the corruption arising from a required religious orthodoxy. At this point one sees clearly that Rousseau's religious feeling leads to *a new method of evaluating religious doctrines and institutions*. At the outset Rousseau sees much of what passes for religion as mere cultural trappings. Why should God have no other way to reach me except through books containing what men have said about what God had said to Moses? Rousseau's "discovery" of culture is therefore accompanied by a discovery of religion as "only culture," made up of human "testimonies" and "ceremonies."[41] This historical religion is debunked as too human in the name of a vital link with God found elsewhere, in the heart.

---

38 Gouhier, *Méditations*, 218.
39 Rousseau, *Nouvelle Héloise*, Part 6, Letter 11: II: 714.
40 Rousseau, *Lettre d'Alembert* (Paris: Garnier Flammarion, 1967), 57.
41 Rousseau, *Emile*, bk. 4, IV: 608, 610. Page 609 cites Charron on the fact that one receives one's religion from other men.

Religious life is therefore completely interiorized by principle. The lived experience of the individual as narrated by the individual to himself is seen to contain the near totality of religious phenomena. Religious themes are desacralized. They become for all practical purposes a dimension of biography.[42] It is also true that Rousseau's new and particular experience acquires henceforth a sacred character. With Rousseau, who has suffered so much, the experience of restored unity, the communing with his deep nature, is experienced as a grace. He repeatedly speaks of it as of a gift of grace. For the traditional scheme of nature and grace, Rousseau substituted that of history and "nature"—"nature" this time meaning the essential goodness with which the self can commune in "gifted" moments. What used to be called human nature in need of redemption is history. What used to be called grace is for such historical man the imaginative return to his own deep nature which is a felt unity. (The "supernatural" is a "super-historical" experience granted by the imagination.) There is nothing in the Christian tradition that would warrant calling such experiences religious. Rousseau, however, convinces many that they are more religious than anything else that passes for religion.

The conclusions seem inescapable. Whether he is reconstituting the origins of inequality or confessing his faith in Providence, Rousseau is creating a literary myth. His imagination provides him with a grasp of the underlying unity both in the history of man and in his own biography. The real and the imagined is reconciled in literature, that is in a manner of writing in which private language and common language merge. The very writing of the myth restores the unity. The nature of this literary activity is most manifest in the autobiographical writing, from the *Confessions*, through the *Dialogues*, to the *Rêveries*. His life is made into more than a novel; it becomes a myth of lost and restored unity. The Rousseau of the *Rêveries* recaptures himself; he invents himself; he is entirely himself. (Apart from the act of writing he is lost, victimized, and beside himself.) As he writes, he keeps lying, i.e., remakes himself into someone other than what he was or passed as, and he keeps finding himself sincere in the process. That is literature as we now know it, an expressive act which is privileged above all other expressions which the self gives of itself.[43] (That is also the only genuine religion he knows: "socialization occurs in the affectivity, translated into a metaphorical writing that borrows the resources of religious language."[44])

---

42   Baczko, *Rousseau*, 233, 249.
43   Starobinski, "La mise en accusation de la société, 37.
44   See M. Eigeldinger, *J.J. Rousseau: Univers Mythique et Cohérence* (Neuchâtel: A la Baconnière, 1978), 163. The author also stresses that Plato uses myth in a manner that supplements reason without contradicting it. With Rousseau myth soars freely, p. 311.

Rousseau the writer is thus what we rather strangely call a "creative" writer. He does not operate within a myth that provides him with an orientation in reality. He does not comment on myths. His own imagination rather provides him with an orientation in reality to which he gives shape by creating a myth. (To call this myth a literary one stresses its peculiarity: it is rooted in autobiographical experience.) The proclaimer of the myth sees himself as master of reality—and over men. There is a side to Rousseau that yearns for the power he attributes to the legislator who founds the institutions of a people "to change, as it were, human nature."[45] The qualification disappears when he speaks of the pedagogue: he "steps in God's shoes"; he "makes a man."[46] (In Book 5 of *Emile*, the teacher, that paragon of sincere virtue, tells his pupil that his new love, Sophie, is dead. This lie is meant to teach him how to sublimate.)

The power of the literary myth and the sweeping powers of the writer can be tested by seeing how the myth transmutes the significance of traditional Christian theological themes.

In his *Profession de foi* the vicar Savoyard bluntly announces that he left all books aside: there is nothing God wishes to teach us in any of them. But one page later we learn that one book still lies open on the table: "The majesty of the Scriptures amazes me, the holiness of the Gospel speaks to my heart."[47] Rousseau speaks most slightingly of the nonsense found in catechisms and of the persecuting bent of the Church. (These, of course, were commonplaces among the *philosophes*.) But he loves Christ and his love has genuine passion. "I am Christian, not as a disciple of the priests, but as a disciple of Jesus Christ."[48]

Two of the testimonies given by Rousseau to the person of Christ indicate exactly what he has in mind. The third of the *Lettres écrites de la Montagne* examines the ethics of the gospel and ends on a statement of what there is that "charms in the character of Jesus." The word charm is to be interpreted strongly; Rousseau confesses himself overcome. There is in Jesus

not only delicacy of mores, simplicity, but also ease, grace and even elegance. He did not shun pleasures and feasts; he attended weddings, saw women, played with children, loved perfumes and ate with financiers. His disciples did not fast; his austerity was not rude. He was at the same time indulgent and righteous, sweet to the weak and terrible to the wicked. His ethics had something attractive, caressing and tender.... Il avait le coeur sensible, il était homme de bonne société.[49]

---

45   Rousseau, *Contrat Social*, III: 381.
46   Rousseau, *Lettres Philosophiques* (Paris: Vrin, 1974), 192.
47   Rousseau, *Emile*, bk. 4, IV: 624-25.
48   Rousseau, *Lettre à Mgr de Beaumont*, IV: 960.
49   Rousseau, *Lettres écrites de la Montagne*, III: 753-54.

This amazing portrait of agreeable, civilized sophistication attributes something winsome, even irresistible, to the lifestyle of Jesus. This moralist has a sternness that attracts whereas everywhere else sternness repels.

The *Morceau allégorique sur la révélation* suggests the source of this extraordinary power. In a dream a philosopher sees a monstrous sanctuary centered on a veiled statue. The temple is a place of illusion and oppression; priests preside over a cruel ritual. The allegory presents then the intervention of three liberating heroes. The second one clearly stands for Socrates; he tears the veil away from the statue, and the figure looks heavenward and tramples upon mankind. But the people in the temple remain caught in the illusion; they keep on worshipping the statue. A third hero, obviously Christ, is announced as "son of man"; he topples the statue and takes its place upon the altar. "He seemed to be taking his rightful place rather than usurping that of another." He then spoke: the priests' power is broken, the people are seized with enthusiasm. "He led all; everything announced a revolution." His mere word confounds his enemies and all are moved by it. "One felt that the language of truth did not cost him anything because he had the source of it in himself."[50] The achievement of Christ is surprisingly similar to that of Rousseau—or of any honest conscience. "Goodness appears in the world through an I that is transparent to it." An immediate presence overcomes all distance, all dissemblance, all misunderstanding, all oppression. It spontaneously surges out of the self.

Mystics before Rousseau had spoken of an inner Christ contrasted to the official one. With Rousseau the writer takes on the mantle of the mystic. Furthermore—and this is quite new—the "authentic" Christ is psychologically redeeming: his word brings just what divided post-enlightenment man needs. The door is open for a whole series of reconstructions of the consciousness of the historical Jesus that make of it a powerful cultural phenomenon that overcomes the evil divisions proper to man in his historical state of culture and that can be recreated by the writer who duplicates this unitive consciousness. So Rousseau does love Christ and the gospels. The "creative" writer honours them. He honours them on his own terms. He recognizes in them an achievement similar to his own.[51]

---

50   Rousseau, *Morceau allégorique*, IV: 1053-54.

51   The contrast between the two Christs is echoed in a contrast between two exegeses. An orthodox exegesis assimilates much erudition but still states what ought to be believed, what authority has to be acknowledge. Rousseau launches an exegesis that lets the texts speak to the heart. Jesus is divine, the gospels sacred, because what they say carries with itself the marks of its own truth. "The content of the texts provides the criterion of their authenticity. Exegesis is a matter of reflexion, not erudition." (Starobinski, *Transparence*, 88. See also 100-101.) Rousseau thus is another one of the rationalist exegetes. He, however, does not measure up the

Does this mean that Rousseau will discard the notion of revelation? The religion of conscience has such an intimate ring, its emotions seem so linked to sentimental reverie alone in nature that commentators have spoken of sentimental piety, pantheistic nature mysticism, or of "spiritualité naturelle." But at the end of a study of what Rousseau has to say about his "extases," Gouhier concludes that even in the *Rêveries*, self, cosmos, and God are always kept distinct. The "extases" are not a swooning of the self but a heightening, a gathering of it.[52] Rousseau does not approve of petitionary prayer. His God is not one to give favours. He is, however, the source of gifts which must be acknowledged as grace. Those who contrasted a sense of the presence of divine immensity with the sense of God's presence as grace made a contrast where Rousseau saw none.

So Rousseau can speak of grace and of revelation because he has experienced them. Rousseau, of course, like all the *philosophes*, brings discredit to the idea that God left a message (embodied in a code of laws or a body of doctrine) with some men of the past so that we are forever held to what was told then. The vicar Savoyard cannot feel the truth of such revelation, nor see its usefulness. The letter to Mgr. de Beaumont, however, can quite rightly claim he has never denied revelation.[53] The truth is that Rousseau rejects one type of revelation, namely, the reified body of truths to be forever believed, and affirms another type, namely, the revelatory moment, where insight and certainty are received as given. Revelation and grace are thus acknowledged; but not because the writer honours what they traditionally taught (what the tradition transmitted in the eighteenth century was in any case singularly perverted); rather, because they are indispensable terms to describe the writer's experience.

Rousseau's pages on the public religion shows that it too, just like the private one, is subordinated to the dominant myth of the "creative" writer. Rousseau ventured into a discussion of civil religion. The problem is extraordinarily complex. Since the sixteenth century, religion in Europe had become socialized, and moral norms had simultaneously been internalized. Each European society acquired its deep cultural unity by the shaping of a moral conscience among all levels of the population. This conscience is both social and religious. In the eighteenth century, the institutional strains caused by the religious elements of this consensus become bothersome to many: the costs of religious intolerance in particular seem too high. Therefore, many come to wish that the civil religion will recede, or that the religious element of the consensus will give way to other elements of equal

content of the Gospels to a rationalist dogma. His is a more literary sort of exegesis: the text is to stir the conscience of a good man.
52   Gouhier, *Meditations Metaphysiques*, 113.
53   Rousseau, *Lettre à Mgr de Beaumont*, IV: 996.

moral and social strength. D'Holbach and his friends emerge as complete secularizers: social unity will gain in strength as religion is shoved aside. Voltaire and d'Alembert are social realists: wise change cannot be sudden. Voltaire and d'Alembert are also class-conscious. They know that upper-class philosophical atheists are virtuous, but they are sure that religion remains necessary to keep the populace moral. Therefore, they envisage a slow ebb of the religious part of the national consensus. Meanwhile they promote among their own the sort of natural religion they believe in. They do not propose to inculcate it to the many or buttress it with legal sanctions. They acknowledge that it lacks spiritual appeal among the many. Rousseau sees the flaws in this position: it provides no basis for a genuine civil, national religion, and it maintains a dishonest compromise between the Christianity of the many and the enlightened religion of the few. The Genevan patriot wants to do better than that. To him religion and civil life are inseparable in a united, moral, egalitarian, national community. So the *Contrat Social* offers a new religious settlement: tolerance for all virtuous cults and a public religion established by law, with as few dogmas as possible and with penalties for public dissenters. The apostle of religious sincerity and tolerance shocks all the *philosophes* by proposing the death penalty for obdurate atheists.[54] Rousseau's pages on civil religion are among the most penetrating ever written. Their only weakness is the inherent contradiction. But Rousseau is forced into the contradiction because he always sees the writer as a giver of unity. There is in his mind no happiness for a group of people apart from a deeply felt unity. A civil religion is the only way this Protestant republican knows toward such unity. He has not yet dreamed up the cohesive force of nationalism. He is however coming close to it; his plan for the rebuilding of the Polish State ask it to "reveal to the Polish people the unique nature of their social identity" and "to strengthen this identity through wise legislation which would establish bonds of affections among the Polish people."[55]

III

I have appreciated the study of Rousseau both in its own right and because it helped me focus issues arising from a look at nineteenth-century attitudes toward religion. New themes emerge in his writings with great clarity and marvelous vigour. Before reducing him to the somewhat undignified position of being a door to the understanding of other people, let me make two points that aim at giving him his due. First of all, this creator of a myth is not entirely bewitched by his

54 Rousseau, *Contrat Social*, III: 460-69.
55 R. I. Boss, "Rousseau's Civil Religion and the Meaning of Belief: An Answer to Bayle's Paradox," *Studies on Voltaire and the 18th Century* 84 (1971), 162.

own magic. He remains endowed with the virtue of moderation most of the time. He knows his limits: a page of *Emile* stresses that the pedagogue is not God and the pupil not king.[56] And, secondly, he remains an admirable example of the courage and dignity of the human being who tries to think while living in modern conditions. The effort is pursued in the context of mental distress. He struggles toward doctrines, truths, that will "save" an otherwise unbearable existence. His doctrine is the product of his disease; it is also, concludes Bénichou, the sign that he did not accept his disease.[57]

This being said, here is our hypothesis. The themes of culture and of imagination together provide the general key to the nineteenth-century, critical approach to religion. Everyone has then discovered culture, namely, sees human life as lived out in a man-made historical social environment. The eighteenth century was highly aware that man can change his environment. The by-products, the unforeseen consequences, are now discovered. Man sees that he does something to himself as he manipulates the natural world and his social environment. Everywhere in chains—man has imposed a fate on himself as he exercised his powers. The moral confidence of the one who acts on his desire for mastering of the world is shattered and a new moral anxiety is felt. The old Aristotelian distinction becomes relevant again. *Praxis (actio)*, the action of man upon his society and himself, must be critically examined and its ends established. *Poiesis (factio)*, the action of man upon inanimate things, or the art of making useful things, offers no guidance at all when it comes to finding the art of living together with one's fellow man.

Man, however, can escape from the prison. His imagination has wings; its flight to the transcendent opens the path to new harmonious realities. Imagination which used to be conceived as a faculty that warps our judgments of reality is perceived now as having an ontological role; it can be creator of a new reality. (*Praxis* then is no longer the coping for the best which Aristotle had in mind; it is envisaged as a dynamic, individual, or corporate self-shaping based on inward creative power.[58]) The discovery of culture precipitates humans into new

---

56   Rousseau, *Emile*, bk. 5, IV: 849.
57   Paul Bénichou, "J.J. Rousseau: De la personne à la doctrine," in *L'Ecrivain et ses travaux* (Paris: J. Corti, 1967).
58   The change can be illustrated by the very shift in the meaning of the agricultural metaphor originally behind the word culture. The Renaissance uses the metaphor of cultivation or culture to speak of an activity aimed at those who are in need of a tutor's attention. Thomas Elyot for instance draws a lengthy comparison between good parents and able gardeners. (*The Governor*, I, 4.) We are still in a world with droughts and garden pests. At the end of the eighteenth century, the affirmation of creative freedom in history seems to have made a clean sweep of such usage. Culture is something the self does for itself, as is illustrated by this passage from Goethe's autobiography: "to labour for his own moral culture is the simplest and most practicable thing which man propose to himself; the impulse is inborn in him:

depths of pessimism: we have maimed ourselves. The discovery of the imagination invites to a new optimism: we can start afresh again. The nineteenth-century criticisms of religion are radical because religion as we know it is seen as culture, as product of our history. Such disenchanting vision is possible because the critic has the underlying confidence that the imagination of the poets—or of religious geniuses—can re-poetize or re-religionize existence.[59] Culture and imagination have emerged as principles of reality, as sources of our sense of reality. What is oppressive is attributed to culture and the imagination is entrusted to guide us to a happier order or a completely happy one.

Many clearly saw in Rousseau the herald of the new dispensation. Hölderlin compared him to the eagle that flies toward approaching gods, and Victor Hugo called him the rising sun of the new world.[60] Rousseau, I must stress, does not just launch a new anthropology. He launches a *powerful* new anthropology. Emile, the man of nature, is admirable, imitable. (Just like Achilles and Alexander were.) John Locke had spoken of the new, modern man but had never tried to paint him as a warm, attractive, obviously authentic human being.[61] A new poetry suffuses politics too. Aristotle said that politics was a combination among needy men to meet their wants. Rousseau says that it is a combination among suffering men to overcome their humiliation and recapture corporate happiness. (Emile in *Emile and Sophie* organizes a rebellion among slaves.)

There is a final point.

As Rousseau writes the history he has just perceived, that of man as creative and as acculturated being, he keeps borrowing from Christian traditional symbols and theological concepts. He tells a story of fall and of redemption. These categories, however, are made to do new work, they tell a purely human story of self-estrangement and

---

while in social life both reason and love prompt or rather force him to do so." (*Dichtung und Wahrheit*, Book 16.) The discovery of historical culture is thereby seen as the prelude to a rationally grounded human self-creating. Goethe speaks of *Bildung*: what he visualizes is not a garden but an artist with a lump of clay.

59   Nineteenth-century English discussions seem dominated by the sense of an underlying similarity between religion and poetry. "Literature is but a branch of Religion, and always participates in its character: however in our time it is the only branch that still shows any greenness; and, as some think, must one day become the main stem." (Carlyle, quoted and commented upon by David J. DeLaura in "Religion, Poetry, and the Rise of Literary Humanism: The 19th Century Matrix," *Journal of the American Academy of Religion* 47/2, Supplement, [June 1979].) Keats sees religion and poetry as basic partners in distress under the conditions of modernity. Matthew Arnold seeks a basic contrast between scientific and literary language and mourns the decline in the status of the imagination as an instrument of cognition" (Nathan A. Scott Jr., "Arnold's Version of Transcendence—The Via Poetica," *The Journal of Religion* 59/3 [July 1979].)

60   Hölderlin, "Rousseau," French translation in *Oeuvres* (Paris: NRF, 1967), 774; V. Hugo, *Océan-Tas de pierres* (Paris: Albin Michel, 1942), 350.

61   Allan Bloom, "The Education of Democratic Man: Emile," *Daedalus* (1978).

self-redemption. The Christian themes appear to acquire fresh relevance: never, it seems, had so many Christian themes been assimilated into man's self-understanding. But the themes are subsumed under an entirely new heading: they are aids toward an autonomous human self-understanding. Rousseau lays the basis of a new art: that of a friendly decoding of Christian "truths" in order to let their profound truth come out. And that decoding is done by someone who offers himself as a sincere Christian who undertakes to "rescue the truth" in an age when priests have masked it.[62] The new anthropology is thus accompanied by a new way of reading Christian doctrines. "Ever mindful of my inadequacy, I will never reason on the nature of God, unless I be compelled to do it by the feeling of his relationship to me," declares the vicar Savoyard.[63] How this prudence contrasts with the confidence (presumption?) of the older theology! One may, however, ask whether the path has not been found to make of theology simply anthropology under another name.

At any rate, the romantic authors exhibit a new mastery: they can manipulate Christian symbols to make them say what the artists want them to say. In a famous passage (significant both in what it says and how it says it), Kleist announces that the gates of Paradise are now closed to us, guarded by an angel with a flaming sword; he adds, however, that there is, perhaps, a back door.[64] In *The Sorrows of Young Werther* (1774), perhaps better translated as *The Passion of Young Werther*, the hero has numerous Christ-like traits—among others he sees his suicide as a sacrifical act to liberate his friends. It is also clear that Goethe intended the novel to be a critique of the religious sentimentalism which he believed was inseparable from Christianity; he emerged from the writing of it a more confirmed pagan.[65] One of the most respected critics of romantic literature (borrowing a phrase from Carlyle's *Sartor Resartus*) entitled a major study *Natural Supernaturalism*; he sees traditional religious ideas assimilated and reinterpreted by the poets "as constitutive elements in a world view founded on secular premises."[66] The nineteenth century abounds in authors who can use the Christian myth to advance their own. There are, of course, also those poets who are great admirers of Christianity and of Christian culture and spend much talent defending them. Kier-

---

62 This sincerity of his belief is crucial. Ever since the Early Renaissance there has been decodings of Christian truths that undertook to show the "real" truth. But such decodings were done on the basis of philosophies rival to Christianity, mainly Epicureanism or Platonism. With Rousseau people who see themselves as disciples of Christ feel the need of decoding.

63 Rousseau, *Emile*, bk. 4, IV: 581.

64 Quoted in Starobinski, *L'Oeil vivant*, 185.

65 Theodore Ziolkowski, "Religion and Literature in a Secular Age: The Critic's Dilemma," *The Journal of Religion* 59/1 (January 1979), esp. 25-28.

66 M. H. Abrams, *Natural Supernaturalism: Tradition and Revolution in Romantic Literature* (New York: W. W. Norton, 1971).

kegaard, who knew something of the poet's ability to create a sentiment of existence, had a firm diagnosis about them: "an admirer of
Christianity is not a live Christian."[67]

---

67   Soren Kierkegaard, *Training in Christianity* (Princeton: Princeton University Press,
     1967), 249.

Walter Benjamin, the Mystical Materialist

CHARLES DAVIS

*Nur um der Hoffnunglosen willen ist uns
die Hoffnung gegeben*

On September 26, 1940, at a hotel in Port Bou on the French-Spanish border, Walter Benjamin, a German-Jewish writer, committed suicide by taking morphia tablets. He died the next morning at the age of forty-eight. He was fleeing France because of the danger of being handed over as a Jew to the Nazis by the Vichy government. He had an emergency visa to enter the United States, but when he reached the Spanish frontier with a party of refugees he was told that the Spanish government had closed the border. Already in ill health because of a heart condition, tired by the journey, in dread of being seized by the Nazis and at the same time unhappy about his future prospects in America, he took the lethal dose of morphine. The next day the rest of the party was allowed to cross the frontier, the Spanish border guards, it is said, being shaken by the suicide.[1]

Benjamin was on his way to join the Institut für Sozialforschung, in exile in the United States from Frankfurt since 1934. Theodor Adorno, the neo-Marxist thinker, whom he had known since 1923 and with whom he had close links, had for some time been pleading with him to come. But Benjamin had remained reluctant, and put off going until there was no alternative. Although he had done some work for the

---

1 For the brief facts of Benjamin's last days, see Martin Jay, *The Dialectical Imagination: A History of the Frankfurt School and the Institute of Social Research 1923-1950* (Boston: Little, Brown, 1973), 197-98.

Institut and was receiving financial support from it, other influences, notably his friendship with Bertolt Brecht, had kept him at a certain distance from it.[2] What would have happened to him and his thought had he succeeded in emigrating to the United States is difficult to say. As it is, we must take his legacy as we find it, the work of a fascinating but difficult, at times esoteric, writer, whom several different groups of interpreters wish to claim for their own.[3] At the time of his death Walter Benjamin was not famous. He was known to the public by his literary essays, but only a few persons, though those of the highest stature, were aware of the originality of his genius. Posthumous fame came to him in Germany with the publication fifteen years after his death of a two-volume edition of his writings.[4] That fame has now spread to the English-speaking world with the successive publication of two selections of translations, *Illuminations*[5] in 1970 and *Reflections*[6] in 1978. An English translation of his early work, *Ursprung des deutschen Trauerspiels* has also been published under the title *The Origin of German Tragic Drama*,[7] but the esoteric character of that work will leave it, I should think, inaccessible to all but the most earnest students of his thought.

As a first description Benjamin may be called a literary critic. That is to say, he wrote on literature, on art, and on literature and art in relation to politics. His style, too, was literary—indeed, it may be termed lyrical. He was not, then, a philosopher in the technical sense. Nevertheless, "Benjamin *was a philosopher*," as Scholem insists.[8] A first

---

2   Cf. the remarks of Phil Slater, *Origin and Significance of the Frankfurt School: A Marxist Perspective*, International Library of Sociology (London: Routledge and Kegan Paul, 1977), xv.

3   For a clear summary account of the different groups of interpreters, see the beginning of Jürgen Habermas' essay, "Bewusstmachende oder rettende Kritik— Die Actualität Walter Benjamin 1972," reproduced in Jürgen Habermas, *Kultur und Kritik: Verstreute Aufsätze* (Frankfurt: Suhrkamp, 1973), 302-44. The relevant pages are 302-305.

4   This edition, which I have not seen, has now been superseded by *Walter Benjamin Gesammelte Schriften*, Unter Mitwirkung von Theodor W. Adorno und Gershom Scholem herausgegeben von Rolf Tiedemann und Hermann Schweppenhäuser (Frankfurt: Suhrkamp, 1974ff). Six *Bände* are planned, each *Band* being subdivided into several parts in separate volumes. So far four *Bände* in nine volumes, containing all the completed writings, have appeared. *Band* 5 and 6 with the *Fragmente* are still to come. The edition is provided with copious notes by the editors on the text and history of each piece of writing, which are indispensable for a study of Benjamin. I will refer to this edition with the abbreviation *G.S.*

5   Walter Benjamin, *Illuminations*, ed. and with an introduction by Hannah Arendt, trans. by Harry Zohn (1st ed., Great Britain: Jonathan Cape, 1970). I have used the Fontana paperback edition (Glasgow: Collins, 1977).

6   Walter Benjamin, *Reflections: Essays, Aphorisms, Autobiographical Writings*, ed. and with an introduction by Peter Demetz, trans. by Edmund Jephcott (New York and London: Harcourt Brace Jovanovich, 1978).

7   Walter Benjamin, *The Origin of German Tragic Drama*, trans. by John Osborne (London: NLB, 1977).

8   Gershom Scholem, *On Jews and Judaism in Crisis: Selected Essays*, ed. by Werner J. Dannhauser (New York: Schocken, 1976), 178. The italics are Scholem's. It may be noted that this collection of essays reproduces three pieces on Benjamin.

reading of any of his essays will reveal that he is a literary critic *sui generis*, and that is so because his thought is philosophical through and through. He writes from a philosopher's experience—though it should be added that he is a philosopher in his own distinctive and incomparable way. My concern here is with his philosophy, though not, I hasten to add, with the full range of his philosophical thought.[9] I am focussing upon his concept of history and upon as much of his philosophy as is necessary to elucidate that concept. I have chosen that theme because I find Benjamin's philosophy of history a provocative challenge to much current thinking, both philosophical and religious.

Since philosophy of history is my topic, the chief text for consideration must be what was—with the exception of a short book review—the last work written by Benjamin, namely, *Theses on the Philosophy of History (Über den Begriff der Geschichte).*[10] This set of eighteen short theses (with two more appended from an earlier draft), only two of which exceed a page in length and then by only a few lines, has already produced quite literally a volume of commentary.[11] Not intending them for publication in their extant form, Benjamin composed the *Theses* between February and April/May 1940. They were the expression of his shocked reaction to the Nazi-Soviet Pact of 1939, which caused him to retreat from political commitment and find a refuge for his revolutionary vision in theology. Theological language now seemed to be the only language available in which to express the ideal of revolution, of transformation, that he had cherished.

Theology in Benjamin's case meant Jewish mysticism. In his student days as a member of Jewish branch of the *Jugendbewegung*, he had met Gershom Scholem, who was already beginning his lifelong study of the Kabbalah. They remained close intellectually from 1916 to 1923.[12] Scholem had been studying Hebrew and was trying to persuade him to join him in Palestine when in 1924 Benjamin met Asja Lacis, a Latvian actress and Communist revolutionary, who dissuaded him from going to Palestine and drew him instead towards Marxism. It was she who introduced him to Bertolt Brecht in Berlin in 1927, a meeting resulting in their friendship which began in May 1929.

In moving to Marxism Benjamin did not simply jettison the Kabbalist mysticism he had received from Scholem. Instead, he en-

---

9   For a comprehensive treatment of his philosophy, see Rolf Tiedemann, *Studien zur Philosophie Walter Benjamins*, vol. 16, Frankfurter Beiträge zur Soziologie (Frankfurt: Europäische Verlagsanstalt, 1965).

10 The German text is in *G.S.* 1/2, 691-704, with textual notes by the editors in *G.S.* 1/3; 1223-66. The English translation is in *Illuminations*, 255-66. Since the theses are all quite short, I shall refer to them simply by thesis number.

11 I have in mind the collection of interpretive essays, Peter Bulthaup, Hrsg., *Materialien zu Benjamins Thesen 'Über den Begriff der Geschichte'; Beiträge und Interpretationen* (Frankfurt: Suhrkemp, 1975).

12 Susan Buck-Morss, *The Origin of Negative Dialectics: Theodor W. Adorno, Walter Benjamin and the Frankfurt Institute* (Hassocks, Sussex: Harvester Press, 1977), 6.

deavoured to shift it into a new context, changing its religious into a
secular illumination, surrounding secular objects with a religious reverence and seeking the origin of mystical concepts in literary rather
than in theological writing. The result was that mysticism and materialism converged in his philosophical thought and produced an original
type of thinking, which, besides its personal expression in Benjamin's
own writings, exercised a powerful influence upon the work of Adorno.[13]

The unusual conjunction of mysticism and materialism is particularly evident in the *Theses*. The problem of interpretation to which the
paradoxical combination gives rise is posed by the very first thesis. This
describes a puppet designed to play chess. Inside the apparatus of
which the puppet was a part was hidden a hunchback, an expert chess
player, who guided the hands of the puppet by means of strings. The
thesis gives the meaning of the symbol: "The puppet called 'historical
materialism' is to win all the time. It can easily be a match for anyone if it
enlists the services of theology, which today, as we know, is wizened and
has to keep out of sight."

How are we going to interpret that? Are we to say with Scholem[14]
that historical materialism is no longer anything but a puppet that can
win the game of history only by calling upon the hidden mastery of
theology, so that in the *Theses* nothing remains of historical materialism
but the name? Or, are we to stress that theology, which is as dried up
and unsightly as the hunchback, is at the service of historical materialism, because, despite what we should have expected from the image
itself, the puppet is said to make use of the dwarf, not vice-versa? In
other words, theology, we must understand, has been brought within
historical materialism. But before entering further into the interpretation of the *Theses*, we must place them in the broader context of the
whole of Benjamin's thought in its development.

The *Theses* were conceived as an introduction to his major, un-
completed project, the so-called *Passagenarbeit* or Paris Arcades work, a
critical study of nineteenth-century culture. When he had written the
Trauerspiel book over a decade before, he had prefaced it with an
epistemological prologue, "probably written last, but almost certainly
conceived first,"[15] in which he reflected what he was doing. The *Theses*
were intended to provide a similar theoretical introduction to the
Passagenarbeit, this time setting forth an epistemology of history, which
means that they attempted to "justify the study of the past by showing
how the interests of liberation impel one to the kind of historical
knowledge represented by the Arcades project."[16] To put the matter in

13   Buck-Morss, *Negative Dialectics*, 21.
14   Scholem, *On Jews*, 231.
15   George Steiner in the introduction to Benjamin, *The Origin of German Tragic Drama*,
      15.
16   Shierry M. Weber, "Walter Benjamin: Commodity Fetishism, the Modern, and the

general terms, the *Passagenarbeit* was an attempt to put into effect a Marxist, materialist version of the philosophical method used in the earlier *Trauerspiel* book. What we must do, therefore, is look at Benjamin's original philosophical programme and then consider how far that programme was modified by his assimilation of Marxism.

Benjamin first set down his goal in writing in 1918 in a then unpublished piece, *On the Programme of the Coming Philosophy*.[17] He had been reading Kant with Scholem, and consequently the discussion proceeds in the framework of the Kantian account of knowledge (*Erkenntnis*). At the same time, Scholem had already begun his study of the Kabbalah, the tradition of Jewish mysticism. Because of that, the question for the coming philosophy was conceived as the relation of knowledge (*Erkenntnis*) to religious experience (*Erfahrung*). Or, more precisely, the programme of the coming philosophy is, "On the basis of the Kantian system to form a concept of knowledge (*Erkenntnis*) such that the concept of the experience (*Erfahrung*) of which knowledge is the articulation will be in correspondence with it."[18] From this standpoint, philosophy and religion or theology are virtually one.[19]

The programme of developing a theory of knowledge that would account for mystical and philosophical experience on a Kantian basis is carried a stage further in the prologue to the *Trauerspiel* book. That prologue is "one of the more impenetrable pieces of prose in German or, for that matter, in any modern language,"[20] but its thought, insofar as it can be discerned, would seem to turn on a distinction between knowledge (*Erkenntnis*) in the Kantian sense, which is cognition as adequate for science, and experience (*Erfahrung*), which is concerned with the revelation of truth.[21] In knowledge the subject constructs a world according to its own concepts; in experience the subject constitutes "ideas." These ideas have an objective structure that, as objective, is determined by the particular phenomena themselves. Despite that contrast between knowledge and experience, knowledge by breaking up reality into its elements does serve to mediate particular phenomena to the ideas. Phenomena do not enter whole into the ideas, but only as conceptually unravelled into their elements. All the same, experience is nonetheless the representation of ideas (*Darstellung der Ideen*) from out of empirical reality itself. The particular phenomena themselves, though conceptually mediated, become the ideas. And so Benjamin

Experience of History" in Dick Howard and Karl E. Klare, eds., *The Unknown Dimension: European Marxism Since Lenin* (New York: Basic Books, 1972), 251.

17   *G.S.* 2/2: 157-71.
18   *G.S.*2/1: 168: *Auf Grund des Kantischen Systems einen Erkenntnisbegriff zu schaffen dem der Begriff einer Erfahrung korrespondiert von der die Erkenntnis Lehre ist.* My translation.
19   *G.S.* 2/1: 171.
20   Steiner in the introduction to Benjamin, *German Tragic Drama*, 13.
21   I owe this line of interpretation to Buck-Morss, *Negative Dialectics*, 91-92.

declares: "Ideas are to objects as constellations are to stars. This means, in the first place, that they are neither their concepts nor their laws. They do not contribute to the knowledge of phenomena, and in no way can the latter be criteria with which to judge the existence of ideas. The significance of phenomena for ideas is confined to their conceptual elements."[22] The ideas, on the one hand, are nothing but the empirical phenomena, and, on the other hand, as constellations they are more. The phenomena, conceptually mediated, are taken up into the ideas and immortalized. Ideas are thus the redemption (*Rettung*) of the phenomena. (Benjamin intentionally used a religious word.) They are redeemed because their elements are caught up into the structure of an idea as an eternal constellation. "Ideas," he writes, "are timeless constellations, and by virtue of the elements' being seen as points in such constellations, phenomena are subdivided and at the same time redeemed (*gerettet*). . . ."[23]

Each idea, it should be noted, is self-contained as a monad. But every single monad contains all the others. As a monad each idea contains the totality and is an image of the world. Nevertheless, each idea differs from every other idea. Ideas are thus discontinuous, each in its own way a complete whole as a monadic image.

What Benjamin is striving for is a "nonmetaphysical metaphysics."[24] He is trying to make the phenomenal world yield noumenal experience. He wants to construct an intelligible world, but on an anti-idealistic, empirical basis. The attempt corresponds to his sensibility as a *littérateur*: his constant concern as a critic with particulars, his extraordinary feeling for detail, and his ability to articulate subtle nuances. At the same time, it also fits in with what Benjmain had assimilated of Kabbalist exegesis. Buck-Morss explains:

The method of Kabbalist exegesis was to decipher both texts and natural phenomena as hieroglyphs in which even the smallest details could be made to reveal truth unintended. The method was through a logic of correspondences across the boundaries of conceptual schema [sic]; the goal was the revelation of truth which took on meaning within a constellation with the present, and this often meant a total overturning of traditional, rabbinical interpretations.[25]

Likewise, Benjamin's method was to scrutinize concrete details in such a way as to see in phenomena more than phenomena and produce a configuration of elements that released a transcendent meaning. We can say, then, that he strove for illumination in a manner similar to the way in which the Kabbalists sought a new revelation of truth. Hence, the illumination he intended was analogously mystical or religious.

---

22   Benjamin, *German Tragic Drama*, 34.
23   *Ibid*.
24   Buck-Morss, *Negative Dialectics*, 93.
25   *Ibid*., 210n.

There was also a further religious dimension to his thought, the theme of redemption. Phenomena were to be rescued from temporal extinction and human experience salvaged from historical oblivion by being transformed into timeless ideas. Ideas may thus be seen as *anamnesis* or remembrance.

The religious theme of redeeming phenomena looks back to an early essay, "On Language As Such and On the Language of Man,"[26] written in 1916, which analyzes the linguistic being of man, who is the one who can name things. That power of naming was realized in Adam in paradise but then damaged by the fall. Language became babble, lost its adequacy, and could no longer express the concrete knowledge of the particular as it does in naming. Philosophy with its contemplation of ideas is a restoration of the divine language of names. As Benjamin writes in the prologue to the *Trauerspiel* book: "Adam's action of naming things is so far removed from play or caprice that it actually confirms the state of paradise as a state in which there is as yet no need to struggle with the communicative significance of words. Ideas are displayed, without intention, in the act of naming, and they have to be renewed in philosophical contemplation. In this renewal the primordial mode of apprehending words is restored."[27] As for the related theme of redemption through remembrance, that, as we shall see, received a more ample development in the *Theses* on history.

While he was writing the *Trauerspiel* book and engaged in the reflections I have outlined, Benjamin met Asja Lacis and began increasingly to identify himself with the Marxist Left. What effect did his move to Marx have upon his philosophical theories?

He seems to have adapted his philosophy to the new context without difficulty. There was, he considered, a common cognitive structure in Marxism, Kantian philosophy, and Kabbalist mysticism. What previously had been religious illumination now became secular illumination, but in fact the mystical illumination given in the ideas had always been an interpretive vision of mundane objects. He spoke now of the constellations, which, I have said, were elements configured so as to release meaning, as dialectical images. These images, the working of dialectical thought, brought together contradictory elements in a new constellation. The difficulty was to achieve a true dialectic. Adorno complained of a draft text of the *Passagenarbeit* that the mere juxtaposition of contradictory elements made the dialectical images just reflect the contradictions rather than critically igniting them.[28] But here we can ask whether Benjamin was going to be able to achieve the desired illumination without theology. Or, again, whether an illumination achieved through theology would be truly dialectical.

---

26   *G.S.* 2/1: 140-57; *Reflections*, 314-32.
27   Benjamin, *German Tragic Drama*, 37.
28   Buck-Morss, *Negative Dialectics*, 144.

On a related point, Benjamin and Adorno reached an agreement in talks they had while staying together in the village of Königstein in September and October of 1929 that materialism implied a relativism that excluded any ontology and all philosophical first principles in favour of a method that took the present as mediating all truth and meaning.[29] But that again simply corresponded to the previous practice of Benjamin.

In regard to the shift to Marxism, it may finally be noted that, whereas in Kantian idealism the structure of consciousness provided the unity and meaning of experience, that unity and meaning was given in Marxism by the structure of society as Marx understood it. In that respect Benjamin was professedly a Marxist, because, as he himself remarked, the politico-philosophic substructure of his essays was provided by Marxism.[30]

Be all that as it may, Benjamin ended with a conception of history which Habermas, rightly I think, regards as incompatible with historical materialism. The *Theses* on history, to which we now must turn, puts forward a radically anti-evolutionist concept of history. There is no way in which that can be reconciled with the progress that historical materialism considers as taking place both in the spheres of productive forces and the structures of power in society. Hence, Habermas concludes with some reason that Benjamin did not succeed in making his messianic theory of experience serve historical materialism.[31]

There is indeed a variety of claims to "historical materialism" as a designation. The historical materialist, said Benjmain in Thesis VII, "regards it as his task to brush history against the grain," and, although Habermas would disagree, Benjamin in here rejecting history as progress speaks in agreement with Adorno and Horkheimer. Under the influence of Benjamin's *Theses*, those two neo-Marxists wrote *Dialektik der Aufklärung* in 1947 against the myth of history as progress. All the same, it must be admitted that their common attitude to historical development simply marks off all three within the Marxist tradition.

Adorno was in fact upset when in the 1930s, under the influence of Brecht, Benjamin took up a more orthodox Marxist stance and wrote in an affirmative way about the course of history, as, for example in his essay, "The Work of Art in the Age of Mechanical Reproduction."[32] Adorno, as is known, did not wish to go beyond critical negation to any positive affirmation of the course of historical development. Benjamin, under Brecht, was moving towards such an affirmation of past and present. However, as we have seen, the shock of the Nazi-Soviet Pact turned him back from political affirmation to a deeply anti-evolutionist

---

29   *Ibid.*, 53.
30   *Ibid.*, 42.
31   Habermas, *Kultur und Kritik*, 332
32   *G.S.* 1/2: 435-69; *Illuminations*, 219-53.

view of history, expressed in theological language. What, then, was the view of history he finally reached in the *Theses*?

In a letter to Adorno's wife, Gretel, Benjamin pointed out that Thesis XVII contained the clue enabling one to recognize the hidden relation of these reflections to his previous work.[33] That suggestion is verified in practice. If read in the context of what we have already learned of Benjamin's thought, the meaning of Thesis XVII comes across clearly and provides a key to the interpretation of the others.

Unlike historicism, the thesis declares, which has no theoretical principle but simply adds data to fill homogeneous, empty time, materialistic historiography has a clear, constructive principle. What is the principle? The thesis continues: "Thinking involves not only the flow of thoughts, but their arrest as well. Where thinking suddenly stops in a configuration (*Konstellation*) pregnant with tensions, it gives that configuration a shock, by which it crystallizes into a monad. A historical-materialist approaches a historical subject only where he encounters it as a monad." Here, then, is Benjamin's cognitive theory of ideas as constellations or timeless monads, applied to historical phenomena by materialist historiography as he understands it.

The theory of constellations (or timeless ideas) as formed out of historical elements by the materialist historian implies the following: first, that in the constellations history is brought to a standstill in a present moment or now-time (*Jetztzeit*), which may be compared to the mystical *nunc stans* or the biblical *kairos*; second, that such constellations break the continuum of history and thus exclude the concept of progress; and third, that, to use religious language, the creation of such constellations is a messianic redemption of the enslaved ancestors or oppressed of the past through a saving remembrance. These three themes form the underlying structure of the following interpretation of the *Theses*.

"A historical materialist," so runs Thesis XVI, "cannot do without the notion of a present which is not a transition, but in which time stands still and has come to a stop." "History," says Thesis XIV, "is the subject of a structure whose site is not homogeneous empty time, but time filled by the presence of the now (*Jetztszeit*)." The thought is expounded more amply in the appended Thesis A, which, with Thesis B, was omitted from the final version prepared by Benjamin, but the content of which is in harmony with that of the other theses:

Historicism contents itself with establishing a causal connection between various moments in history. But no fact that is a cause is for that very reason historical. It became historical posthumously, as it were, through events that may be separated from it by thousands of years. A historian who takes this as his point of departure stops telling the sequence of events like the beads of a

---

33   *G.S.* 1/3: 1223.

rosary. Instead, he grasps the constellation which his own era has formed with a definite earlier one. Thus he establishes a conception of the present as the "time of the now" (*Jetztzeit*) which is shot through with chips of Messianic time.

The intelligibility of history, therefore, does not lie in a continuous course of events, filling a period of homogeneous time, but in a grouping of historical elements in a constellation with the present in a new revolutionary "Now," which shatters the continuity of history and brings its ongoing movement to a standstill.

Thus, the materialist grasp of history breaks the continuum of history. "The awareness," asserts Thesis XV, "that they are about to make the continuum of history explode is characteristic of the revolutionary classes at the moment of their action." That thesis goes on to tell the story that during the July revolution in France, the clocks in towers were fired on simultaneously and independently from several places in Paris. Revolutions produce new calendars, and calendars do not measure time as clocks do; they record days of remembrance. "Thus, to Robespierre," we read in Thesis XIV, "ancient Rome was a past charged with the time of the now (*Jetztzeit*) which he blasted out of the continuum of history." Again, Thesis XVI says, "The historical materialist leaves it to others to be drained by the whore called 'Once upon a time' in historicism's bordello. He remains in control of his powers, man enough to blast open the continuum of history."

The insistence that the continuum of history must be burst asunder means the rejection of the concept of progress. Such a rejection is set out explicitly in Thesis XIII. There it is pointed out that the fundamental reason for opposing the concept of progress is a critique of the understanding of history as a flow through homogeneous, empty time. The two conceptions of history, namely, as a progression through homogeneous time and as a constellation of past events in remembrance, are contrasted in Thesis B with regard to their different visions of the future. "The soothsayers who found out from time what it had in store certainly did not experience time as either homogeneous or empty. Anyone who keeps this in mind will perhaps get an idea of how past times were experienced in remembrance— namely in just the same way." The thesis goes on to observe that the Jews were prohibited from investigating the future, though instructed in remembrance by the Torah. This stripped the future of its magic: "This does not imply, however, that for the Jews the future turned into homogeneous, empty time. For every second of time was the strait gate through which the Messiah might enter." In other words, the future to be hoped for, or, in religious language, the coming of the Messiah, was not the end of a continuous progressive flow, but the effect of a flash of remembrance.

For Benjamin redemption broke the continuity of history, because that continuity represented the victory of the oppressors or ruling class. What has to be called in question is "every victory, past and present, of the rulers" (Thesis IV). Historicism, on the contrary, empathizes with the victor. "And all rulers," we read in Thesis VII, "are the heirs of those who conquered before them. Hence, empathy with the victor invariably benefits the rulers. Historical materialists know what that means. Whoever has emerged victorious participates to this day in the triumphal procession in which the present rulers step over those who are lying prostrate." The spoils are cultural treasures, and the historical materialist regards such treasures with a cautious detachment, because, as the same Thesis VII states, "There is no document of civilization which is not at the same time a document of barbarism." The revolutionary spirit is nourished, according to Thesis XII, "by the image of enslaved ancestors rather than that of liberated grandchildren." The redemptive aim must be to rescue those enslaved ancestors from the forgetfulness to which the victorious ruling class would assign them. "There is," argues Thesis II, "a secret agreement between past generations and the present one. Our coming was expected on earth. Like every generation that preceded us, we have been endowed with a *weak* Messianic power, a power to which the past has a claim. That claim cannot be settled cheaply" (Benjamin's italics). The task, says Thesis VI, is "to seize hold of a memory as it flashes up at a moment of danger. Historical materialism wishes to retain that image of the past which unexpectedly appears to man singled out by history at a moment of danger." The thesis goes on to articulate the danger. It is the danger "of becoming a tool of the ruling classes." Every age must try to wrest traditions away from conformity with the rulers. That conformism threatens to overwhelm not merely the living but also the dead. "Only that historian," Thesis VI continues, "will have the gift of fanning the spark of hope in the past who is firmly convinced that *even the dead* will not be safe from the enemy if he wins. And this enemy has not ceased to be victorious" (Benjamin's italics). Hence, the Messiah in coming as redeemer comes also as the subduer of Anti-Christ.

The coming of the Messiah is what occurs through a redemptive remembrance. On the one hand, as Thesis V states, "every image of the past—which is to say, only for a redeemed mankind has its past become citable in all its moments."

The vision of history presented in the *Theses* receives a particularly vivid expression in Thesis IX, which gives an interpretive description of a painting by Paul Klee, entitled *Angelus Novus*. Benjamin acquired the painting in 1921 and used it, as it were, as a meditation picture. The angel is said to be the angel of history. "His face is turned toward the past. Where we perceive a chain of events, he sees one single catastrophe which keeps piling wreckage upon wreckage and hurls it in front of his feet." The angel, it is said, would like to bring redemption, to achieve a *restitutio in integrum*, but he is caught in a

storm blowing from paradise, that is, from the origin, which irresistibly propels him into the future. "The storm is what we call progress."
Redemption, in other words, is not to be given by history, the continuous flow of which piles ruin upon ruin, but in a messianic
standstill of history.

No redemption, Benjamin avers, is to be found in the onward
course of history. The continuity of history is the persistence of the
unbearable. "Progress" is the eternal return of catastrophe upon
catastrophe.[34] In a short note, "Theological-Political Fragment,"[35]
wrongly given a late date by Adorno, but belonging in fact to the years
1920-21,[36] Benjamin had already insisted, against the then-prevalent
political interpretation of Messianism among Jewish thinkers, that
"the kingdom of God is not the *telos* of the historical dynamic; it
cannot be set as a goal." It is for that reason that the secular or
profane order cannot be based upon the idea of the Kingdom of God.
Therefore, "theocracy has no political, but only a religious meaning."
The messianic realm, according to the "Fragment," is not a goal to be
realized politically within history. The Messiah comes bringing all
history to an end, and he alone can establish a relationship to the
Kingdom.

The "Fragment" goes on to state that the order of the profane
should be built upon the idea of happiness (*Glück*). The quest for
happiness runs counter to the messianic direction, and yet is related to
it: "just as a force can, through acting, increase another that is acting
in the opposite direction, so the order of the profane assists, through
being profane, the coming of the Messianic Kingdom." What is it to be
profane? It is to be in time as transient. Happiness, consequently,
since it is realized in time, is bound up with a totally transient existence; it shares the eternal rhythm of a total going-under or perish-
ing. Messianic intensity arises in the other direction from unhappiness
or suffering. It is found in the heart or inner life of the isolated
individual. This intensity, an energy derived from suffering, intro-
duces immortality and the idea of a spiritual reintegration or *restitutio
in integrum*. Some indication of what Benjamin meant by immortality
may be found in an essay on Dostoevski's *The Idiot* published at this
time (1921), though he wrote it in 1917.[37] There he identifies the
immortal with the unforgettable. Immortality is not the same as the
eternity of nature, but is what compels remembrance. The immortal
life is the life that cannot be forgotten.

Admittedly somewhat enigmatic, the "Fragment" would seem,
then, to present us with the following vision. Profane, political exis-

---

34   Cf. Habermas's account of Benjamin, *Kultur und Kritik*, 313.
35   *G.S.* 2/1: 203-04; *Reflections*, 312-13.
36   *G.S.* 2/3: 946-49.
37   *G.S.* 2/1: 237-41.

tence is a quest for happiness as realized in time within the limits of finitude. Its rhythm is a ceaseless movement into nothingness. Thrusting across it comes the messianic movement, an intense energy arising from suffering and directed towards an immortality of remembrance. The goal of messianism, the Kingdom of God, is outside history and only realized in a breaking of the continuity of history.

Happiness reappears in Thesis II of the *Theses* on history. Reflection shows, Benjamin there argues, that our image of happiness is thoroughly coloured by the time in which we live. In other words, what determines our image of happiness is not some inconceivable future state, but the past which might have been but was not: it exists "only in the air we have breathed, among people we could have talked to, women who could have given themselves to us." But what does that imply? It implies that "our image of happiness is indissolubly bound up with the image of redemption." To put it in another way, the desire for happiness expresses itself in the context of suffering as a desire for redemption, which means a desire for the transformation of the past, of what has been. The thesis goes on to assert in a passage already quoted that the past is indeed open to transformation by the messianic power of each generation.

The suggestion that the past is still open and can be transformed by remembrance is contained in an exchange which Benjamin had with Horkheimer in 1937.[38] Benjamin asserted that the work of the past is not finished and closed off; it cannot be reified and possessed like a piece of property. Horkheimer disagreed. The past is finished. Past injustice has happened and is done with. The slain are truly slain. He said of Benjamin's assertion, "In the last analysis your statement is theological." In an unpublished manuscript of the *Passagenarbeit* Benjamin quotes the letter from Horkheimer and comments:

Remembrance (*Eingedenken*) can make of the unfinished (i.e. happiness) something that is finished and, conversely, it can make the finished (i.e. past suffering) into something that is unfinished. This is theology. Yet in remembering we gain the knowledge that we must not try to understand history in fundamentally a-theological terms, just as we would not want to write history in straightforwardly theological terms.

Probably that exchange with Horkheimer stimulated the thinking that led a few years later to the *Theses* on history.

In conclusion, let me now sum up what we have gathered of Benjamin's understanding of history.

---

38   An account of the exchange with quotations from the unpublished material is to be found in Rolf Tiedemann, "Historischer Materialismus oder politischer Messianismus?" in Peter Bulthaup, Hsrg., *Materialien*, 86-89. An account is likewise given in Christian Lenhardt, "Anamnestic Solidarity: The Proletariat and its *Mores*," *Telos* 25 (Fall, 1975), and I have taken from Lenhardt the translation of the quotation from Benjamin.

The first thing we should notice is that he writes as an historical materialist. How far his insights are compatible with a consistent historical materialism is another matter. But he is not returning to traditional religion nor putting forward in any literal sense a coming of the Messiah and redemption. He is bringing theology within historical materialism, insofar as he is using theological language to express a secular redemption, a profane illumination. Hence the paradoxical character of his thought as mystical materialism. As he wrote in his comment upon Horkheimer, neither straight theology nor a flat exclusion of theology would do. It is a question of incorporating theological, which means mystical, insights into historical materialism.

The basic framework of Benjamin's view is a negative, pessimistic vision of the ongoing course of history. He sees it as the endless return of catastrophe after catastrophe—in other words, he presents the negative side of Hegel's dialectic without the positive counterpart, the slaughter-bench of history without the unfolding of absolute Spirit. Further, history in its continuity is the history of the victors, not of the conquered, of the oppressors, not of the oppressed, of the rulers, not of their subjects, of the successful, not of the failures. The myth of progress must be rejected, and the historical materialist must dissociate himself from the triumphal procession of ongoing history.

How, then, are the enslaved ancestors to be redeemed, and the past history of suffering opened up and transformed? By remembrance. This creates constellations or paradigmatic configurations, uniting scattered events of the past with the present, joining the slain, the victims of the past, with the oppressed of the present. It is in these discontinuous constellations as ideas or centres of meaning that history is intersected by a saving power that brings its ongoing destructive course to a standstill in a set of timeless "Nows" and transforms the past by remembrance.

Thus, what we have, I think, in Benjamin, is a secularized apocalyptic. To put it in an admittedly oversimplified fashion, we may regard mainstream historical materialism as the secularization of prophetic eschatology, which embodied the conviction that God was working within history and that redemption would take place within the historical arena. Apocalyptic eschatology arose when there was a loss of confidence in political or historical forces in general—a shift from any expectation of a redemption within history to hope for a direct action of God breaking asunder the continuum of history and bringing history to an end. Hence, in Benjamin there is a loss of confidence in political forces, a loss of hope for any change in the onward course of history, and a turning instead to a redemption that would cut across history, bringing it to a standstill in a mystical *nunc stans* or *Jetztzeit* of remembrance.

Is it a religious vision? Yes, indeed; but a religious vision for those who live in a period of hopelessness when no positive action within history seems possible. "Only because of the hopeless is hope given to us."[39] And what is that hope? It is that flashing across history through a transforming remembrance of the suffering of the oppressed a reality and intelligibility that is not history is revealed.

39   From the essay, "Goethes Wahlverwandtschaften," *G.S.* 1/1: 201.

Some Underlying Issues of Modern Jewish Philosophy

MICHAEL D. OPPENHEIM

INTRODUCTION

The study of modern Jewish philosophy is a very complex pursuit. The cast of characters, as it were, is not large, especially in comparison with modern Protestant and Catholic philosophy. However, the central figures encompass a great diversity of positions. There are philosophers who take their point of departure from the following standpoints: eighteenth-century Rationalism, nineteenth-century Idealism, Romanticism, Existentialism, Pragmatism, Jewish mysticism, and secularist currents that range all the way to "God is Dead" theology. These classifications are, obviously, inexact; but they do have value in indicating the diversity and richness that is present in modern Jewish philosophy. The student of this area must at some time wonder whether it is presumptuous to speak of modern Jewish philosophy at all. Not only is there the aforementioned diversity, but there is very little discussion among the philosophers. One cannot point to the whole of modern Jewish philosophy as a tradition of thinkers who were strongly influenced by their predecessors and sought either to develop or reject the systems or doctrines that had been handed down. Most of the major Jewish philosophers do not evaluate the positions of their predecessors or endeavour to place themselves in the "stream" of modern Jewish philosophy.

Yet, the common core of questions that modern Jewish philosophers address provides the tradition of modern Jewish philosophy with a unity and integrity. These questions arise from the philosophers' struggle with modernity, identification with the Jewish experience, and commitment to the Jewish community.[1] Modern Jewish philosophers have not repudiated the Emancipation, the Jewish entrance into the stream of Western culture in the third quarter of the eighteenth century. While noting the problems that beset modern life, they have affirmed that there is meaning and value in the modern world. Modern Jewish philosophy has taken seriously modern man's self-understanding that has been influenced by religious pluralism, modern philosophy of religion, biblical scholarship, the disciplines of history, psychology, and sociology, and the natural sciences. However, one must speak of an *encounter* with modernity, because modern Jewish philosophers have not allowed their self-understanding as modern men to wipe away their consciousness of themselves as Jews. These thinkers identify with a body of literature, values, and ways of life that have come together to form an ongoing religious tradition. This identification with the Jewish experience has made them intensely aware of the necessity of discovering or creating a continuity between the Jewish past and present. Finally, modern Jewish philosophy brings together a group of people who possess a deep commitment to a particular community. Modern Jewish philosophers have a basis and a history that extends beyond their own life spans. They are conscious of being part of a people defined by the Call to Abraham, Exodus, Sinai, Exile, etc. Many of their questions arise from their community's paradox-filled life within the course of modern history. Thus, the stance of modern Jewish philosophers in both present and past, as well as their commitment to the Jewish community, has forced them to struggle with a common core of questions.

While many philosophers, historians, and general commentators on Jewish history have isolated one or more questions that they found to be central to modern Jewish philosophy, a careful enumeration of these questions is not to be found. The following list of some of the underlying issues in modern Jewish philosophy is offered as a beginning. The overriding concerns here are to enumerate the major issues and to characterize them briefly. On both of these accounts the listing is only provisional. First, there are probably other issues that should be included, and it may be better in particular cases to divide one issue into two, or to compress two into one. Second, in defining issues one is doing more than just collecting already "given" facts. Every definition, as the philosopher knows, is a *midrash*, that is, an interpretation. Philosophers differ not only in how they answer particular questions, but,

---

1   Prof. David Hartman of Hebrew University in Jerusalem, in the summer of 1973, spoke of the modern Jewish philosopher in terms of his affirmation of the modern world, identification with the Jewish heritage, and commitment to the Jewish community.

more fundamentally, in how they perceive and formulate the questions which they wish to address. Thus, there can be no presuppositionless or unbiased formulation of the questions, and legitimate differences about definitions must be expected. The attempt has been made to formulate the questions in as open a way as possible, so that common features in various definitions will be recognized. Finally, in order to further clarify the issues, some characteristic solutions offered by Jewish philosophers are brought forward.

The issues selected reflect the two dimensions of Judaism's encounter with modernity that have preoccupied modern Jewish philosophers. The writings of these philosophers are permeated with discussions about the integrity, continuity, and meaningfulness of Jewish communal life, and about the possibility of the modern Jew retaining religious belief. In reaction to these concerns, the list of issues is divided into two groups. The first group gathers together those issues that appear in the literature of Jewish philosophy from the beginning of the process of Emancipation in western and central Europe. The era of Emancipation began with the breakup of the autonomous Jewish communities and the weakening of the power of the rabbis over such areas as education, law, and even religious worship. Eventually, the Jewish communities were transformed into voluntary organizations. This process was completed in Western and Central Europe by 1880, at the time when Jews finally acquired the rights of citizenship in the countries in which they resided. These changes dramatically challenged the Jewish community and its institutions. In response to the new social and political situation of the Jews, Jewish philosophers sought to answer such questions as the following: "What is Judaism?" and "What does it mean to be a modern Jew?"; "Why is Judaism still important for the individual Jew as well as the wider society?"; "How can continuity with the past be maintained?"; and "What types of changes in religious practice are legitimate?"

Modern Jewish philosophers also recognized that belief in the biblical God who created the world and directs history was being radically challenged. The challenges arose from two sides. First, Jewish philosophers responded to the general critique of religious belief that arose from such disciplines as philosophy, psychology, and sociology. Second, they understood that the tragedies of modern Jewish history had brought many Jews to seriously question God's power over human affairs. The event of the Holocaust brought this question to the fore and made it almost unavoidable. In addition, the establishment of the modern state of Israel forced Jewish thinkers to re-examine the issue of God's presence in history.

MODERN JUDAISM—THE COMMUNITY
AND THE INDIVIDUAL

---

1. The Essence (or Character) of Judaism[2]

The question of the essence of Judaism has often been raised by Jewish philosophers in modern times. Those who have struggled with this question have sought to isolate one element or a small group of elements from the totality of Jewish life in the past. Once a philosopher determines the essence of Judaism, the claim is then made by him that throughout the ages and in spite of all the transformations that Judaism has undergone, the essence has both remained the same and provided Judaism with its *raison d'être*. The preoccupation of Jewish thinkers with this question reflects, among other things, their understanding of the historical dimension of Judaism, that is, its life as a "cumulative tradition," and the pivotal position that an inquiry into the essence or nature of Judaism takes in arriving at solutions to other related questions, such as questions of continuity and identity.

The first modern Jewish philosopher, Moses Mendelssohn, was also the first to seek a solution to this question. In *Jerusalem, or On Religious Power and Judaism*, Mendelssohn held that the essence of Judaism is its "divine legislation—Laws, commandments, statutes, rules of conduct, instruction in God's will and in what they [the Jews] are to do to attain temporal and eternal salvation."[3] This divine legislation had been revealed to the Jewish people at Sinai, and it continued to be both the foundation of Jewish life and the unique possession of the Jewish people. Mendelssohn regarded as constituents of Judaism those eternal truths about God and man that are necessary for man's salvation. However, he contended that these were the heritage of all men and accessible to all through reason.

Beginning with Mendelssohn's younger contemporary, Saul Ascher, most Jewish philosophers in western and central Europe turned away from the view that Jewish Law, Halacha, was the essence of Judaism. They described Judaism as a religious tradition and proposed that particular religious beliefs or moral ideals should be understood as its essence. Ascher saw religious doctrines or "dogmas as the essence of Judaism," for he believed that "only they can preserve Judaism in its purity, at times when the law is or has to be neglected."[4]

---

2   Like their non-Jewish counterparts, many contemporary Jewish philosophers have abandoned the earlier quest for essences in general, and the essence of Judaism in particular. Although the goal of finding one element or a common core of elements is now thought to be ill-conceived, Jewish thinkers still endeavour to elucidate the character of Judaism.

3   Moses Mendelssohn, *Jerusalem*, trans. and ed. by Alfred Jospe (New York: Schocken Books, 1969), 61. The book was originally published in 1783.

4   Saul Ascher, *Leviathan oder über Religion in Rücksicht des Judentums*, 172-73, cited by

The stream of liberal Jewish philosophers, which began with Ascher, continued to the twentieth century. Leo Baeck, for example, in the book appropriately titled *The Essence of Judaism*, wrote that Judaism's "predominant aspect from the very beginning was its ethical character, the importance it attached to the moral law. Ethics constitute its essence. Monotheism is the result of a realization of the absolute character of the moral law; moral consciousness teaches about God."[5] Baeck believed that these essential teachings of Judaism were the "religious legacy" of the prophets.

Jewish thinkers in eastern Europe, who lived in a vastly different social, political, and intellectual environment from the Jews of the West, usually understood Judaism as more than a religious tradition. They spoke of it as the total spiritual or cultural expression of the Jewish people. This approach to the character or essence of Judaism is well represented by Mordecai Kaplan, the twentieth-century American Jewish philosopher. Kaplan indicated both the importance of the quest for the essence of Judaism as well as his solution to that quest in the title of his work of 1934, *Judaism as a Civilization*. He proclaimed that Judaism "includes the nexus of a history, literature, language, social organization, folk sanctions, standards of conduct, social and spiritual ideals, aesthetic values, which in their totality form a civilization."[6] Thus, Kaplan continued to take part in the enterprise to define an essence of Judaism, although he saw it as a mistake to isolate one element out of the total "nexus" of elements that constitutes Judaism, since Judaism was for him a living and evolving civilization.

2. Identity

The familiar question, "Who is a Jew?" and the somewhat wider question, "What does it mean to be a Jew?"[7] emerge out of the struggle for Jewish identity. The issue of Jewish identity comes to life whenever Jews engage in significant personal, social, and intellectual contact with other cultures and religious traditions. In the absence of either contact with others or internal schism the question of identity does not arise. In modern times the identity issue has been crucial from the beginning of the Jewish emancipation. Most modern Jewish philosophers have addressed the question of Jewish identity in such a way that neither Jewish

---

Ellen Littmann, "Saul Ascher: The First Theorist of Progressive Judaism," *Leo Baeck Institute Year Book 5* (London: East and West Library, 1960), 114.

5   Leo Baeck, *The Essence of Judaism*, trans. by Victor Grubenwieser and Leonard Pearl (New York: Schocken Books, Schocken Paperback Edition, 1970), 59. The book was originally published in 1905.

6   Mordecai Kaplan, *Judaism as a Civilization* (New York: Schocken Books, 1972), 178. The book was originally published in 1934.

7   The question "What does it mean to be a Jew?" requires an answer that includes more than just the issue of identity. This question about meaning alludes to the issues of value and continuity.

particularity nor the thrust of Emancipation are repudiated. In other
words, Jewish philosophers affirm the uniqueness, separateness, or
distinctiveness of Judaism and reject full assimilation into the wider
culture. On the other hand, they do not define Jewish identity in such a
way that Jews will have to renounce all participation in the wider
culture.

The traditional definition of who is a Jew, a definition based on
birth,[8] has been retained in discussions of Jewish identity. However, the
wider question of the meaning of being a Jew has elicited many different types of responses. Emil Fackenheim in his essay, "In Praise of
Abraham, Our Father," offered a modern adaptation of the traditional
understanding of Jewish identity, an adaptation that recognizes that
"Jewishness" no longer has an exclusively religious meaning. He
writes: "a Jew is anyone who by his descent is subject to Jewish fate (the
"covenant"); whether he responds to Jewish fate with Jewish faith
(whether he is "obedient" or "stiff-necked") does not affect, though it is
related to, his Jewishness."[9] Discussions of what it means to be a Jew
parallel the usual answers to the question of the essence of Judaism.
Jewish philosophers have described the meaning of being a Jew in
terms of subscribing to particular religious beliefs or observing specific
practices, on the one hand, or, on the other hand, participating in the
life of the Jewish nation or civilization.

The contemporary Israeli philosopher, Eliezer Schweid, in his
book, *Israel at the Crossroads*, proposed that there were actually three
"directions" that Jewish philosophers have taken to the question of
Jewish identity: religious, national, and cultural. Schweid found that
the common denominator of the different religious definitions of what
it means to be a Jew was a "belief in a God who is revealed to Israel and a
way of life to which one is obligated according to that belief."[10] National
definitions focus on the "consciousness of unity against a background
of common origin and common fate."[11] The cultural direction, which is
usually an outgrowth of the national definition, describes the Jew's
participation in the Jewish culture through his ties to its past and his
commitment to its future.

Schweid's own attempt to address this question, in *Judaism and the
Solitary Jew*,[12] brings together elements from all three of the "di-

8   According to Halacha, if an individual is born to a Jewish mother, then he/she is
    Jewish. Modern Jewish philosophy has not examined the issue of identity in connec-
    tion with converts to Judaism. It seems that the infrequency of such conversion has
    resulted in this not being a "live" issue.
9   Emil Fackenheim, "In Praise of Abraham, Our Father," in *Quest for Past and Future*
    (Boston: Beacon Press, Beacon Paperback, 1970), 64. This essay was first published
    in 1948.
10 Eliezer Schweid, *Israel at the Crossroads*, trans. by Alton Meyer Winters (Philadelphia:
    The Jewish Publication Society of America, 1973), 22.
11 *Ibid.*, 23.
12 Eliezer Schweid, *Judaism and the Solitary Jew* (in Hebrew) (Tel Aviv: Am Oved
    Publishers, 1974), 31-112.

rections." He begins by examining the questions "Who am I?" and "From where do I come?" He regards these questions as the foundation of any inquiry into identity. Those constituent elements that appear in answer to the above questions include the individual's relationships to the family, people, history and culture of that people, and origins of that people. According to Schweid, the fact that religion is interwoven with all of these elements is distinctive to the issue of *Jewish* identity. For example, Judaism powerfully shapes the ways that members of the family understand their relationships to other members, and it stands as the foundation of the coming together of the Jewish people as a people.

Martin Buber offered a dynamic portrait of Jewish identity by describing the unique nature of the Jewish people. Buber discovered that definitions of Jewish identity since the Emancipation have taken an understanding of the Jewish people as a starting point. Those philosophers who characterized Jewish identity in terms of religious beliefs or practices often described the Jewish people as a religious community. In this case, it is held by these thinkers that individual Jews were open to God's revelation, but the recognition of the life of the Jewish people in history was missing. On the other hand, those who offered national definitions of Jewish identity sought to portray the Jewish people in history, but they ignored the element of revelation, or the covenant between God and the people of Israel. Buber described the Jewish people as both a nation and a religious community. He understood the meaning of being a Jew in terms of the individual's participation in the unique destiny of that people:

Israel receives its decisive religious experience *as a people*.... The community of Israel experiences history and revelation as one phenomenon, history as revelation and revelation as history. In the hour of its experience of faith the group becomes a people.... The unity of nationality and faith which constitutes the uniqueness of Israel is our destiny....[13]

Finally, while contemporary approaches to the problem of Jewish identity continue to reflect the earlier discussions, two radically new elements have both intensified the quest for the meaning of being a modern Jew and have introduced new dimensions to the discussion. These events, the Holocaust and the establishment of the state of Israel, will be examined at another point.

3. Value

The question of value has both a communal and a personal dimension. Jewish philosophers have found themselves asked, both by those within and outside their community, "Does Judaism have a role to play in the

---

13   Martin Buber, "The Jew in the World," in Arthur Hertzberg (ed.), *The Zionist Idea* (New York: Atheneum, 1969), 455. The essay was originally published in 1934.

modern world?" and "Why should someone remain a Jew?" There is a pronounced apologetic thrust to the modern Jewish philosophical endeavour. Jewish philosophers have understood—from the time of Moses Mendelssohn's forced reply to Lavater's challenge that he either renounce Judaism or prove its superiority to Christianity—that Judaism is under attack by exponents of other religious traditions as well as by atheistic philosophers. In addition, they have recognized that the ongoing secularization of Western society provides a hostile environment for all religious traditions.

The major works of modern Jewish philosophy have constantly affirmed that Judaism had an important role to play in the modern world. Abraham Heschel contended, in fact, that this was an essential task of modern Jewish philosophy when he wrote: "The task of Jewish philosophy today, is not only to describe the essence but also to set forth the universal relevance of Judaism, the bearings of its demands upon the chance of man to remain human."[14]

There are three factors behind the endeavour of Jewish philosophers to affirm the universal relevance of Judaism, that is, its role in the modern world. First, as explained above, Jewish philosophers have recognized that Judaism was under attack. Second, they believed that by describing Judaism's role in the modern world they could help the individual and the community in their encounter with modernity. Philosophy could reinforce the individual's will to remain Jewish, and it could help the community to overcome the forces of assimilation and fragmentation. Third, the very fact that Jewish thinkers engaged in the enterprise of Jewish philosophy implied that they saw an important relationship between Judaism and the modern world. Jewish philosophers "translated" the Jewish experience into the categories of the wider culture. They saw that this process of translation would be valuable for both the Jewish community and for the outside world. Through their work the community could be revitalized and the non-Jewish world could gain the benefit of Judaism's enduring spiritual and intellectual resources.

While Jewish philosophers have agreed that the "teachings" of Judaism had significance for non-Jews as well as Jews, the nature of these teachings have been depicted in very different ways. For example, many of the Jewish philosophers of the nineteenth century were influenced by German Idealism and responded, in particular, to the thought of Schelling and Hegel. Such philosophers as Solomon Formstecher and Samuel Hirsch utilized Idealist categories in their explanation of Judaism, but they saw that Judaism broke with the current philosophy over one detail. In the face of an all-encompassing philosophical system that undermined the reality of human freedom,

---

14   Abraham Heschel, *God in Search of Man* (New York: Harper and Row, Harper Torchbooks, 1955), 421.

these philosophers found that Judaism's significance for modern man lay in its message of man's freedom and the corresponding importance of the individual's moral action.[15]

On the other hand, against the backdrop of twentieth-century society's glorification of knowledge, power, and social success, Joseph Soloveitchik wrote about the "loneliness" of the religious life. In his essay, "The Lonely Man of Faith," Soloveitchik sketched a portrait of the Jewish understanding of the religious life. He held that while Judaism did not disparage man's dignity and power, it understood that these were not the final *telos* of man. The religious man believes that to live authentically he must at times stand alone before God and let "himself be confronted and defeated by a Higher and Truer Being."[16] In this way Soloveitchik depicted Judaism's understanding of what it means to be human, an understanding that could stand as a corrective to the prevailing views about the nature of man.

Often the inquiry into the issue of value takes its point of departure from the philosopher's view of the essence or character of Judaism. For example, Hermann Cohen in *Religion of Reason Out of the Sources of Judaism*[17] declared that Judaism was a religion of reason. Cohen meant by this that Judaism is an authentic stream through which one of man's highest rational expressions, i.e., religion, is manifested. In defining Judaism in this way he, at the same time, answered the value question in the affirmative. Cohen held that all expressions of reason, whether philosophy, science, or religion, have eternal validity. Judaism's particular importance in the modern world was underscored by Cohen when he pointed out its continuous task of teaching and guarding the monotheistic and messianic concepts of the religion of reason.

Franz Rosenzweig provides another important illustration of the apologetic thrust in Jewish philosophy. Rosenzweig, who early in his life was on the road to conversion to Christianity, expressed both his personal commitment to Judaism and his understanding of its value in the modern world in his magnum opus *The Star of Redemption*.[18] Rosenzweig even regarded this book as his "armour" against the stings of Christianity and philosophy.[19] In the *Star* Rosenzweig gave philosophic answer to both the communal and the personal dimensions

---

15 For a presentation of the philosophies of Solomon Formstecher and Samuel Hirsch, see Julius Guttmann, *Philosophies of Judaism*, trans. by David W. Silverman (London: Routledge and Kegan Paul, 1964), 308-21.

16 Joseph B. Soloveitchik, "The Lonely Man of Faith," *Tradition* 7/2 (Summer, 1965), 24.

17 Hermann Cohen, *Religion of Reason Out of the Sources of Judaism*, trans. by Simon Kaplan (New York: Frederick Ungar Publishing Co., 1972). The book was originally published in 1919.

18 Franz Rosenzweig, *The Star of Redemption*, trans. by William Hallo (New York: Holt, Rinehart, and Winston, 1970). The book was originally published in 1921.

19 From a letter by Rosenzweig. The letter is included in *Franz Rosenzweig: His Life and Thought*, ed. by Nahum Glatzer (New York: Schocken Books, 1970), 107.

of the question of the value of Judaism. He wrote that there are two covenants with God through which his plan for history is being realized. Both the Jewish community and the Christian community participate in the plan of divine redemption. The role of the Jewish community is to withstand the attacks of others and the vicissitudes of history by witnessing to the element of eternal life that God has placed in its midst. Rosenzweig hoped to give support to the individual's determination to remain a Jew by describing the *living* reality of the Jewish people's covenant with God. Obviously, the power of Rosenzweig's answers is contingent on the questioner's religious stance, just as Cohen's efforts are based on a particular view of the relationship between reason and religion. However, Rosenzweig's combination of commitment to Judaism and philosophic exposition represents one of modern Jewish philosophy's most dynamic answers to the question(s) of the value of Judaism.

Finally, in the twentieth century some philosophers have rejected the attempt to justify the value of Judaism or the continued existence of the Jewish people. Mordecai Kaplan in *Judaism as a Civilization* held that the Jewish civilization has the same right to exist as any other great civilization, and he refused to justify this right of existence by speaking of its value or mission to the nations. He wrote, "as a civilization, Judaism possesses the prerogative of being justly an end in itself."[20] However, Kaplan still saw that one must give answer to the question of the Jew remaining a Jew, to the personal dimension of the value question. He argued that only by participating in the civilization into which one is born can the individual achieve a this-worldly "salvation," that is, integrity and authenticity.

4. Continuity

The effort to maintain or to re-establish continuity with the religious life and values of the Jewish past has permeated the work of the modern Jewish philosopher. It has been understood that the dramatic changes and challenges that were ushered in from the period of the Emancipation brought the perplexing question of continuity in their wake. Franz Rosenzweig believed that one of his major tasks as a Jewish philosopher was to foster the community's *trust* in itself, its belief and confidence in its ability to participate in the on-going Jewish tradition. He wrote in the essay "The Builders" that the feeling of being in continuity with the Jewish past, "the feeling of being our fathers' children, our grandchildren's ancestors," was nothing less than "the very basis of our communal and individual life."[21]

---

20   Kaplan, *Judaism as a Civilization*, 181.
21   Franz Rosenzweig, "The Builders," in N. N. Glatzer (ed.), *On Jewish Learning* (New York: Schocken Books, Schocken Paperback Edition, 1965), 91. The essay, which was originally a letter to Martin Buber, was first published in 1923.

At least two factors are fundamental to the endeavour of the modern Jewish philosopher to address the question of continuity. First, in exploring the issue of continuity one must also take up the question of the essence or character of Judaism. Obviously, the issue of continuity can only be treated if one already has some understanding of that with which one desires continuity. If, for example, one agrees with Leo Baeck's position concerning the essence of Judaism, then the effort to achieve continuity will focus on the ethical teachings of the prophets, rather than on some other feature of the past that lies at the periphery of Judaism. The second factor is the philosopher's understanding of the nature of the barrier that stands between the present community and its past. The more radical the gap between past and present, the more radical must be one's efforts to find continuity with that past. Thus, the philosopher's understanding of the extent of the gap determines whether continuity is to be achieved through passively accepting something that has been handed down, creatively working with the past heritage, or radically transforming the fragments or shreds from the past.

The dynamic between one's conception of the barrier and the endeavour to achieve continuity is forcefully brought out in the following examples. Martin Buber in the essay "Renewal of Judaism" suggested that "Judaism can be no longer be preserved by mere continuation," that is, by passively taking up what had been handed down.[22] For Buber the modern world was so different from the past that the Jewish heritage was quickly losing its meaning and relevance. Since "mere continuation" would lead to a dead end, Buber called for a renewal that could only be accomplished through active "intervention and transformation."[23] In *Judaism as a Civilization* Mordecai Kaplan perceived the barrier in an extreme way. He wrote: "The differences between the world from which the Jew has emerged and that in which he now lives are so sharp and manifold that they almost baffle description."[24] Kaplan demanded nothing less than a "reconstruction" of Judaism as a consequence of his portrait of this rupture between past and present. Finally, Hannah Arendt in *Men in Dark Times* described the modern paradox that for many Jews "the past spoke directly only through things that had not been handed down, whose seeming closeness to the present was thus due precisely to their exotic character, which ruled out all claims to a binding authority."[25] To establish her view she turned to the work of Gershom Scholem, the great historian of Jewish mysti-

---

22   Martin Buber, "Renewal of Judaism," in Nahum Glatzer (ed.), *On Judaism* (New York: Schocken Books, Schocken Paperback Edition, 1972), 36. This lecture was first delivered in 1911.
23   *Ibid*.
24   Kaplan, *Judaism as a Civilization, 511.*
25   Hannah Arendt, *Men in Dark Times* (New York: Harcourt, Brace and World, Inc., 1968), 195. The essay was first published in 1968.

cism. Arendt held that Scholem saw that the break between past and present was so drastic that he made the "strange decision to approach Judaism via the Cabala, that is, that part of Hebrew literature which is untransmitted and untransmissible in terms of Jewish tradition, in which it has always had the odor of something downright disreputable."[26]

In order to further indicate the dynamic between a philosopher's perception of the break with the Jewish past and the nature of the quest to establish continuity with that past, a selection of the philosophers previously mentioned will be reintroduced at this point. For illustrative purposes the break or barrier between past and present can be pictured as a pane of glass. The glass is transparent at the top and completely opaque at the bottom. As one looks from the top to the bottom of the pane, the glass becomes less and less transparent, more and more frosted. A number of philosophers' positions can be delineated in terms of their ability to look from their standpoint in the present, through the glass, to the Jewish tradition of the past. We will begin with those who, looking through the top of the glass, have no difficulty in seeing the past. An ultra-Orthodox thinker would hold that the so-called break between past and present is really an illusion, and, thus, that there ought to be no changes in Jewish life in our times. Of course, since the encounter with modernity is a foundation of modern Jewish philosophy, there are no ultra-Orthodox *modern* Jewish philosophers. Moses Mendelssohn might be a good representative of the next position. At the point where he would look at the past, the pane of glass would be just beginning to become frosted. Mendelssohn held that there were certainly some differences between the past Jewish environment and the present. Still, for him it was not difficult to have a continuity with the past, for one lived as the "fathers" did by accepting the totality of that "divine legislation" which was given to Moses on Sinai. Thus, the Halacha, which Mendelssohn regarded as the essence of Judaism, continued to give direction to one's way of life, just as it had in the past. Looking through the pane of glass further down, Leo Baeck's vision of the relation between the Jewish past and present could be appropriately described. For Baeck many of the past patterns of life had become obscured and this resulted in a different conception of modern Judaism than that which was offered by Mendelssohn. According to Baeck, the modern Jew could no longer find meaning in taking up the totality of Jewish law, but he did not see this as disastrous. The core of Judaism had always been the moral ideals of the prophets, and since these ideals could still be appropriated and lived out by the present community, a firm continuity with the past was possible.

At the next standpoint, since the past is even further obscured, philosophers no longer hold that there is something left intact from the

26   *Ibid.*

past that need only be preserved. Martin Buber is a good example of this position. As we saw, Buber said that continuity with the past can only be founded on the creative endeavours of the present generation. The things that had been passed down could not merely be preserved, they had to be transformed. At the next stage, Hannah Arendt's understanding of the rupture between past and present can be grasped. She held that this gap was so great that only those things that had never been central in the past could be recast into a new foundation for the present. By radically overturning the past hierarchy of Jewish values and styles of life one could come upon something that, when brought into the new context of the present, would serve as a paradoxical link with the past. Finally, at the bottom of the pane of glass, where there is no possibility of seeing anything by looking back from the present, stand those who believe that Judaism died when it came into contact with the modern world. Of course, there are no examples of modern *Jewish* philosophers who have taken this standpoint on the question of continuity.

There is one further dimension to the issue of continuity that should be examined. Some Jewish philosophers have sought to formulate a criterion of selection that could provide a true continuity with the past. Thus, rather than isolating a "one thing" that brings forth continuity, these thinkers have tried to create a principle of selection that would guarantee that what is maintained from the past is truly alive for the present and future generations.

In the essay "Herut"[27] Martin Buber struggled with the problem of formulating a criterion or method of selection to aid the modern Jew in finding a truly living and vibrant foundation for his Jewish life. Buber stated that a legitimate method of selection consisted of two steps. First, the individual must examine every aspect of the Jewish past. The modern Jew must divest himself of all prejudices about what might be essential and inessential in Judaism and thus open himself to all of the possible richness of the tradition. Second, he should take from the past and transmit to the present and future everything that can be both appropriated by him and transformed into a force or power in his own life. Thus, the category of "inner power" is offered by Buber as the criterion of selection and transmission.

5. Legitimacy/Authority

The legitimacy/authority issue is a component of the wider issue of continuity. However, in light of the significance of the specific focus here—Halacha and the fundamental religious institutions and beliefs tied to it—and the importance that Halacha has had for the Jewish past

---

27   Martin Buber, "Herut," in Glatzer (ed.), *On Judaism*. This essay was first published in 1919.

and present, the legitimacy/authority issue merits special treatment. The subject of Halacha appears in all of the major works within modern Jewish philosophy. While some philosophers have called for fundamental changes within Halacha, all have understood that changes could not be made without looking into two related questions. First, in what manner can proposed changes be given legitimacy? Second, which people have the authority to determine what is legitimate and what is not?

Samson Hirsch in *The Nineteen Letters* held that the validity of Halacha should not be challenged. For Hirsch, as well as Moses Mendelssohn, no fundamental changes should or could be made to the divine commandments. There could be some adaptation, just as Judaism had always adapted to changing conditions. Whatever adaptations or interpretations that might be made had to be determined by the traditional rabbinic authorities. Thus, for Hirsch, wholesale "reform" of Halacha was illegitimate, and only the consensus of authorized rabbis of a generation had the authority to deal with questions of Halacha. In referring to the call for reform of Halacha by other thinkers, Hirsch wrote:

The only object of such "reform," however, must be the fulfillment of Judaism by Jews in our time, the fulfillment of the eternal idea in harmony with the conditions set by the time. It must be the education and progress of time to the high plane of the Torah, not the lowering of the Torah to the level of the age....[28]

A different approach was taken by Franz Rosenzweig. Rosenzweig accepted Martin Buber's category of "inner power" and applied it to Halachic matters. In "The Builders" Rosenzweig proposed that whatever elements of Halacha could be appropriated by the modern Jew and transformed into "inner power" were both binding and legitimate. The modern Jew has the task of "keeping" all of those laws through which the divine voice can be heard, and rejecting whatever fails to show itself as a vehicle for the divine. Rosenzweig added the further stipulation that one must be open to the possibility of finding new vehicles for the divine within the Jewish tradition and thus of adding to the body of Halacha. In proposing the category of "inner power" as the criterion of legitimacy, Rosenzweig saw that *every* Jew stands as an authority in this matter. He wrote that, as a consequence of this criterion, "no one can take another person to task, though he can and should teach him; because only *I* know what *I* can do; only my ear can hear the voice of my own being which I have to reckon with."[29]

In *Judaism as a Civilization* Mordecai Kaplan presented one of the most distinctive and interesting approaches to Halacha. As discussed

---

28   Samson Raphael Hirsch, *The Nineteen Letters*, ed. by Jacob Breuer (New York: Feldheim Publishers, 1969), 113. The book was originally published in 1836.
29   Rosenzweig, "The Builders," 91.

above, Kaplan held that the radical gap between the Jewish past and present demanded that Judaism be reconstructed. One of the consequences of this understanding of Judaism is the substitution of the word *minhagim*, customs or folkways, for the word *mitzvoth*, commandments. Kaplan affirmed that Judaism must retain its distinctive ways of life even though the modern Jew can no longer believe that these ways come from God. Jews who viewed the commandments as customs would not dismiss them even if the divine sanction was absent. In addition to establishing a harmony between the Jew's understanding of Halacha and his scientific understanding of the universe, Kaplan believed that this standpoint would allow the Jewish law to be seen in a more positive and dynamic way. Finally, addressing the question of a criterion for deciding what changes in Halacha were necessary, Kaplan offered the following suggestion:

In the last resort, one's Jewish selective sense must be the final arbiter. There need be no fears about anarchy resulting from diversity in the practice of folkways. Diversity is a danger when we are dealing with law. But, on the assumption that Jews would accept the *miswot* not as laws, but as folkways, spontaneity would not only help to foster the *miswot* but would also give rise to an unforced uniformity which would be all the more valuable because it was not prescribed.[30]

Finally, it is important to note that despite the great variety of positions that are taken by modern Jewish philosophers concerning the role of Halacha in the present, almost all believe that it does indeed have significance for the modern Jew. For example, although Hermann Cohen was sympathetic to the vast reform of Jewish law suggested by some thinkers, he still thought that the concept of Law and some specific laws had to be maintained as a bare minimum. In his discussion of "The Law" in *Religion of Reason Out of the Sources of Judaism* Cohen affirmed that "the continuation of the religion of the Jewish monotheism is therefore bound to the continuation of the law...."[31]

JEWISH FAITH-MODERNITY AND
HISTORY
---

1. Teshuvah or The Second Immediacy[32]

Some challenges that modernity has hurled at religion seem to have destroyed the possibility of religious faith. These challenges have ari-

---

30 Kaplan, *Judaism as a Civilization*, 439. According to Kaplan, the word *minhagim* was to be substituted for the word *mitzvoth* in the case of those commandments that refer to the relationship between man and God.

31 Cohen, *Religion of Reason Out of the Sources of Judaism*, 366.

32 Emil Fackenheim first used the term "second immediacy," which he borrowed and adapted from the work of Søren Kierkegaard, in the essay "Two Types of Reform," in *Quest for Past and Future*. The essay was first published in 1961.

sen out of many sources: modern philosophy of religion, biblical criticism, the disciplines of history, psychology, and sociology. The modern Jew, as well as the modern religious person in other traditions, seems incapable of taking an unreflective or unquestioning religious stance toward God and Torah.

The "first immediacy" refers to those traditional beliefs about God and Torah that were held within the context of pre-modern society. Although religious people have always had what one might call "moments of doubt," it is only in modern times that sustained questioning by such thinkers as Marx, Nietzsche, and Freud has brought the individual to doubt radically both the reality and the value of his religious belief. Religious belief is not something that one just takes for granted in this age. Emil Fackenheim, who explores this issue in many of his writings, sees the modern challenge to faith as something unprecedented in religious history. In the book *God's Presence in History*. Fackenheim characterizes the threat as "subjective reductionism" that is, a "stance of *critical reflection* which dissipates every supposed divine Presence into mere feeling and appearance."[33] However, some modern Jewish philosophers have answered this challenge by stating that although a faith that is identical with the faith of one's "fathers" is impossible, a "second immediacy," that is, a self-conscious and questioning faith, is still possible.

Philosophers such as Mordecai Kaplan and Gershom Scholem have held that if the modern challenge to faith is taken seriously, there is no honest way to retain belief. In *Judaism as a Civilization* Kaplan finds that he must "reconstruct" Judaism because the traditional views about God, Torah, and salvation have been destroyed. Scholem's essay "Reflections on Jewish Theology"[34] includes the contention that Jewish philosophers have repudiated the naïve realism of the biblical view of the God who speaks to man and who directs history. He observes that even the so-called existentialist Jewish philosophers have abandoned the biblical understandings of creation, revelation, and redemption.

On the other hand, Franz Rosenzweig, Abraham Heschel, and others affirm that a "second immediacy" is truly possible. Rosenzweig maintains that whatever doubts one may have about the reality of God or the efficacy of Torah to bridge the gap between God and man, these doubts are dissipated in the *immediacy* of living out the commandments. He writes of this immediacy: "Psychological analysis finds the solution to all enigmas in self-delusion, and historical sociology finds it in mass

33 Emil Fackenheim, *God's Presence in History* (New York: Harper and Row, Harper Torchbooks, 1970), 43.
34 Gershom Scholem, "Reflections on Jewish Theology," in Werner Dannhauser (ed.), *On Jews and Judaism in Crisis* (New York: Schocken Books, 1976). This lecture was first delivered in 1974.

delusion. . . . We know it differently, not always and not in all things, but again and again. For we know it only when—we *do*.[35]

Abraham Heschel's book *God in Search of Man* is nothing less than an instrument designed to lead one to a "leap" of faith. Heschel endeavours to sensitize the modern person to the possibilities of recognizing God beyond the mystery that permeates nature and behind the power that inflames the words of the biblical prophets. Thus, for both Rosenzweig and Heschel, religious faith *can* withstand the unprecedented challenge of modernity.

2. God's Presence in History

In reaction to such unique events as the destruction of European Jewry and the creation of the state of Israel, contemporary Jewish thinkers have been forced to address the question of God's presence in history. While the issue of "the second immediacy" points to the confrontation between Jewish belief and the modern secular world, the issue of God's presence in history refers to the challenge that modern *history* poses for Jewish belief. Modern Jewish philosophers have asked whether the religious person could reaffirm the meaning of modern history and God's direction in the present in light of the radically evil and destructive event of the Holocaust. Yet, on the other hand, the founding of the state of Israel after two thousand years has appeared to many as a proof of God's concern and guidance in the present.

Richard Rubenstein was one of the first Jewish philosophers to recognize the importance of the Holocaust for modern Jewish thought. In the autobiographical essay "The Making of a Rabbi" he wrote, "I am convinced that the problem of God and the death camps is the central problem for Jewish theology in the twentieth century. The one pre-eminent measure of the adequacy of all contemporary Jewish theologies is the seriousness with which they deal with this supreme problem of Jewish history."[36] In response to the Holocaust, Rubenstein concluded that our age witnessed the "death" of the traditional Jewish concept of God.

Of all contemporary Jewish philosophers, Emil Fackenheim has been the most persistent in wrestling with this issue. In his book *God's Presence in History* Fackenheim indicates that the attempt to find meaning in the present is, in fact, a life and death struggle for the preservation of Judaism in the modern world. Fackenheim explains: "For the God of Israel cannot be God of either past or future unless He is still God of the present."[37] Fackenheim contends that the basis for belief in

---

35   Rosenzweig, *Franz Rosenzweig: His Life and Thought*, 245.
36   Richard L. Rubenstein, "The Making of a Rabbi," in *After Auschwitz* (Indianapolis: Bobbs-Merrill Company, 1966), 233.
37   Fackenheim, *God's Presence in History*, 31.

the God who acted in the past (biblical history) and who will act in the future (the Messianic age) is gone, if God has nothing to do with the present period. The God who spoke in the Bible was a God of history. This does not mean that he is responsible for whatever happens or that his plan is always clear. Yet, to say that God directs history is to say that at no time does he completely turn his back on the world. Thus, the religious person must somehow affirm that there is meaning in the present.

In light of the threat that the Holocaust poses for Jewish faith, Fackenheim refuses to follow in Martin Buber's steps when Buber says that there are times when God is silent. He admits that Buber's image of the silent God is able to sustain Jewish faith in its confrontation with secularism, but he also believes that it "fails to sustain us in our confrontation with the Nazi holocaust."[38] Fackenheim continues, "if *all present* access to the God of history is *wholly* lost, the God of history is Himself lost."[39] However, Fackenheim believes that one can glimpse a fragment of meaning, and he refers to this in his controversial statement that there is a "Voice of Auschwitz [which] manifests a divine Presence."[40]

Jewish philosophers have recognized that it is necessary, both as individual Jews and as leaders of the Jewish community, to struggle with the religious dimensions of the existence of the state of Israel. However, as with the event of the Holocaust, they acknowledge that only fragmentary responses are possible in reflecting upon the relationship between Israel and God's direction of history. In the book *Israel: An Echo of Eternity* Abraham Heschel hints at the religious significance of Israel, while concluding that "no single answer can exhaust its meaning."[41] Heschel writes:

We have not even begun to fathom the meaning of this great event. We do not fully grasp its message for us as a community and as individuals. It has not penetrated our capacity for representing its meaning in our daily lives. . . . For all who read the Hebrew Bible with biblical eyes the State of Israel is a solemn intimation of God's trace in history. It is not fulfillment of the promise, it is not the answer to all the bitter issues. Its spiritual significance, however, is radiant. . . .[42]

The Jewish philosopher has not turned his back on the compelling issues of modern Jewish life in order to contemplate the questions that scholars, rather than living people, hold dear. Modern Jewish philosophers have tried to follow in the task that Maimonides set for himself through the title of his great work, *The Guide to the Perplexed*. The title of

---

38 *Ibid.*, 78.
39 *Ibid.*, 79.
40 *Ibid.*, 88.
41 Abraham Heschel, *Israel: An Echo of Eternity* (New York: Farrar, Strauss, and Giroux, 1967), 219.
42 *Ibid.*, 219-20.

the magnum opus of Nachum Krochmal, *Guide to the Perplexed of our Time*, thus characterizes the work of more than one man. In the encounters with Emancipation, modernity, and the course of modern history, Jewish philosophers have struggled to affirm the meaning of Jewish existence.

It should be obvious that the issues identified above are not just Jewish issues. All the major religious traditions of the world have, more or less, been thrust into the modern world and into encounter with each other. In addition to giving guidance to those within the Jewish community, modern Jewish philosophers should be of help to philosophers in other religious traditions. In most cases Jewish philosophers have struggled with the modern challenges to religious life and religious belief in a more extreme way than have those in other traditions. The radical manner in which the Emancipation thrust the Jewish community into the modern world forced Jewish thinkers to take stock of that world in an unprecedented way. The paradoxical and sometimes terrifying course of modern Jewish history has accentuated the challenges to religious belief.

The establishment of the modern state of Israel has been mentioned in connection with the issue of God's presence in history. However, this does not exhaust its influence on the issues that have been examined in this paper. The impact of Israel's existence on such issues as identity, continuity, and value has yet to be fully explored by modern Jewish philosophers. The state of Israel is a revolutionary *novum* which has brought out new dimensions within these issues and has made some earlier solutions obsolete.

The dynamic quality of modern Jewish philosophy is inescapable. The preceding pages have been filled with such words as encounter, challenge, struggle, and confrontation. This choice of words is neither accidental nor a stylistic eccentricity; it truly reflects the state of modern Jewish philosophy. In light of its being virtually ignored by both modern philosophers of religion and scholars of Jewish studies, modern Jewish philosophy remains an unexplored mine of richness and diversity for those who wish to plumb the depths of modern Jewish life.

Reflections on the "Whig" Interpretation of Jewish History: *Ma'assei banim siman le-'avot*[*]

GERSHON DAVID HUNDERT

My motive in publishing these remarks is a desire to initiate and stimulate discussion of a series of questions related to being a national historian, and in my case, a Jewish historian. The use of the term "reflections" in the title is quite deliberate. I sought a term connoting thoughts and ideas as well as a certain subjectivity. There will be, of necessity, an almost confessional character to this essay, because the subject of historiography is inseparable from the standpoint of the situation of the historian. Thus, everything that I shall say here will have a certain self-revealing or self-reflecting character. The term "reflections" also serves as a warning to the reader that this short essay is far from being a thorough analysis of contemporary Jewish historiography.

Those who undertake the study of their own nation's history have a certain custodial, even proprietary attitude toward that history. In seeking and discovering what the historian deems to be his past, or, to put it another way, in publicly declaring what he defines as important and significant in his nation's past, the historian perforce asserts that

---

[*] In somewhat different form, these remarks were first presented to the Faculty Seminar in Jewish Studies, McGill University, in November 1978. I have also shared early drafts of this paper with some friends and colleagues including Ruth Wisse and Harry Bracken of McGill, David Biale of SUNY, Binghampton, and Paula Hyman of Columbia University. All of these made important and useful comments and criticisms, for which I thank them most heartily, but none of them is to be implicated in the responsibility for my remarks.

others with different understandings are mistaken. These polemics, however, implicit or explicit, are not conducted on a plane where contrary assertions can be verified by recourse to empirical tests. Such differences in interpretation are the product of subjective, ideological, even psychological factors. They have to do, finally, with history itself, namely, the situation, the environment, the *sitz im leben* of the historian.

Let me illustrate this with an example which may seem to be rather distant from the present subject of Jewish historiography. One of the most influential works in the field of English historiography has been Herbert Butterfield's *The Whig Interpretation of History*.[1] In that short book Butterfield elegantly and mercilessly attacked the school of historians for whom,

Whether we take the contest of Luther against the Popes, or that of Philip II and Elizabeth, or that of the Huguenots with Catherine de Medici; whether we take Charles I versus his parliaments, or the younger Pitt versus Charles James Fox, it appears the historian tends in the first place to adopt the whig or Protestant view of the subject, and very quickly busies himself with dividing the world into friends and enemies of progress.[2]

On the crudest level Butterfield's critique could be translated for the field of Jewish history into an attack on those Jewish historians who have divided the non-Jewish world as it impinged on the Jews into two categories—those individuals and classes who benefited the Jews, and those who were hostile or worse. But this is a straw man; no sophisticated contemporary Jewish historian would be capable of such a simplistic viewpoint.[3] Still, there is a "whig"-like interpretation of Jewish history represented by a strong and influential school which tends to examine all of the events, institutions, and movements in Jewish history in the light of a single criterion—the degree to which these phenomena anticipate or partake in the national revival of the Jewish people or signal its continuity. I speak of the Jerusalem school of Zionist historians which was founded by Ben-Zion Dinur and Yitzḥak (Fritz) Baer.[4] Before proceeding to some remarks about the achievements and shortcomings of that school, I should like to return to Butterfield for a moment. In his book, which was published first in

---

1 Herbert Butterfield, *The Whig Interpretation of History* (London, 1959).
2 *Ibid.*, 5.
3 In the minds of some general historians, though, this is still the perception of Jewish historiography. See Richard Pipes' remarks at the beginning of his essay on "Catherine II and the Jews," *Soviet Jewish Affairs* (1975).
4 In addition to the works cited below, see: Morris R. Cohen, "Philosophies of Jewish History," *Jewish Social Studies* 1 (1939), 39-72; Benjamin De Vries, "On *Yisrael ba-amim*," *Beḥinot* 10 (1957), 21-27; Jacob Katz, "Between National History and Nationalist History," *Beḥinot* 9 (1956), 3-6; Michael Meyer, *Ideas of Jewish History* (New York, 1974), esp. 36-37; Pinchas Rosenbluth, "Yitzchak Baer," *Leo Baeck Institute Yearbook* 22 (1977), 175-88; Leni Yahil, "Dinur and Baer," *Molad* 183-84 (1963).

1932, Butterfield wrote that "the study of the past with one eye, so to speak, upon the present is the source of all sins and sophistries in history. . . . It is the essence of what we mean by the word unhistorical."[5]

What Butterfield condemned is precisely what has been extolled about the writing of one of the founders of the Jerusalem school. Ernst Simon, in a talk on Ranke, claimed that Yitzḥak Baer was the clearest continuer of Rankian traditions in the sphere of Jewish history. He went on to say that Baer, though he may have been less "tolerant" than Ranke, was not a dogmatic historian. On the contrary,

> There is in Baer continuity which accepts surprise and accepts novelties unanticipated by our forefathers. . . . If the dogmatic historian follows only the at once fruitful and dangerous principle that the deeds of the fathers prefigure those of the sons [ma'asei 'avot siman le-banim], the believing and undogmatic historian also follows the reverse principle that the deeds of the sons configure those of the fathers [ma'asei banim siman le-'avot] in the sense of realizing what was only historical potential in earlier generations.[6]

In this passage Simon has captured, I think, the essence of Zionist historiography, namely, the interpretation of the past in the light of a particular understanding of the present, ma'asei banim siman le-'avot. It is the sense that all of Jewish history has been moving toward a particular goal or telos—the regaining of sovereignty by the Jewish nation.

This can be seen most clearly in the writings of Baer's colleague, Ben-Zion Dinur, who divided all of Jewish history into three stages: Israel in its homeland, to 636; Israel in dispersion, 636 to 1948; and the present era of renewed national sovereignty.[7] Dinur was the prototypical Palestino-centric historian viewing the land as central to the historical experience of the Jews and finding in the periodic 'aliyot and other expressions of rebellion against the exile—especially messianic movements and speculation—the most important elements in Jewish history.

A brief summary of Dinur's argument in support of his contention that 1700 should be considered the beginning of the modern period in Jewish history will serve as a convenient example of his perspective.[8] While other Jewish historians have tended to identify the beginning of modern Jewish history with the Haskalah or emancipation, Dinur contended that neither of these phenomena reflect the "real historical

---

5   Butterfield, Whig Interpretation, 11, 31-32, quoted in E. H. Carr, What Is History? (New York, 1962), 50.

6   Ernst Simon, "The Significance of L. Ranke for the Development of Historiography" (Hebrew), in Historians and Historical Schools: Lectures Delivered at the Seventh Convention of the Historical Society of Israel (Jerusalem, 1962), 70.

7   Ben-Zion Dinur, "Jewish History—Its Uniqueness and Continuity," Journal of World History 11/1-2 (1968), 27. Also in H. H. Ben-Sasson, ed., Jewish Society Through The Ages (New York, 1972).

8   Ben-Zion Dinur, "Modern Times in Jewish History" (Hebrew), in Be-mifneh ha-dorot (Jerusalem, 1972), 19-68.

content" of the life of the Jews in the modern period, indeed, neither is to be identified with the realm of Jewish historical activity ['asiyah historit] in modern times. At the beginning of modern times in Jewish history, according to Dinur, stands the 'aliyah of a thousand Jews led by Yehudah he-ḥasid in 1700. He made this claim not so much because of the importance of the event itself, but because it is rich in symbolism with reference to the essential content of Jewish history. The immigration of those Sabbatian Hasidim adumbrated the pattern which followed. It demonstrated the continuity of messianic tension and marked the beginning of a more realistic form of messianic activity. Dinur tried to establish that there was a hidden messianic agenda in every 'aliyah between 1740 and 1840. The 'aliyah in 1700 was thus both an ideological symbol and a social-realistic symbol of what followed. It gave ideological expression to the will to migrate which was affecting significant sectors of east-European Jewry at that time. Dinur also pointed to the novelty in the form of leadership and organization of the 'aliyah in 1700. It was not shaped by the traditional communal organization, but it was an ideological movement with charismatic leadership. In this way it was an anticipation of Beshtian Hasidism.

There is no other event which is so interpenetrated with the historical paths of Israel in modern times in all their variety. . . . This period, it seems to me, which culminated with international recognition of Jewish independence in the land of Israel, which succeeded the great holocaust which destroyed the European Jewish communities, necessarily begins with that first 'aliyah which saw itself as a harbinger of redemption.[9]

This is history as exegesis, as midrash, finding symbols of the present in the past, "looking at the past with one eye, so to speak, on the present," ma'asei banim siman le-'avot.

It seems to me that Zionist historiography has tended to emphasize two main themes in Jewish history aside from the land of Israel, namely, messianism and the communal institutions of the Jews. In a sense these two themes are both static and dyanmic expressions of the continuous national existence of the Jewish people, and this is the reason for their centrality in the deliberations of the Zionist school. No one would argue that these are unimportant dimensions of the Jewish historical experience. I do want to suggest, however, that at times the depiction of these phenomena has been distorted in a variety of ways as a result of the modes of inquiry and the presuppositions of the Zionist school.

Let us return for a moment to Dinur and his attempt to show that the Hasidic movement "was a movement for redemption and its Torah was entirely a Torah of redemption."[10] One element in Dinur's argu-

---

9   Ibid., 29.
10 Ben-Zion Dinur, "The Beginnings of Hasidism: Its Social and Messianic Bases" (Hebrew), in Be-mifneh ha-dorot, 81-227.

ment is that Hasidism was the culmination of a shift in the source of authority in the Jewish community to the prophetic plane. This he traces to pre-Beshtian Hasidim whose goal was to be infused with the holy spirit, with prophecy. The significance of this trend toward the renewal of prophecy, for Dinur, was that it was the key to a deliberate redemptionist programme. Citing Maimonides, Dinur pointed out that the *halakha* is clear on this subject; the renewal of prophecy is an indication of the imminent arrival of the messiah. "Therefore," he concluded, "each story of the appearance of Elijah, and each story and tale of the descent of the *shekhinah* in that generation should be seen as signs that the days of redemption were near."[11] Dinur then went on to interpret the famous letter of the Besht to his brother-in-law, R. Gershon Kutover, as a kind of manifesto of the messianic agenda of Hasidism. The reference to the Besht's guide—Ahijah the Shilonite, who was also the teacher of Elijah—had particular significance for Dinur. He suggested that it is to be interpreted to mean that the Besht had appropriated Elijah's role as the harbinger of redemption.

Dinur's views, in this particular case, have been amply refuted by Gershom Scholem, Israel Halpern, and others, and there is no need for me to take up the cudgels.[12] These scholars have demonstrated that Hasidism, in its early stages, had no messianic agenda, and that no hint of a messianic programme can be detected either in the Besht's letter or in the early emigration of Hasidim to the land of Israel. The point here is the centrality of messianism in the Zionist conception of Jewish history. It is central because it is understood as the expression *par excellence* in pre-modern times of Jewish national consciousness. Therefore, there is a tendency to see messianism even when it was not there, particularly in major social and religious movements.[13]

Dinur is perhaps an easy target. But even Gershom Scholem, who is certainly to be distinguished from the Baer-Dinur school though not from Zionist historiography, had similar predilections.[14] In his desire to assert that the Sabbetian movement was a revolt of the *whole* Jewish people against their pariah status, against the *galut*, Scholem undoubtedly went too far.[15] The movement at its crest in 1665-67 had very little impact indeed on what was the largest Jewish community at the time and the home of the overwhelming majority of Ashkenazi Jewry, namely, the Jewish community of Poland. As Weinryb has shown, and

---

11 *Ibid.*, 171.
12 G. Scholem, "The Neutralization of the Messianic Element in Early Hasidism," *Journal of Jewish Studies* 20 (1969), 25-55. Also in his *The Messianic Idea In Judaism* (New York, 1972). I. Halpern, *Ha-'aliyot ha-rishonot shel ha-ḥasidim* (Jerusalem, 1947).
13 See, for example, Raphael Mahler, *Ha-kara'im* [A Medieval Jewish Movement For Redemption] (Merhavia, 1949). Also in Yiddish (New York, 1947).
14 David Biale, *Gershom Scholem: Kabbalah and Counter-History* (Cambridge, Mass., 1979), esp. 36-37.
15 G. Scholem, *Sabbatai Sevi* (Princeton, 1973).

my own research confirms, there is no convincing evidence that the movement caused any interruption whatsoever in the day-to-day affairs of that Jewry.[16] No reliable source indicates abandonment of businesses or property, or widespread movements of repentance. Polish archival sources, which record real estate transfers, commercial transactions of various kinds, taxes, and so on, indicate that the Jews carried on "business as usual" during the crucial years 1665-67. These records are doubly weighty because they are absolutely trustworthy.

Just as messianism has been elevated and magnified to serve the ideology of the Jerusalem school, so, too, another element in Jewish history has been placed at the centre of historical concern by Zionist historians. There is, though, less novelty in this second case. Shimon Dubnow, a non-Zionist, but certainly a nationalist, was probably the first to emphasize the significance of the communal organizations of the Jews, seeing in them the *sine qua non* of Jewish existence. In his introduction to the minute book of the Jewish Council of Lithuania, Dubnow asserted that that body was "one link in the chain of autonomy—the independent rule of the communities of Israel in all lands. If it were not for this chain which links all the scattered Diaspora, Israel could not have existed in the generations following the destruction of its kingdom and its land."[17]

Yitzhak Baer, in a very important article in which he was at pains to demonstrate the continuity of the conception of a Jewish community from Graeco-Roman times, suggested that the community preserved and embodied the hidden unity of the Jewish nation and the instruments of Jewish sovereignty. More, he asserted:

The same religious-political purpose and goal which opens the history of the people of Israel caused the formation of the local *kehilla*, organized around the synagogue . . . and after the dissolution of the last institution of leadership of the whole people, the local community remained the last political expression of the invisible unity of Israel.[18]

Israel Halpern, who edited the minute books of the Council of the Jews of Moravia and of the Council of Four Lands, wrote the following in his introduction to the former:

The preparation of this book and its publication have continued intermittently for a number of years. It was begun under the rule of strangers and appeared in the State of Israel. It is certain that we would not have been so privileged were it not for the reverence and determined preservation of the Jewish

---

16 B. D. Weinryb, *The Jews of Poland* (Philadelphia, 1973), 206-35. G. D. Hundert, "Security and Dependence: Perspectives on Seventeenth-Century Polish-Jewish Society" (Ph.D. dissertation, Columbia University, 1978).

17 S. Dubnow, *Pinkas ha-medinah* (Berlin, 1935), xi.

18 "The Bases and the Beginnings of the Organization of the Jewish Community in the Middle Ages" (Hebrew), *Zion* 15 (1950), 1.

character and Jewish independence which characterized the various exiled communities of Israel through the generations and which found clear expression . . . in these ordinances.[19]

In a sense, what Dubnow, Baer, Halpern, and others who have expressed similar sentiments are saying is that the *kehilla* preserved the Jewish national spirit or idea so that it could re-assert itself in our own day—*ma'asei banim siman le-'avot.*

The *kehilla*, then, is viewed as a unique expression of Jewish destiny. The continuity of Jewish national life is to be sought in the Jews' own autonomous institutions, that is, in the one domain in which Jews were captains of their own fate, in which they controlled their own destiny, in which they were not carried along like so much flotsam and jetsam on the larger historical currents of majority history. The *kehilla* did provide, in Yerushalmi's phrase, a "substructure" for Jewish civilization.[20] It was the stage for the inner history of the Jews, though Yerushalmi probably went too far in calling it a sovereign national state in microcosm.[21]

That the search for the plane on which the history of the Jews in the Diaspora "possesses dynamics all its own" should have led to the *kehilla* was both inevitable and correct. The history of the Jews must indeed focus on the institutions which were shaped and, in large measure, created and governed by the Jews. This position has been taken by both Diaspora and Zionist historians. It is precisely here, however, at the very nerve-centre of Jewish history, that the need for a supplementary or complementary dimension becomes clearest and most pressing. Even when the Jews were "at home," the institutions they created were shaped in significant ways by the "outside."

The task confronting the Jewish historian—I might almost say his duty—is the identification of what is endogenous and what is exogenous in Jewish civilization. What I am suggesting is not the abandonment of the focus on the institutions and actions of the Jews themselves, but the broadening of that focus to include a comparative dimension. The implicit claims of uniqueness, the sense that the *kehilla* was exclusively the product of the Jewish spirit, of an inner Jewish dynamic, will, perforce, be modified, but will not be vitiated. Indeed, in significant ways the claim that the *kehilla* is the locus of Jewish history will ultimately be strengthened by a more clear-sighted view of the context in which it arose. Although in some ways the tunnel-vision of Jewish historians of the past has been expanded, in others the insular school still rules. Where are the comparisons of Jews and Muslims in Christian Spain, of Jews and Italians in sixteenth- and seventeenth-century

---

19 *Takkanot medinat Mehrin* (Jerusalem, 1952), Introduction.
20 Yosef Hayim Yerushalmi, "Introduction," *Bibliographical Essays in Medieval Jewish Studies* (New York, 1976), 11.
21 *Ibid.*

southern German cities, of Jews and Scots in pre-partition Poland? Without thorough investigations of those groups and others we cannot fully understand and recover the story of the Jewish experience in those lands.

One cannot but be struck by the note of national pride which permeates the quotations cited from the writings of Dinur, Baer, Halpern, and Dubnow. I feel some discomfort (guilt to use the accurate term), because what I have been saying tends to deflate some of the implicit and explicit claims of these scholars. Let me express this in a different way by returning to Butterfield. It will be recalled that he attacked those who study the past, "with one eye, so to speak, on the present." During the 1940s,

> Professor Butterfield's country was engaged in a war often said to be fought in defence of the constitutional liberties embodied in the Whig tradition, under a great leader who constantly invoked the past "with one eye, so to speak, on the present." In a small book called *The Englishman and His History* published in 1944, Professor Butterfield not only decided that the Whig interpretation is the "English" interpretation but spoke enthusiastically of "the Englishman's alliance with his history" and of "the marriage between the present and the past."[22]

E. H. Carr, in pointing out this inconsistency, chose to interpret Butterfield's reversal as an example of the way in which the historian is influenced by his environment. Perhaps Carr underestimated the self-consciousness of the contemporary historian. Perhaps Butterfield had a deliberate and conscious desire to perform his national duty as an historian. Even if this desire was unconscious it is more significant than simply a question of the influence of the environment in a general way. Historians do influence their nations. Fritz Stern has attributed the collapse of German democracy in the 1930s "in some measure at least . . . to the misunderstanding of Western Liberal thought which German historians perpetuated and to their inadequate representation of Germany's own history and society."[23]

What then is the task of the Jewish historian today—should he emphasize themes and subjects which nurture and salve the national consciousness of his people? Dinur, writing at the same time as Butterfield (1944), delivered his views on Dubnow's conception of the movement of Jewish history from one "centre" to another:

> What is the real content of that phenomenon which our historiography is wont to call changing centres if not the destruction of those exilic communities (*galuyot*) and the appearance of other exilic communities? And do not those new exilic communities also stand on the brink of destruction? And have they not lived with the sentence of destruction from the beginning? Is the path in

---

22   Carr, *What Is History?*, 50-51.
23   F. Stern, *The Varieties of History* (New York, 1956), 19.

fact so long, from an historical point of view, from the appearance of those exilic communities to their end? . . . Destruction (*ḥurban*) is the very shadow of the exile, of every exile.[24]

Here is the anguish of a Jew, a Jewish historian, and a Zionist, speaking when word of the Holocaust had only just arrived in the Yishuv. Those terrible tidings served to confirm Dinur's understanding of the Jewish past.

There is then, in Zionist historiography, a sort of teleological fallacy which I have been alluding to by repetition of the phrase, *ma'asei banim siman le-'avot*. History has been written to conform with Zionist ideology—with the implicit claim that the regaining of national sovereignty by the Jewish people is the culmination, even the goal, toward which all of Jewish history has been moving. A component of this interpretation is the tendency to exaggerate the incidence, the extent, and the importance of messianic movements—this because messianism is seen as the expression of the "dynamic nationhood" of the Jews. Similarly, the tendency toward seeing in the autonomous institutions of the Jews the expression of "static nationhood" has narrowed the historical field. It has militated against comparative studies of those institutions by magnifying and thus obscuring what is Jewish about the Jews' history. In a word, my point is that ideology, any *system* of theories, axioms, or faith assumptions about human society or culture, and the pursuit of truth do not mix.

My remarks, of course, are those of a Jewish historian in the Diaspora. My goal here has been to initiate discussion and self-criticism by illustrating the central question for a national historian, namely, the definition of his responsibility to his nation. If, as I believe all will agree, the Jewish people faces urgent problems of self-definition, political action, and education, and since the historian un-avoidably influences at least the perception of these problems, the question I have raised here must be addressed. Surely we shall want to avoid falling into the error of ideological history-writing, but just as surely we shall want to escape infection by the comfortable complacency of the North American Jewish Diaspora.

---

24 Ben-Zion Dinur, "Exiles and Their Destruction" (Hebrew), in his *Dorot ve-reshumot* (Jerusalem, 1978), 175, 188. See also H. H. Ben-Sasson, "Religion and Society in the Teachings of the Honourees" (Hebrew), in *Religion and Society: Lectures Delivered at the Ninth Convention of the Historical Society of Israel* (Jerusalem, 1964), 30-31.

Between Dignity and Redemption: A Critique of Soloveitchik's Adam I and Adam II

JEROME ECKSTEIN

INTRODUCTION

Joseph B. Soloveitchik is the foremost contemporary rabbinic scholar in modern Orthodoxy. He is also thoroughly learned in philosophy and other secular disciplines. But he has published relatively little, and even less on theology. Consequently, his published writings are significant events. In this essay, I deal with only one of them, "The Lonely Man of Faith."

My first section represents his categories of Adam I and Adam II and shows how, according to Soloveitchik, they explain the unique ontological loneliness of the man of faith. The second section analyzes and criticizes these categories. In the final section I present a new set of related categories, interestedness and intraestedness, and try to show how it overcomes the difficulties encountered by the two Adams.

I

Soloveitchik focusses on the loneliness of the man of faith. This loneliness, though perhaps partly formed by the general sense of alienation in Western society, is special. The man of faith

looks upon himself as a stranger in modern society which is technically minded, self-centered, and self-loving, almost in a sickly narcissistic fashion, scoring honor upon honor, piling up victory upon victory, reaching for the distant

121

galaxies, and seeing in the here-and-now sensible world the only manifestation of being.

But there is in addition a loneliness that is intrinsic to faith, and this "interpenetration of faith and loneliness . . . goes back to the dawn of the Judaic covenant."[1]

To explain this type of loneliness, Soloveitchik develops two typological categories, Adam I and Adam II, which he traces to the Bible's two divergent accounts of the creation of man. Unlike most Bible critics who attribute the divergent accounts to different sources and traditions, he takes them as a consistent description of "a real contradiction" in the nature of man. Each version represents an opposite dimension of humanity.[2]

God commanded Adam I to subdue nature by a unique means, his creative and practical intellect. Adam I is interested only in the functional and not the metaphysical; "he is completely utilitarian as far as motivation, teleology, design and methodology are concerned." He, unlike the relatively helpless beast, achieves dignity and majesty by controling the environment; and his charge extends to the realms of law and beauty as well as to nature. He manifests in these activities "obedience to rather than rebellion against God."[3]

Adam II, however, seeks the world's purpose and wonders about God's elusive presence. In these quests he does not apply Adam I's functional method; "he does not create a world of his own"; "he does not mathematize phenomena or conceptualize things"; he is not "dynamic and creative"; he does not explore "the scientific abstract universe." Instead, "he encounters the universe in all its colorfulness, splendor and grandeur"; he studies the cosmos with the "naivete, awe and admiration of the child who seeks the unusual and wonderful in every ordinary thing and event"; he is "receptive and beholds the world in its original dimensions"; he explores "the irresistibly fascinating qualitative world where he establishes an intimate relation with God." Both Adams strive to understand the cosmos and fulfill their nature as God ordained—but in incommensurate ways.[4]

The dignity of Adam I is a "social and behavioral category, . . . a technique of living, a way of impressing society"; it is measured by the accomplishments of the "surface-personality"; it "confronts mute nature—a lower form of being—in a mood of defiance." In contrast to Adam I's dignity, Adam II approaches the world redemptively. Unlike dignity, redemption is an "intrinsic existential quality" rather than "just an extraneous, accidental attribute . . . of being"; it is a "definitive mode

1   Joseph B. Soloveitchik, "The Lonely Man of Faith," *Tradition* 7/2 (Summer, 1965), 7-8.
2   *Ibid.*, 10.
3   *Ibid.*, 11-12, 13-16.
4   *Ibid.*, 16-17, 18.

of being itself" that does not have to be acted out in the "outside world";
it can be experienced privately in one's "in-depth-personality"; it is
attained through control over oneself rather than control over the
environment; it is achieved "when humble man makes a movement of
recoil, and lets himself be confronted and defeated by a Higher and
Truer Being."[5]

Only Adam II, as a member of the covenantal faith community,
can discharge the biblical command to love God with all of one's heart,
soul, and might; for he alone can concentrate completely on that task
without being distracted by "peripheral interests, anxieties, and problems." But the Bible also commands man to participate in the majestic
community, which is preoccupied with the peripheral interests of con-
quering the world. There is a "staggering dialectic" implied in these
commands: God forbids man to rest in either the covenantal or the
majestic community. God wills that "complete human redemption be
unattainable" in this world. The man of faith is only a visitor in the two
communities. He must move back and forth to avoid striking roots in
either community. His loneliness is integral to his being; his is an
"ontological loneliness," not reducible to modern or societal conditions.[6]

Only a few suffer this loneliness. Even the religionists seldom visit
(let alone belong to) a covenantal faith community. Instead, they usually belong to a religious community, which is a subclass of the majestic
community. A man of the religious community "values religion in
terms of its usefulness to him and considers the religious act a medium
through which he may increase his happiness." That the happiness and
success of Adam I will thus be augmented, Soloveitchik believes, is
"very certain and self-evident." But ontological loneliness rarely pre-
vails, for Adam I has dominated Adam II in the nature of man.[7] The
highways are almost empty between the majestic city and the redemptive hamlet. Only a few solitary travelers feel the ontological loneliness
of roadside inns.

Even these uncommon travelers, however, cannot have their two
Adams in perfect harmony. For the man of faith does not compromise,
and his covenantal undertaking eludes rational analysis. "There are
simply no cognitive categories in which the total commitment of the
man of faith could be spelled out," because the commitment rises from
his whole personality. His in-depth personality accepts the covenant
immediately, "before the mind is given a chance to investigate the
reasonableness of this unqualified commitment." For example, Adam I
may find prayer to be pragmatically rational—uplifting, integrating;
but Adam II experiences prayer "as the awesome confrontation of God

---

5   *Ibid.*, 18-19, 23-24.
6   *Ibid.*, 50, 54-55.
7   *Ibid.*, 56-58.

and man, as the great paradox of man conversing with God as an equal
fellow member of the covenanted society, and at the same time being
aware that he fully belongs to God and that God demands complete
surrender and self-sacrifice." The paradox and awesomeness of Adam
II's prayer conflict in the man of faith with the practical rationality of
Adam I's prayer. Most people do not have this problem, though, since
they suppress the Adam II dimension of their nature. Thus the contemporary man of faith is especially lonely. "He experiences not only
ontological loneliness but also social isolation, whenever he dares to
deliver the genuine faith-*kerygma*."[8]

II

A sentence haunts me on reading Soloveitchik. "Out of my distress I
cried: 'Lord!' ['Redeemer!']."[9] I am deeply moved by Soloveitchik's
lonely odyssey and the enlargement of soul forged in its course. My
brief philosophic description of the two Adams hardly conveys a sense
of this scholar's religious ordeals; for that (and for other reasons) one
should read his article. But he does interpret his journey in terms of
philosophy, and to that aspect I now respond.

Soloveitchik maintains that only Adam II is "receptive and beholds
the world in its original dimension"; only Adam II "does not create a
world of his own," but wants rather "to understand the living, 'given'
world"; and only Adam II can meet God "face to face."[10] Thus, Adam
I's cognition distorts reality, while Adam II knows the cosmos purely
and God intimately. Two claims are hereby made: Adam II's knowledge is superior to Adam I's, and Adam II's knowledge is pure,
undistorted—absolute.

I think that the second claim is meaningless rather than false. The
Kantian revolution forces me to recognize that perspectival and contextual dimensions are intrinsic to the *meaning* of the terms "knowledge" and "sense perception." I cannot imagine how a pond would
appear in itself, from no perspective; nor can I conceive the nature of
evidence in itself, pure or apart from rules of evidence; for visual
perspective is part of the meaning of vision, and rules of evidence are
part of the meaning of evidence. A smoking pistol is evidence in one
legal system but not in another because the systems have different rules
of evidence. (Therefore, to call something "self-evident," as Soloveitchik does, is a contradiction in terms.) The same is true of all signs,
tokens, indications, and testimonies.

Hence, sight without perspective and evidence without rules are
not merely hard to produce or even, regrettably, empirical impos-
sibilities due to human limitations. Claims of such sight or evidence are

---

  8 *Ibid.*, 60, 62-63, 65.
  9 Psalm 118:5
 10 Soloveitchik, "Lonely Man of Faith," 33-34.

not merely false; they are absurdities, nonsense. One might as well rue the absence of a round square. The same is true of all knowledge and sensation—indeed, all experience: context and perspective, though mostly unnoticed, even by the dictionary, are integral to their meaning. Adam I need not envy Adam II on this score; neither can he behold any part of the world absolutely or pristinely, for that is logically impossible.

No wonder, then, that for Maimonides the word "knowledge" has a completely different meaning when attributed to God. For if God's knowledge and man's knowledge were essentially similar, then even God's knowledge could not be absolute or pure. But Maimonides does not want to say that. He says, instead, that we can know nothing affirmative about what God's knowledge means; we know only what human knowledge means. Consequently, he does not denigrate Adam I's knowledge; on the contrary, he believes that it can become the highest form of divine worship.

Why should we, then, accept even Soloveitchik's first claim? I find no justification for evaluating Adam II's knowledge as plainly superior to that of Adam I. Since all human knowledge, including Adam II's, is symbolic, contextual, and perspectival, none should be considered unqualifiedly better. Symbols, forms, and categories as well as contexts and perspectives reveal the world truly, even if incompletely and differently. They are integral to what knowledge means; they ought not to be accepted sadly as necessary distortions. We should, rather, delight in the diversity afforded by the distinctive approaches of the two Adams. Each of them truly reveals respectively different dimensions of the inexhaustible *reality*; or, as the Talmud might put it, "the words of both are the words of the living God." In some situations and for some purposes we prefer the one over the other, but neither's knowledge is simply superior.

Soloveitchik's widespread favouritism toward Adam II weakens his humanism and religiousness as well as leads to error. To say, as Soloveitchik does, that only Adam II can love God fully has such consequences. Love of a person, whether human or divine, requires the knowledge of both Adams to be adequate. Both Adam I's techniques of practical care and Adam II's modes of intimacy are essential to love. The traditional Jew needs to love God by engaging the Halakha's abstract, quantitative reasoning about service to God, as well as by joyful dancing with the holy scroll on Simhat Torah. The physician needs to love by rigorous study of science as well as by sympathy for the sick. And if God is conceived as requiring human aid, then Adam I's pragmatic methods can constitute love of God even more vitally.

Soloveitchik rightly says that love bids a "complete concentration and immersion in the focus," but he is mistaken in ascribing such power only to Adam II; Adam I can centralize his concerns of utility as much, and they are equally necessary for a solid love. I do not agree that the biblical command to love God with all one's heart and soul and might is

directed exclusively to Adam II; the vigour and breadth of this charge
seems to call for a response from man's entire nature. Exaggerating
Adam II's power of love and underestimating Adam I's capacity
weakens the two Adams as metaphysical categories by misrepresenta-
tion. This error also diminishes the humanism and religiousness of
both Adams, for it saps idealism by unrealistic expectations as much as
by unappreciated possibilities.

Soloveitchik's favouritism is on the whole intense enough to be
restrictive. He unjustifiably relegates to each Adam separate powers,
attitudes, and subject matters—inferior, for Adam I, and superior, for
Adam II. This is true not only of love. He also restricts dynamic activity
to Adam I, and "receptivity" to Adam II. Indeed, when Adam II seeks
redemption from God, his receptivity supposedly melts into a sense of
"defeat." But this exclusivity is unwarranted. Adam II is frequently
"active" in searching for God or in exploring the "qualitative world," as
when he tours a strange city on foot; and Adam I is frequently "receptive" in his concerns, as in the observation of a malformed hoof.
Qualities often require dynamic activity to be perceived, while quantities often require receptivity to be controlled. There is no adequate
basis for confining activity to Adam I and receptivity to Adam II.

Just as a parent's partiality often deprives the "favoured" child of
important capabilities, so with Soloveitchik does it unfairly and exclusively deny to Adam II the powers to "create a world of his own,"
"mathematize phenomena or conceptualize things," and investigate
the "scientific abstract universe." The impression given is that these
powers are less valuable, but this is debatable. A more serious objection
is that Adam II does, indeed, have these powers. We have seen that all
experience entails forms, symbols, and perspectives; hence, to some
extent, people are continually creating a world. Adam II "creates a
world of his own" as much as Adam I does; only they do it differently,
and their worlds are different.

Adam II cannot only enter the realms of mathematics, concepts,
and abstract science, but he can also work there. He is not barred from
meeting concepts or from conceptualized thinking. On the contrary,
he is invited to explore these realms for the "splendor and grandeur" of
their topographies. He is welcome not only to survey these areas for the
"unusual and wonderful" surface qualities of concepts, but to wander
into the deep, winding caverns of abstract thought and delight in their
unique qualities—provided that neither level is searched for the practical purpose of controlling the environment. Many a religious scientist
or idealist philosopher or mystic discovers there an "irresistibly fascinating qualitative world where he establishes an intimate relation
with God."

On first meeting the concepts of Adam I and Adam II, for example, the imagination, if not occupied with utility, immediately perceives
distinctive qualities of personality, colouration, and drama. On extend-

ing the definitions of the two Adams into abstract and noncommercial thought, we discover other qualities. The concepts reconcile contrary biblical accounts in a traditionally religious way; they describe a special kind of loneliness; they have rough edges that often do not cut along fault lines; and they are laden with value. There is thus no sufficient reason for excluding Adam II from the realms of abstract thought, thereby diminishing his humanistic and religious potencies.

Soloveitchik's restrictive policy produces other puzzlements. He says that only Adam II attains redemption, through "control over himself." But he also says that Adam I's dignity is achieved through "control of his environment." Yet the attitudes and modes of behaviour are similar whether one controls the environment or oneself! Further, control of oneself ranges from treating oneself as a commodity to disciplining oneself, and Soloveitchik connects redemption with the latter. Yet self-discipline is hardly an inactive and "receptive" attitude or a redemptive posture that is "defeated!" I can understand Soloveitchik's desire as a Jew to involve man's active participation in (at least non-Messianic) redemption. But were he free of his exclusionary tendency, he could avoid contradiction and give a more adequate account by conceiving man's role in redemption as a particular mixture of the involvements of both Adams.

Soloveitchik's exclusionary policy leads him to another, similar, predicament. Only Adam I acquires dignity or majesty, he says, because only Adam I has a majestic or glorious posture vis à vis the environment; but only Adam II, he says later, can encounter the grandeur of the universe. Considering that the words "majestic" and "grandeur" are synonymous, this is strange. If only Adam I has a majestic posture, why would only Adam II encounter the grandeur of the universe? If anything, cosmic majesty would be discovered through a majestic posture. Actually, however, man's dignity, the world's grandeur, and God's glory are best achieved or perceived by a particular mixture of the involvements of both Adams. My impression is that Soloveitchik's Judaism saves him from an exorbitant denigration of Adam I, and pushes him into saving contradictions with regard to majesty and redemption.

There are two more troublesome cases of Soloveitchik's favouritism. Adam I's dignified existence, he says, "confronts mute nature—a lower form of being—in a mood of defiance"; but Adam II's humbly redeemed life is "confronted and defeated by a Higher and Truer Being [God]." This contrast raises several problems. The phrases "lower form of being" and "Higher and Truer Being" are respectively lower case and upper case in both typescript and value. What does this signify?

Does this mean simply that God is more valuable than nature? But then dignified Adam I also meets God—for instance, in prayer, as a member of the religious community; and I doubt that Soloveitchik deems this aspect of God—a granter of petitions—to be less "High," less worthy, than any other divine aspect. Hence, Adam I encounters the "Higher Being" as much as Adam II meets nature.

Does this mean, rather, that God has a greater degree of reality than nature? If so, I cannot fathom Soloveitchik's meaning. I can understand that, compared to nature or anything else, God is wiser, better, more powerful, etc.; but I cannot understand how God or anything can be more real than something else. Anything encountered is real, whether it be a stone, poem, idea, mirage, or a novel; though they are located in different orders of reality, they are "equally" real. Sometimes a stone is more valuable than an idea, or a novel more precious than history, or one order of reality more relevant than another; but each is "as much" real as the others. There is an ontological parity—not an ontological priority—among and within all the orders of reality.[11]

The same difficulty arises from Soloveitchik's claim that Adam II encounters a "Truer Being." I understand that one truth can have a greater degree of probability than another, but this is not what Soloveitchik means here. The two Adams are never distinguished in terms of the probabilities of their truths.

Does the claim mean that Adam II's truths are more valuable than Adam I's? Well, I agree that at times truth A is more precious than truth B, but in other circumstances or perspectives truth B is more precious than truth A. I doubt that Soloveitchik deems the truths Adam II discovers to be always more precious than those discovered by Adam I. What would be his sources in the Jewish tradition for this value judgment?

Indeed, the main point of Psalm 19 is that man has two sources of knowledge of God—nature and Torah—but no ranking of their value or verity is even suggested. Verse 2 says: "The heavens declare the glory of God, and the firmament showeth His handiwork"; while verse 8 says: "The law of the Lord is perfect, restoring the soul; the testimony of the Lord is sure, making wise the simple." This Psalm may have influenced Immanuel Kant when he wrote: "There are two things that fill my soul with holy reverence and ever-growing wonder—the spectacle of the starry sky that virtually annihilates us as physical beings, and the moral law which raises us to infinite dignity as intelligent agents." The last verse (15) of this Psalm seems to emphasize the equality of value between the concerns of Adam I and Adam II. It says: "Let the words of my mouth and the meditation of my heart be acceptable before Thee, O Lord, my Rock, and my Redeemer." God, as Rock, is the reality, truth, and value that Adam I pursues; while God, as Redeemer, is the reality, truth, and value that Adam II seeks.

---

11 For a thorough discussion of ontological parity see Justus Buchler, *Metaphysics of Natural Complexes* (New York: Columbia University Press, 1966).

Apart from the above considerations, I cannot imagine how one truth can be truer than another, or one reality more real than another. There is no way in which I can accept Soloveitchik's claim that Adam II meets a "Higher and Truer Being" than does Adam I. The two Adams encounter "equal" truths and realities.

Furthermore, Soloveitchik's statements about the moods of the two Adams and the responses of God and nature are not accurate. I have already illustrated that, contrary to Soloveitchik, Adam II is not necessarily "defeated" or even "passive." Neither is Adam I, as Soloveitchik asserts, always defiant and never humble. As a true scientist, for example, Adam I accepts the results of experiments humbly, especially when they oppose his wishes; and, when nature is silent, he modestly admits to limited powers. He is also humble in the sense and manner of Levi Yitzhak of Berditchev: confronting the majesty of the universe, he "forgets his ego and is no longer aware of his selfhood at all."[12] At other times, contrary to Soloveitchik's characterization, nature is not mute; it replies clearly when addressed with suitable questions—whether defiant or humble. Indeed, in recent generations, God has been much more silent than nature.

I find that a miasma of existential and oriental phraseologies cheaply envelops large sections of the country. In the marshy regions of East Hampton, Esalen, the bar at Teachers, ecclesiastic and academic pulpits—places of intentional and unintentional seduction—the sentimental fog is especially thick. One cannot see whether the Goal is on the mountain or in the valley, but that doesn't concern most citizens; they are equally comfortable in describing it as the "higher being" or the "in-depth personality." As Ecclesiastes says, "all is vapor." Even a brilliant mind, such as Soloveitchik's, sometimes does not penetrate the haze.

Thus his troublous favouritism is also expressed in misty concepts of personality echelons. Adam I's activities emanate solely from the surface personality, while Adam II's activities emanate solely from the in-depth personality. Dignity is a behavioural and social event, whereas redemption is felt privately in the "very hidden strata of the isolated 'I' who knows himself as a singular being." In solitude, man "has no opportunity to display his dignity and majesty, since both are behavioral social traits"; but man can "live a redeemed life" in solitude.[13] Soloveitchik's value judgment throughout this discussion is that the in-depth personality is worthier than the surface personality.

The terms "surface" and "depth" are applied metaphorically to the word "personality," and they generally function normatively—their descriptive meaning is at best vague. Most people are hard put to

12   Quoted in Louis Jacobs, *Hasidic Thought* (New York: Behrman House, Inc., 1976), 118.
13   Soloveitchik, "Lonely Man of Faith," 24, 20.

describe, or even illustrate, these stations of personality. The stations are usually used for praise or blame; for instance, "I keep none of its traditions, yet deep down I am a good Jew." A common declension: I am integrally good; you are bad on the surface, but good deep down; he is rotten to the core. Often, the phrase "true personality" replaces that of "in-depth personality"; but though the substitute is equally amorphous in description, it sharpens a difficulty. For all of a person's judgments—whether by doing, saying, or making—have a revelatory dimension;[14] they all exhibit to some degree the "true" personality. But we are not offered descriptive criteria for distinguishing the "true" personality from the "false," the "in-depth" personality from the "surface" personality; we are only given additional honourific and pejorative terms. All of these terms purport to be handles for discriminating facts, but on grasping them they evanesce into puff and puffery.

Soloveitchik, however, does invest these terms with factual distinctions, but his matrix of value dulls their usefulness. He identifies the surface personality with Adam I's activities and the in-depth personality with Adam II's activities. And since he depicts both types of activities concretely, his stations of personality are not mere whiffs. They become boggy, though, with normal use. Were I to employ such language, I would define "in-depth personality" in terms of relatively pervasive, permanent, and dominant behaviour; and I would define "surface personality" in terms of relatively insular, transient, and attenuated behaviour. These definitions, I believe, are commonsensical and not as troublesome as those of Soloveitchik.

Since all of Soloveitchik's references to the in-depth personality are favourable, and since he is partial to Adam II's activities, he suggests that nothing immoral can emanate from the "centre" of our being. That suggestion is generally considered false. Not only did many of Hitler's unspeakable crimes originate from his in-depth being, but some of our own shameful acts are manifestations of pervasive, permanent, and dominant aspects of personality. By colouring the echelons of personality with value, Soloveitchik misrepresents ordinary experience. In contrast, I believe that colour-blind descriptions match better the common encounter with evil.

Soloveitchik also opposes ordinary experience and language by characterizing the surface personality (Adam I) as social, behavioural, concerned with "peripheral interests," and by characterizing the in-depth personality (Adam II) as private, conscious, concerned with man's "know[ing] himself as a singular being." Most people would also reject these characterizations. Whether something is experienced socially or privately, behaviourally or intuitively, consciously or uncon-

---

14   Justus Buchler, *Toward a General Theory of Human Judgment* (New York: Columbia University Press, 1951); *Nature and Judgment* (New York: Columbia University Press, 1955).

sciously, is not normally connected to its scope, persistence, or force—and the form of the experience is thus usually irrelevant to the station of personality. Nor does the general importance of the interest's content necessarily determine that station. Sometimes the in-depth (pervasive, permanent, dominant) personality is expressed in trivial, peripheral concerns, and sometimes the surface (insular, transient, attenuated) personality is manifested in interests of the utmost gravity. The in-depth personality is involved in business and frolic as well as redemption, while the surface personality is involved in solitary prayer and private speculation as well as majestic control of the environment. The search for one's own uniqueness, also, occurs in the activities which Soloveitchik ascribes to Adam I as well as Adam II. I may discover some part of my uniqueness in play as well as in spiritual meditation, in a business meeting as well as in the covenantal faith community. Soloveitchik gives us no reason to abandon this common language and experience.

Thus the weaknesses of the two Adams as categories in the metaphysics of human judgment originate largely from a tendency to assign them exclusive domains, and from a religious bias in favor of Adam II. But their weaknesses as metaphysical categories necessarily impair their explanation of the ontological loneliness of the man of faith. Indeed, one begins to wonder whether the loneliness felt by the man of faith is ontologically or psychologically unique. One is certain that Soloveitchik's loneliness differs from the typical, or even from a refined, perception of the general sense of alienation in Western society. But is it essentially different from the loneliness of a sensitive man who has sadly lost faith?

This sensitive man also regularly journeys along the nearly deserted highways between the majestic city and the redemptive hamlet. Once in a while he meets at the roadside inn a solitary traveler of faith; sometimes, they greet each other; on rare occasions they converse and even commune. Then he continues on the way to his native hamlet, though in all his travels he never finds it. He encounters the familiar landmarks, but the hamlet has vanished. He returns to the city, of which he is not a citizen. His trips to the hamlet become increasingly infrequent. He is lonely. Eventually he journeys only to the roadside inn, hoping to meet his friend.

III

The categories of Henri Bergson (intellect vs. intuition, or the mechanical vs. the mystical) and Martin Buber (I-It vs. I-Thou) had adumbrated the categories of Soloveitchik (Adam I vs. Adam II). The three sets of categories are roughly comparable in the metaphysics of human judgment or in philosophic anthropology. Further, the three

sets are, in varying degrees and ways, weakened by an ethical or
religious bias toward one category, or by the assignment of exclusive
domains to each category. The scope of this article does not permit me
to examine the philosophies of Bergson and Buber. Instead, I shall
propose a fourth set of categories (interestedness vs. intraestedness) in
the metaphysics of human judgment which, though roughly comparable to the other three, is, I believe, free of the above impairments; and I
shall compare it solely to the two Adams. I shall not in the present
article extend this fourth set into the fields of theology or philosophy of
religion, though I think that it has some relevance there. I wish to
suggest only that if philosophy is sometimes to be a handmaiden to
theology, then she should perform her proper duties as well as possible.

The adjective "interested" characterizes an involvement, conscious or unconscious, that is directed to something other than itself
(from *inter* and *esse*—"to be between"). For instance, one walks down a
country lane: the walk is the involvement; it is directed toward meeting
a friend; and the motive, the source of the involvement and the direction, may be loneliness or love or any other want. Only the involvement's direction is pertinent to the judgment of interestedness; the
motive is irrelevant to the determination. The walk is interested because it is directed away from itself, toward meeting a friend. There are
several synonyms for the term "interested," such as "means," "utile,"
and "practical," since interestedness may be directed either to the
useful or the merely instrumental (e.g., the construction of an imprac-
tical machine that is geared only to an attempted production of perpetual and useless motion).

But we have no word to designate an involvement, conscious or
unconscious, that is directed at itself. Hence, I have devised for such
involvements the adjective "intraested" (which I pronounce ĭn-träst'-
ĕd), with its adverbial and substantive modifications (from *intra* and
esse—"to be within"). Intraestedness can prevail, for instance, when one
walks down a country lane: the walk is the involvement; it is directed
toward the walk's sights, smells, sounds, touches, or tastes, or to the feel of
the body walking; and the motive may be curiosity, pleasure, beauty,
or the desire to experience intraestedness. Only the involvement's
direction, and not its motive, is pertinent to the judgment of intraestedness. This walk is intraested because it is directed toward itself.

One is never purely (exclusively) interested or purely intraested;
one is always somewhere on a continuum between their poles. Sometimes, interestedness dominates from the beginning of the involvement, while intraestedness is attenuated; at other times, the reverse
occurs; and the involvement is characterized by the dominant mode.
Thus the interested walker may have been from the start subordinately
directed to see and hear a waterfall intraestedly, while the intraested
walker may have been from the beginning subordinately and interestedly directed to improve his health.

Another factor intensifies the "impurity" of these categories. For during the course of all interested instances there arise impromptu constituent involvements which are intraested. For example, the interested walker ineluctably encounters trees and clouds on the way to his friend. They are not then instrumental for him. He just sees them. His vision, even if fleeting, is at those moments intraested; these impromptu constituent involvements are directed at themselves. Even in the very interested case of seeking to escape from a burning room, one inevitably perceives shapes, colours, and sounds that are then neither useful nor instrumental. One dimly sees the door's yellow rectangularity and indistinctly hears street noises though they are then not relevant to one's plight or any other interest. These impromptu constituent involvements, also, are intraested, for they are directed at themselves.

The reverse, however, is not necessarily true; not all instances of intraestedness have impromptu constituent involvements which are interested. One can listen intraestedly to a melody uninterrupted by interest. On the other hand, the intraested walker may chance upon a log and have to step over it to avoid tripping; this is a case of an impromptu constituent involvement that is interested, though the walk as a whole is dominated by intraestedness.

There is an opposition of quality, though, in the two categories. Intraestedness is spontaneous ("wild"), whereas interestedness is anticipative ("tamed"). Since intraestedness is not domesticated for a specific outcome, it moves freely in the wilderness of the present. It is not constrained to focus narrowly on an expected result, but unrestrainedly explores the current situation's wonderfully iridescent actualities and teeming possibilities. The "wildness" of intraestedness is a consequence of its direction.

John Dewey suggests another special quality of intraestedness when he speaks of "the underlying qualitative character that constitutes a situation,"[15] that is, the pervasive and permeating trait which gives unity to the whole situation or subject matter. Even when we are interested, part of us vaguely senses this quality. (This is yet another type of the compression, or "impurity," of these two categories.) But interestedness itself concentrates only on the involvement's anticipated sequel; it ignores the essential qualitative presence of the variegated situation. The interested walker may even largely neglect the spread of autumn in an Adirondack wood because he is intensely directed toward meeting a friend.

Let those be wary who lean toward restricting interestedness and intraestedness to active and passive involvements, respectively. Bird watching that aims at the hunt is interested, while dancing barefoot in the meadow to touch the softness of ground and wind is intraested. On the other hand, watching birds just to watch them is intraested, while

---

15   John Dewey, *Philosophy and Civilization* (New York: Minton, Balch and Company, 1931), 99.

dancing for a prize is interested. These categories differ in their direction, but not in their energy or locale. Both categories can be involved with anything, in any domain. We cannot tell simply by its name whether an involvement is interested or intraested; every involvement can be either. It all depends on the direction of the involvement,

Neither category is absolutely superior in epistemology or in ethics. Only relative to certain contexts, perspectives, or purposes may one category be preferred over the other. The directional and qualitative differences between the two categories will be prime factors in our choice; some situations will favour one, while different situations will favour the other. Neither interestedness nor intraestedness is absolutely superior in the metaphysics of human judgment.

Epistemologically and ethically, intraestedness is free in a unique way: to wander, experience spontaneously, and be generally sensitive to novelty. Interestedness is also free in a special way: to lead the situation toward a specific result—to control. Thus there are two discrete kinds of freedom, each appropriate to its own mode of involvement. The paradox of freedom—that it is both order and spontaneity—is clarified by this relativity. Since we are never purely interested or purely intraested, our distinct states of freedom or unfreedom are always compresent—though one is dominant. Our constant challenge is to establish a satisfactory balance.

Ethically, in addition to determining what is a *satisfactory* balance, we must always evaluate the natures and contexts of the particular involvements at hand. For, ethically, there is a time to be interested and a time to be intraested. Most people would agree that to look intraestedly at a tree instead of returning the birdling to its nest, is unethical, but looking at the tree interestedly, to return the birdling to its nest, is ethical. Most people would also agree that walking intraestedly in the forest when no duty presses otherwise is ethical (at least in the sense of not being unethical), but an interested walk in the forest that is a preliminary to theft is unethical. Ethically, neither category is absolutely superior to the other.

Not only do these categories have their own appropriate modes of freedom, but they also have, correspondingly, their own appropriate modes of dignity. (The primary definition of the word "dignity" is: "the quality or state of being worthy.") Dignity is derived from freedom and strength. The dignity of intraestedness is the unique sense of worthiness that comes from the freedom and strength and confidence to explore the present situation spontaneously, while the dignity of interestedness is the special sense of worthiness that comes from the freedom and strength to control. The meek may inherit the earth, but they do not possess the dignity of those who subdue it. Yet the subduers of the earth do not possess the dignity of those who, undirected to consequences, rove its beauty. The dignity of climbing a mountain to rescue a comrade is different from the dignity of climbing a mountain "because it is there."

If interestedness and intraestedness have in general no absolute ethical or epistemological superiority, then neither do their special modes of freedom and dignity. Yet our society has been overwhelmingly interested. It has so utterly neglected intraestedness that we have not even had a word for such involvements. Society has thereby repressed unique forms of freedom and dignity and knowledge; it has in that way diminished us. Can we right the balance; is an earthly redemption possible?

Metaphysics provides some encouragement. For intraestedness is ubiquitous. Even when not dominant, it is trebly present in subordinate or attenuated form: as another involvement compresent from the beginning, as an impromptu constituent, and as a perception of the situation's underlying unity. Hope is raised because we need only reinvigorate intraestedness and summon it from the underground. Salvation is available everywhere, because nowhere on earth is there either absolute purity or absolute simplicity. The impurity of interestedness and intraestedness, always comingling in the person, can ease the return of intraestedness to ascendancy; while the infinite complexity of all that is encountered beckons intraestedness to the unending wilderness in everything.

Paradoxically, technology also offers some hope. I tend to agree with Henri Bergson when he writes:

> So let us not merely say . . . that the mystical summons up the mechanical. We must add that the body, now larger, calls for a bigger soul, and that mechanism should mean mysticism. The origins of the process of mechanization are indeed more mystical than we might imagine. Machinery will find its true vocation again, it will render services in proportion to its power, only if mankind, which it has bowed still lower to the earth, can succeed, through it, in standing erect and looking heavenwards.[16]

I believe that a contented belly disposes us more to intraestedness than does starvation. On such grounds, our society has a better chance of righting the balance than any other society in history. On the other hand, since I am anti-utopian to the marrow, I agree with Soloveitchik that complete redemption is impossible in this world.

The similarities between Soloveitchik's categories and mine are: Adam I's involvements, like those of interestedness, are directed to something other than themselves—he is "functional," "utilitarian," and "controls the environment"; Adam II's involvements are like those of intraestedness in being directed at themselves—he is nonfunctional and seeks a situation's qualitative presence.

Unlike Adam I and Adam II, however, neither interestedness nor intraestedness functions absolutely or purely—not epistemologically, not ethically, and not in any other way. Neither can perceive God or the

---

16   Henri Bergson, *The Two Sources of Morality and Religion* (Garden City: Doubleday Anchor Books, 1935), 310.

world except through the framework of contexts, perspectives, purposes, and symbols. Hence, neither is inherently superior to the other.

Unlike Adam I and Adam II, neither interestedness nor intraestedness has exclusive domains. Neither is barred from the social or private realms, from "lower" or "higher" stations of personality, from peripheral or central concerns, from mathematics or mysticism. No domain is closed to either of them. Here, too, neither category is inherently favoured.

Unlike Adam I and Adam II, neither interestedness nor intraestedness is assigned exclusive powers. Neither is solely conscious or unconscious, active or passive, defiant or humble, behavioural or intuitive—neither can alone reveal the uniqueness of a person. Neither is exclusively dignified or redemptive. Here, also, neither category is inherently favoured.

I think that all of these differences enable interestedness and intraestedness to overcome the obstacles encountered by the two Adams.

Our Torah, Your Torah, and Their Torah: An Evaluation of the Artscroll Phenomenon

B. BARRY LEVY

INTRODUCTION

In the past three years a small group of dedicated writers has produced and marketed a dozen volumes of an anthologized commentary that will eventually cover the entire Bible. Preliminary success, determined from the number of copies in circulation and their relative popularity among Jewish readers, indicates that Mesorah Publications has undertaken what may amount to the most extensive Jewish effort on the Bible in this century and surely what to date represents the largest American Orthodox contribution to Bible study ever. In the following pages we will describe and evaluate some aspects of this project and the volumes that have so far appeared.[1]

---

1 Traditionally, the issues of biblical interpretation have been reserved for initiates, but many of the important texts are available in English. We will refer to English translations of works wherever possible in order to allow maximum exposure for readers not able to read the original languages. Also, for purposes of clarity, we have refrained from using the accepted scientific notation for transliterations, preferring a simpler one in some cases. When inconsistencies between Sephardic and Ashkenazic usages occur, the latter are consistent with the Artscroll spellings, which it seemed more appropriate to retain in certain contexts. Appreciation is gratefully expressed to my student Rabbi Menahem White and to my colleague Dr. Lawrence Kaplan for their comments and suggestions as well as to Mr. Joel Linsider whose critical eye has helped eliminate many stylistic flaws.

I. DESCRIPTION

Begun in the early part of 1976, the Artscroll series now includes *The Megillah* (Esther), *Ruth*, *Eichah* (Lamentations), *Koheles* (Ecclesiastes), *Shir haShirim* (Song of Songs), *Bereishis I* (Genesis 1-11), *Bereishis II* (Genesis 12-22), *Yonah* (Jonah), *Tehillim I* (Psalms 1-30), *Tehillim II* (Psalms 31-55), *Yechezkel I* and *Bereishis III*.[2] All of the volumes follow the same general design and literary format. Each biblical book is presented in easily read, vocalized Hebrew (beginning with the third volume, with the cantillation signs) together with a rabbinic anthology-commentary and various additions. The source of the Hebrew text is not indicated, but readers acquainted with the Koren Bible will recognize some of the features popularized there: omission of notes on massoretic irregularities, marking of *aliyoth*, having the *Kethib* unvocalized while the *Qere* is properly vocalized in the margin, etc. For the most part, the Hebrew is a routine exemplar of the Massoretic Text; any abnormal deviations are the result of printing errors.[3]

One's initial impression of the work is that the rabbinic anthology-commentary is the essence of the project, and this is correct. But in reality there are several different interpretative genres woven together in every volume, and each deserves individual treatment. At the top of the odd numbered pages, facing the Hebrew text, is an English translation. As explained in the prefaces to various volumes, "the standard JPS translation—which very often is at odds with the Talmudic translation of the Hebrew—simply would not do" (*The Megillah*, p. x). Whether this refers to the old 1917 translation or the new one, which began to appear in 1962 (Esther: 1969), is not clear, but the first obvious exegetical endeavour was a translation of each verse.[4] Usually translations see as their goal the rendering of the text into the target language in a manner that comes as close as possible to the original. In this case, because a multiplicity of potentially correct meanings is available from the commentaries consulted and independent decision is eschewed, the translation has been designed to follow the commentary of Rashi or, in a few cases, one of the other classical writers; doubtful cases are

---

2   *Yechezkel I* and *Bereishis III* have not been available for this study. *Tehillim I-II* were done by Rabbi A. C. Feuer and the remaining volumes by Rabbi Meir Zlotowitz; Rabbi Nosson Scherman has provided the overviews. A volume on Daniel has also been announced. Italicized titles of biblical books refer to the Artscroll volumes; other citations refer to the Bible itself.

3   E.g., Ps. 21:2. It should be noted, however, that the biblical passages cited in the commentaries are frequently not vocalized correctly, e.g., Gen. 1:29, 1:30 (2x), 2:4, 3:11, and many more. Perhaps it would be better if these remain unvocalized in future volumes.

4   As will become clear later, the Artscroll position includes a negative response to the commentaries accompanying these translations. Since no commentaries have yet appeared with the new *JPS* translation, this seems to be a rejection of the 1917 one, long ago declared in need of replacement by its own press because it is out of date. However, Rabbi White has pointed out to me a significant number of close parallels between Artscrolls' "new" translation and the 1917 *JPS* one. A careful comparison may conclusively demonstrate a substantial amount of borrowing, at least in Esther.

sometimes left untranslated. Readers who know Hebrew may not appreciate how greatly some of these renderings differ from those translations generally in use, and a comparison is strongly recommended. What has been created, following the models of some of the non-literal Palestinian *targumim*, is a rabbinic translation dependent on and containing rabbinic interpretation. As much as this type of translation may resemble or differ from the other English versions of the Bible, the Artscroll volume on *Shir haShirim* is virtually unique, but again the Aramaic *targum* of the book may be seen as a model for the effort.[5]

Accompanying both the text and the translation is the major contribution of the series, the anthologized comments that have been collected from dozens of traditional Jewish writers. Unlike other contemporary efforts that have relied on the contributions of non-Jews or non-observant Jews, or observant Jews who adhere to views that are suspect, this anthology claims to consult only approved sources. One should not think that this limitation of sources has in any way lightened the burden of the writers, for their efforts have merely been redirected to combing the rich resources of the *midrashim*, *talmudim*, and *targumim*, as well as approved classical and modern commentators, linguists, and philosophers for a selection of relevant materials on each verse, frequently each phrase or word. The results have effected, among other things, the resurrection of dozens of important works that contain or bear directly on the exegesis of the Bible, many of which have been forgotten or ignored in almost all circles interested in the Bible, including Orthodox ones. Each source is paraphrased and explained and its origin noted, thus, the interested reader may check the original if he so chooses.

Accompanying the commentaries on the volumes published after *Ruth* (the second published) is what appears to be an ever growing collection of footnotes containing, for the most part, related midrashic and homiletical materials. Here we also find stories of the great rabbis of ancient and modern times and how their lives and teachings exemplified the ideas expounded in the text and commentary. While not always essential to the commentary and its message, the presence of this material adds an attractive dimension to the work, both in contents and appearance. Interestingly, the layout of these sources across both columns of the commentary and at the ends of pages (even when associated with the commentary a page or two earlier) creates a feeling of depth not unlike that achieved by the artistic layout of a page of *Miqra'ot Gedolot*.

Each book and, in the case of the Torah, each *sidrah* is further elucidated by the lengthy overviews that precedes it. Unlike the transla-

---

5 English translations of the Palestinian *targumim* to the Torah and the *targum* to The Song of Songs are available in A. Diez-Macho, *Neofiti 1*, vols. 1-5 (Madrid: 1968ff.); J. W. Etheridge, *The Targums of Onkelos and Jonathan Ben Uzziel on the Pentateuch With the Fragments of the Jerusalem Targum* (reprint: New York, 1968); B. Grossfeld, ed., *The Targum to the Five Megilloth* (New York, 1973).

tion, notes, and commentary described above, the overviews are not an interpretative genre. They are comprised of a host of materials of a quasi-philosophical or homiletical nature that relate to, but do not actually explain, the biblical text.[6] Culled from the earlier and later writers, with particular preference for spokesmen of the *mussar* literature, these overviews present some of the related religious issues and themes that the authors have chosen to serve as the guidelines of their work and the issues of the commentaries. In the case of *Tehillim*, there is a brief introduction for each individual chapter. At the end of each volume that completes a biblical book is a list of the authorities cited in the commentary on that book. Each author or work is briefly described, the information varying, in some cases, from one volume to another. Complete lists for incomplete books (The Torah, *Tehillim*, etc.) are promised for the final volume of each. Preceding each volume is a very important preface that outlines the goals of the series and of individual volumes, specific problems, procedures, editorial policies, etc. In addition, the volumes are accompanied by approbations from Rabbi Moses Feinstein and greetings by other noted rabbinic leaders as well as occasional brief Hebrew statements by Rabbi Mordechai Gifter. The volumes are bound in covers or encased in dustjackets that depict medieval or modern illuminated Hebrew manuscripts, a factor that serves to enhance their appearance. The inside is equally attractive, displaying a wide range of type faces, both in Hebrew and English. In short we have here a beautiful publishing job, appropriately called "Artscroll."

II. EVALUATION

Any commentary reflects a series of perspectives on various issues. These perspectives represent both the exegetical history from which the commentary draws and the ideological context to which it is addressed, and an analysis of both is essential for a close appraisal of the work. Accordingly, we shall address the purpose of the Artscroll volumes, the sources on which they draw, and describe their intended readers, goals, methods, etc. Simultaneously, we will attempt to evaluate the success of the effort.

In carrying out this task, we have had to decide whether to judge Artscroll in the context of contemporary biblical scholarship or that of contemporary Orthodox Judaism. The former is so different from Artscroll's approach that comparison is virtually impossible. Many contemporary Jews have a biblical hermeneutic that is close to Artscroll's, but it is difficult to use these unpublished ideas to evaluate the work, and, in any case, to do so would amount to comparing a thing

---

6 We have discussed some aspects of the overviews as they relate to various methodological and exegetical issues, but they have not been treated exhaustively. See James Barr, *Fundamentalism* (London, 1977), 160.

with itself. Accordingly, we will attempt to evaluate Artscroll from the perspective of the history of Jewish interpretation of the Bible. This allows both the scholar and the lay reader to evaluate Artscroll's contribution in its historical context and to judge its status as an accurate and authoritative interpretation of the tradition it claims to represent.

A. The Intended Readers

What is the purpose of the Artscroll series? For whom was it written? Begun as a commentary on Esther in memory of Rabbi Meir Fogel, the Artscroll volumes seek to fill a perceived void in the traditional literature on the Bible that is available to the English reading world.[7] Though various types of commentaries are available, all, it would seem to the editors, suffer from being scientific, apologetic, critical and/or untrustworthy. These faults extend to the translations on which they are based as well as the exegetical attitudes they express. They are not even authentically Jewish, it is claimed, as they often use the contributions of non-Jewish writers. One major purpose of the Artscroll volumes is to replace these unacceptable commentaries.

To whom are these volumes addressed? The prefaces of the various volumes list early teenage day-school students, Hebrew teachers, college students, housewives, uninitiated adult readers, *kollel* scholars, and *yeshiva* students: in short, everyone who can read except small children and rabbis, and we suspect that more than one member of the last group will derive a great deal of information from the volumes. Briefly, then, the series is aimed at everyone in the traditional Jewish community with the exception of those whose expertise in the subject would necessitate fluent knowledge of most of the primary sources on which it is based. Interesting, by way of comparison, is the reaction of Rabbi Moses Feinstein in his letters of approbation affixed to the beginnings of the books. In *The Megillah* he recommends the work for students, but in the other volumes he omits any reference to the intended readers, simply noting that the volumes collect materials from the rabbis and present them in English for the purposes of arousing a love of Torah and observance of the *mitzvot* and strengthening of faith in God. He further notes that they can serve to attract those who have strayed somewhat. It may be pushing the point, but it seems

---

7 It should be noted, though, that many volumes of primary texts, traditional commentaries, and philosophical writings of biblical import are available in English translation and others are in progress: Mishnah, Babylonian Talmud, Tosefta (in progress), *The Mechilta, Midrash Rabbah*, The Zohar, Ibn Ezra on Song of Songs and Isaiah, Nachmanides on the Torah, *Midrash* on Psalms, *Pesikta* of *Rav Kahana, Pesikta Rabbati, MeAm Loez* (in progress), Menasseh ben Israel's *Conciliator*, Hirsch on the Torah and Psalms, Maimonides' Writings (some in progress), Rashi on the Torah, Albo's *Sefer HaIkkarim*, Saadia's *Beliefs & Opinions*, selections from Radak on Psalms, Onkelos, Pseudo-Jonathan, and many, many more. While the number of potential users of the Hebrew originals seems to be increasing, virtually an entire library of translations is available.

that he envisioned a much smaller reading population for the books. The editors' attitude is what is important here, though, and it would appear that their purpose is to address the entire English-speaking (or reading) population of the Orthodox community and anyone else who is interested. We have here no high-school reader or adult study-group anthology, but rather a major work, intended for a wide readership that includes many people who are at home with Bible study and can appreciate the comments included. As obvious as it may seem, this point is important, for it means that the analyses presented must withstand the tests of readability, sophistication, reliability, and accuracy. In spite of the editors' repeated appeals that the volumes are not the final word, must not be used for halachic decisions, and should, if properly used, lead to further study of the original sources, the extent of the effort, the size of the projected series, the range of the audience addressed, and the project's initial success lead us to believe that the editors are consciously working to produce *the* official, authoritative, English Bible commentary for religious Jews, one that will remain for generations as the base of Bible study for all but the few who have the ability, time, and inclination to probe further into the original sources.

B. The Sources: Plusses and
Minuses

The best way to grasp the extent of the Artscroll effort is to examine the lists of authorities whose works have been excerpted. A quick glance at these bibliographical entries may lead some readers to the conclusion that everyone of significance has been consulted, an observation that would be only partly true. Nonetheless, for simple bibliographies of traditional works on each biblical book, they are quite fine, and the list for the Torah promised at the conclusion of Deuteronomy is sure to be a document of independent importance, possibly worthy of independent publication. Various data on the commentaries are scattered around in the volumes as well and, together with the careful listing of the source for almost every comment, give the reader a very suitable base for further study.

While the editors have been scrupulous in noting the sources of the ideas anthologized in the commentaries and overviews, and even the bases of specific translations, the sources for the data on the commentators themselves have not been listed. Whatever the sources of these pages, they should receive the same credit given the commentators whose works were excerpted. Comparison of some of the entries with the corresponding entries in the *Encyclopaedia Judaica* reveals a remarkable similarity in the formulation of some sentences.[8] We hasten

---

8   While there are many such unnoted citations, one unquestionable example is the
    entry for "Ibn Aknin, Rav Yosef ben Yehudah" in *Shir haShirim*, 212, borrowed from
    "Aknin, Joseph Ben Judah Ben Jacob Ibn," *Encyclopaedia Judaica*, 2, cols. 501-03.
    Several modifications have been introduced into some of the *EJ* material, but the

to add, however, that some of the entries that do not appear to have made use of the *EJ* would have benefitted from doing so, for some of the data that they contain are incorrect.

Most blatant is the error concerning the authorship of the *targumim*. In the list of the commentaries on Esther (p. 146) we are told that "*targum*" means "the Ancient Aramaic translation of the Bible. Usually referring to the *Targum Onkelos*." The error, i.e., the sentence-fragment, has been removed in the subsequent volumes. The matter is dealt with more fully in *Yonah* (p. 155) where, though hardly appropriate, we find some talmudic sources on Onkelos, as well as the observation that "The *Targum* to the rest of the Scripture—called *Targum Yonasan*—is by the first century *tanna*, R. Yonasan ben Uziel . . . *Megillah* 3a." A careful reading of this talmudic passage will yield the following information: (a) Onkelos translated the Torah; (b) Yonasan ben Uziel translated the Prophets and wanted to translate the Hagiographa also but was prevented from doing so. It is therefore reasonable to assume, contrary to the statement on p. 155, that Yonasan did not translate the rest of the Bible. Since his efforts were limited to the Prophets, he also did not produce the translation of the Torah transmitted and cited in his name (e.g. *Shir haShirim*, p. 135). That the attribution of this text to the same Yonasan ben Uziel is incorrect has been known for a long time.[9] Actually, Onkelos is to be considered the author only of a *targum* to the Torah, and we have no idea who composed the *targumim* on the *megillot* or that on the Torah attributed to Yonasan ben Uziel. Notwithstanding problems of authorship, there are several different *targumim* on the Torah, so references to "*Targum*" (*Tehillim*, p. 118, *Bereishis*, p. 75, etc.) are hardly very helpful.

In addition, there are several other bibliographical errors. Ibn Ezra composed not one but two commentaries on Esther, both of which are available and might have been consulted.[10] Bachya's commentary on Esther should properly be noted as a part of *Kad HaKemach*, not as a separate work.[11] In the notes on *Ruth* and *Eichah*, we are told that the second edition of Radak's *Michlol* became known as *Sefer HaShorashim*; in fact it is a second part of his work that bears that name, *Michlol*

---

change of "He and Maimonides met each other during the latter's sojourn in Fez and Aknin wrote a sad couplet on the sage's departure for Egypt" to "He and The Ramban met each other during the latter's sojourn in Fez, and Ibn Aknin wrote a sad couplet on the sage's departure for Egypt" is hardly an improvement. Artscroll's desire to change Maimonides to "The Rambam" resulted in the error of "The Ramban." Yinglishizing the *EJ*'s language should be a lesser priority than identifying it as the source of this material.

9   Cf. Azariah De Rossi, *Meor Einayim: Imrei Binah*, chap. 9; Leopold Zunz, *Die gottesdienstlichen Vorträge der Juden Historisch entwickelt* (Berlin, 1832), chap. 5. It is assumed that the Artscroll editors would not consider these to be approved sources, but they do approve of Rabbi Z. H. Chajes who makes a similar observation in *Iggeret Biqqoret*, vol. 2, *Kol Sifrei HaMaharats Chajes* (henceforth, *Collected Writings*), 573.

10   In addition to the generally known Italian version found in most Rabbinic Bibles, a French one was published by Joseph Zedner (London, 1850).

11   This error has been corrected with respect to Bachya's commentary on Jonah.

(published in 1525), popularly referring to his grammar, and *Sefer HaShorashim* (published in 1479) to his dictionary.[12] Though born in 1489, Joseph Caro, author of the *Shulchan Aruch*, should be seen as a sixteenth-century figure, not fifteenth century as stated in *Eichah*, p. 150. The extant commentary on The Song of Songs that bears his name is attributed to Nachamides only with the greatest difficulty,[13] and the commentary on Chronicles attributed to Rashi (*Bereishis*, p. 330) is generally ascribed to some other medieval writer.[14] Also, what is Rashi's "introduction" referred to in *Bereishis*, p. 288? Is it Gen. 3:8? We know of no introduction of his to the Torah, and those brief ones that do exist for other books do not discuss the theoretical deviation from *halachah*, the subject of this paragraph.

The bibliographies are also incomplete, as some writers have been cited but not listed, for example: *Otzar HaAggadah* (*Eichah*, p. 92); Ibn Latif (*Kohelles*, p. xii); *Michlol Yofi* (*Yonah*, p. 100); Yefes ben Ali (*Yonah*, p. 111). Comments of Rabbi Chavel on Nachmanides' commentary on the Torah are cited (*Bereishis*, p. 234), but we have no way of knowing if this refers to the English or Hebrew editions of that work. Similarly, we are presented with a host of comments on Genesis that have been taken from "midrash" but there is no way to know which of the many *midrashim* on that book is intended unless, which appears to be the case most of the time, "midrash" refers to the volumes collected in the *Midrash Rabbah*, as noted in the bibliographical entries of the *megillot*. A lengthy passage has been quoted from Josephus' *Contra Apionem* (*Ruth*, p. xxix), but neither a source for the translation nor its exact location has been indicated.[15]

The general selection of writers contains few surprises. While one might miss the occasional commentary or text with which he is familiar, and more frequently a favourite comment on one or another verse by the writers used, for the most part there is a sample of the various schools and periods of biblical interpretation. A large sampling of *mussar* points to a particular interest in recent inspirational writing, and the frequent appearance of Hasidic writers is further evidence of their impact on American Orthodoxy, but, together with these, we find the comments of Rabbis S. R. Hirsch and David Hoffman, surely of a more Western bent. Needless to say, there is a full complement of *midrashim* and medieval writers, as well as a very broad sample of talmudic and targumic materials.

Conspicuous by its absence is what one might call the Italian school. While the Italian Jewish community is one of the oldest continuous communities in existence and has a distinguished history of

---

12   Cf. Frank E. Talmage, *David Kimhi: The Man and The Commentaries* (Cambridge, 1975), 191-92.
13   Cf. C. D. Chavel, ed., *Kitvei Rabenu Moshe ben Nachman*, vol. 2, 473-75.
14   See, for example, H. Y. D. Azulai, *Shem HaGedolim, Maarekhet Gedolim*, *s.v.* Rashi.
15   This passage comes from *Contra Apionem*, vol. 2, 165-66.

involvement in biblical studies, only Norzi (*Minhat Shai*) and Seforno receive attention.[16] Renaissance influence may have pointed modern Italian writers in a direction that differed from that of their east-European colleagues, who in turn expressed no little dismay at some of their writings. Nevertheless, we share the admiration expressed by Rabbi Z. H. Chajes for Azariah de Rossi (in spite of the criticisms of the Maharal of Prague) and regret that his work has been omitted from consideration.[17] Similarly, S. D. Luzzatto of Padua, one of the best known modern Jewish commentators, is totally ignored, and U. Cassuto, of the famous rabbinic family and a commentator whose writings are well known in Israel, is not considered worthy of mention.[18]

There are several possible reasons for these omissions. First (with a few marked exceptions), is a general lack of absorption of Italian writers into the east-European world, perhaps because of a cultural gap between the groups. Also, within Judaism, even rabbinic Judaism, there have always been modes of biblical interpretation that were highly rabbinic, based in large part on earlier rabbinic writings and constituting part of an ever-growing corpus of Talmud-based and *midrash*-based exegesis. The Bible was seen almost exclusively through earlier rabbinic literature, obscured by and, in some extreme cases, even ignored because of it.[19] This approach obviously saw little of value in contemporary religious exegesis that was equally extreme in being non-rabbinic, allowing the Bible much (but not total) freedom to speak for itself. The Italians, who identified more with this latter approach (popularized by authoritative writers of earlier centuries), were rarely accepted by the rabbinic writers of the former persuasion. In addition, men like Luzzatto and Cassuto may have been found guilty of dabbling in some unacceptable intellectual trends of their times. Although they succeeded in resolving the conflict between religion and the science of their day, the fact that they were not part of the *yeshiva* world has rendered them unfit to serve as contributors to the Orthodox anthologies of the twentieth century. American Jews may be descended from northern or eastern Europeans and are indebted to their forefathers for the fervour that has enabled them to remain committed Jews until today, but intellectually they have a great deal to learn from those scholars of the Italian peninsula who marked out the road for a

---

16 Bertinora is mentioned occasionally, but his work on the Bible is less important than his other writings.

17 On the attitude of the Maharal toward De Rossi see J. Elbaum, "Rabbi Judah Loew of Prague and his Attitude to the Aggadah," *Scripta Hierosolymitana* XXII, 28 ff. Chajes' positive attitude to De Rossi is evident from the many places he refers to him and even praises him, e.g., *Imrei Binah*, Introduction, vol. 2, *Collected Writings*, 872-73.

18 An important sample of Luzzatto's work has been translated into English under the title "A Critical and Hermeneutical Introduction to the Pentateuch," published by Sabato Morais in *Italian Hebrew Literature* (New York, 1926), 93-152. Some of Cassutto's works have been published by Magnes Press in Hebrew and in English translation and include commentaries on Genesis and Exodus, two volumes of collected essays, *The Goddess Anat*, and *The Documentary Hypothesis*.

19 Cf. Salo Baron, *A Social and Religious History of Jews*, vol. 16 (New York, 1976), 56 ff.

serious rapprochement between a traditional understanding of scripture and the challenges of the modern biblical sciences.

While the modern Italians are omitted, Josephus, an ancient Italian of sorts, and unquestionably not a religious authority, is quoted frequently. In *Ruth* (p. xxix) there is a passage from *Contra Apion* in which he explains that other nations place their trust in various types of governments while the Jews obey only the rule of God.[20] In *Bereishis* (p. 265) we are informed that Josephus mentioned that in his time Noah's ark was still in existence; again on p. 327 we learn, in the name of Rabbi David Hoffman, that Josephus associated the names Arpachshad and Kasdim. In *Bereishis* (p. 472) Josephus is again cited for his report that a large tree near Hebron has existed since the creation of the world. Abraham's rescue of Lot received some further amplification in Josephus, and this is reported in the commentary on Gen. 14:15; similarly the report is given that the pillar of salt formed by Lot's wife was seen by Josephus (*ibid.*, p. 708).

The manner in which Josephus is used raises several important questions. Almost all of the passages for which he is cited are reports of the contemporary status of items or places mentioned in the Torah. Given the apologetic nature of Josephus' work and the possibility that his statements on the tree and ark represent pious tales rather than confirmed information, it is rather doubtful that one should rely on all of his reports.[21] Of course, if he is trustworthy, why isn't his information used more frequently? And what are Orthodox Jews supposed to learn about proper method in the exposition of the Torah from these citations? One's first reaction to the problem might be to see the inclusion of such passages as simple apologetics, designed to confirm the reports of the Torah or sages. The clearly stated attack on apologetics notwithstanding, (*The Megillah*, p. x), this seems the best explanation of Artscroll's procedure. Alternatively, we might attribute this interest in Josephus to the reported interest of the Vilna Gaon in this writer, but what about the host of other ancient texts? Why were these not used? If religious Jews may consult some works that were neither written by religious writers nor preserved by trustworthy sources, why should they ignore other similar texts that are now available?[22]

---

20   This passage comes from *Contra Apionem*, vol. 2, 165-66 (Loeb edition, 358-59). The Artscroll editor follows this citation by the observation, "Josephus' description of Jewish government is often mistakenly described as theocracy but it is not that at all." This bears explanation in light of the Greek term theocracy used here, which, according to Thackeray (the Leob editor), "was apparently coined by Josephus!"

21   On the method of Josephus' *Antiquities* see most recently Harold Attridge, *The Interpretation of Biblical History in the Antiquitates Judaicae of Flavius Josephus* (Missoula, Montana, 1976), and the literature cited there.

22   As an example of the logical progression that Artscroll's use of Josephus requires, let us examine the reference to the existence of Noah's ark in his time. Josephus noted, as quoted by Artscroll (*Bereishis*, 265), "Its remains are shown there by the inhabitants to this day" (*Antiquities* I: 3:5 borrowed without citation from Whiston's translation; in the Thackery edition, 45). A few lines later, Josephus cited Berosus' observa-

Also of note is the source of the Artscroll comment on Jon. 2:4. In dealing with the apparently plural form of *ymym*, "seas," the editor cited the explanation of the famous Karaite exegete Yefes ben Ali, cited, in turn, by Ibn Ezra. To be sure, Ibn Ezra was anything but a Karaite partisan, but it has been shown that there are significant parallels between some of his explanations and those of the anti-rabbinite group.[23] We might expect that Ibn Ezra would refer to Karaite writers, even in a positive way, but why is one cited in a publication that claims to contain only authoritative religious teachings? The slip occurred only once, though, and no bibliographical entry for Yefes ben Ali is to be found at the end of the book, so that the unsuspecting reader will have no way of identifying the author.

We will return to the limitations of working only with approved authorities later. For now, let us examine the Artscroll treatment of the documents that it has analyzed and presented.

C. The Lack of Linguistic Precision

1. Philological Errors in Treating the Bible Text

Any one who sets out to study what the traditional Jewish writers have said about any verse of the Bible will find an overwhelming array

---

tion: "It is said, moreover, that a portion of the vessel still survives in Armenia on the mountain of the Cordyaeans and that persons carry off pieces of the bitumen, which they use as talismans." He then added that according to Nicolas of Damascus, "relics of the timber [of the ark] were for long preserved" (Thackery, 45-47). It stands to reason that Josephus' statement, which was cited by Artscroll, was based on these earlier sources, and we must judge *them* and not Josephus if we are to avoid apologetics as Artscroll wishes. Thus we must now admit the statement of Nicolas, Herod's biographer and undoubtedly not an approved religious writer, as well as that of Berosus, a Babylonian priest (born ca. 350 B.C.E.) who, like Josephus, wrote his national history in Greek for the hellenized world.

Of course a pre-Christian Babylonian source is a good testimony to what may have happened in ancient Mesopotamia, but by Berosus' admission his report was hearsay. But what was Berosus doing? The above statement is part of an account of the flood that Josephus, as was his wont, correlated with the biblical account (*ibid.*). Most scholars agree that Berosus' version is related to the flood story that was preserved in the Babylonian text *Atra-hasis*, related, in turn, to the Epic of Gilgamesh and the Sumerian flood legends. Most modern scholars perceive the biblical flood story as a conscious rejection of (if not a polemic against) the Mesopotamian versions of the flood story. Riding on Josephus' syncretistic desire to correlate hellenistic world history and the Torah, Artscroll has admitted the pagan priest Berosus into its canon of approved writers and very possibly permitted the violation of one of the primary messages of the biblical flood story! And, moreover, what is Artscroll's position on equating the biblical flood with that described in Mesopotamian literature? Are they identical? Did Noah also bear the names Xisouthros and Utnapishtim?

23   Some of this material has been noted by I. Krinsky in the introduction to his commentaries on Ibn Ezra (*Mehoqeqei Yehudah*), Genesis, Introduction, 12a ff.; cf. M. Friedlaender, *Essays on the Writings of Abraham Ibn Ezra* (London, 1877). More recently, see Moshe Sokolow, *The Commentary of Yefet Ben Ali on Deuteronomy XXXII* (Ph.D. dissertation, Yeshiva University, 1974).

of ideas. Determining the correct position as defined by the tradition, particularly if one seeks the unanimous agreement of all authoritative spokesmen of that tradition, can be frustrating if not impossible. Since unanimity is frequently nonexistent, a selection of appropriate possibilities is in order, but one of the most serious deficiencies in the entire Artscroll project lies in the fact that the editors selected whatever appealed to them without any objective criteria for determining whether a particular comment is linguistically possible. Anyone who investigates the history of Hebrew linguistic science will surely discover that one of the most important periods of research was during the Middle Ages and included the writings of Ibn Janach, Ibn Ezra, and Radak.[24] The ability to evaluate the linguistic materials produced by the various writers and commentators over the centuries undoubtedly would have placed these men at the center of any serious attempt to grapple with the Bible text and most other commentators in a range of secondary positions. These writers knew a solid linguistic argument when they saw it, and they knew linguistic distortion when they saw it. Their dictionaries, grammars, and commentaries have stood the test of time and are still highly regarded by all philologists and students of the Bible. They may not be perfect, but they are great, and they stood, in some cases, almost a millenium ahead of what has become the modern discipline of comparative Semitic philology.

These writers are frequently cited in the Artscroll series, but, consciously or unconsciously, the work has made the approach of Rabbi S. R. Hirsch the basis of its philosophy of language. Hirsch's linguistic ingenuity is sometimes remarkable and was obviously supplemented by a creative mind and (for some people) appealing doctrines, but it is totally unacceptable to any scientific appreciation of the dynamics of language. Indeed, it has much in common with some of the very approaches that many of the medieval linguists and commentators attacked as unfounded. Such fanciful philology is legitimate only as another form of *midrash*, which, like the *midrashim* of old, is unrestrained by any limits of grammar and lexicography and can do almost anything to the Bible text in the name of religious edification.[25] Since Hirsch's philology has not been presented as *midrash*, we must assume that this is not the editors' position and that in citing such materials they consider themselves to be presenting the simple mean-

---

24 English studies on the history of Hebrew linguistic science include H. Hirschfeld, *Literary History of Hebrew Grammarians and Lexicographers* (London, 1926); S. Baron, *A Social and Religious History of the Jews*, vol. 7 (New York, 1958), chap. 30; N. Sarna, "Hebrew and Bible Studies in Mediaeval Spain" in R. D. Barnett, ed., *The Sephardi Heritage* (New York, 1971).

25 Thus we find the alleged relation of *ṣnh* and *ṣn'h* (*Tehillim*, 423); *rš'* and *r'š* (*ibid.*, 58); *rḥb* and *rhb* (*ibid.*, 501); *'rṣ*, *rṣ* and *rṣṣ* (*Bereishis*, 34, 51; *ṣl* and *ṣlm* (*ibid.*, 69-70); and many, many more. To be sure many of these words have one weak letter (usually a guttural), but they are not related, and the theory on which such notions are based is incorrect, notwithstanding the fact that some writers have favoured this position; cf. Malbim to Lev. 2:14, note 152.

ing of the text. It is necessary to test Artscroll's linguistic principles with the grammatical and lexical tools that are available. Unfortunately, the range of linguistic inaccuracies is extensive. The editors should have taken more seriously the advice of Rabbi Y. M. Epstein, "Every sage must possess some knowledge of Grammar" (*Aruch HaShulchan, Orach Hayyim* 61:9), as the following paragraphs should demonstrate.

The first of many problems lies in understanding the role of the prepositions. People who know modern Hebrew are frequently surprised to learn that the meaning of a preposition in biblical Hebrew is not always constant. Thus, for example, while the accepted convention of modern Hebrew (and of most premodern dialects as well) has *'el* meaning "to" and *'al* meaning "on," in the Bible the two are interchangeable. Attempts to force the more common meaning into those passages where the alternate meaning is more appropriate have generated many interesting *midrashim* and interpretations, but, from the standpoint of the simple meaning, the two words are sometimes equivalent. This is best illustrated by the interchange of the two words in the parallel passages in Samuel-Kings and Chronicles and was noted in various places by Rashi, Ibn Janach, Radak, and most of the other early commentators and linguists.[26] The editors' preference for a one-to-one correspondence between the words and their English equivalents, rather than this more flexible understanding (probably the result of influence from the "Teitsch school" of translation) has led them to errors of judgment in Lam. 4:21, Jon. 3:2, etc. As is the case with *'el* and *'al*, we also find routine interchanges of the prepositions *b-, m-, 'im, 'et*, etc. This phenomenon might be explained simply that a preposition may have several meanings rather than one, but the fact remains that these words or prefixes overlap in meaning and may substitute for each other. Additional examples of misinterpretation and unnecessary confusion surround the understanding of prepositions in Jon. 2:4, Ps. 28:6, etc. One of the most blatant misunderstandings lies in the attempt to designate the "literal" meaning of various prepositions in the commentaries in contrast to what has been offered as the idiomatic meanings in the translations. In many of these cases, the idiomatic translation *is* the literal one, and many passages in the commentaries and translations should be corrected in this light, e.g., Gen. 2:2, 4:11, 8:20, 22:3.

Another apparent lapse in the editors' knowledge of grammar relates to the tenses of verbs, particularly to the prefixed forms of the verbs known in various grammars as future or imperfect. While the

---

26   E.g., 1 Sam. 31:3-1 Chron. 10:3; 2 Sam. 6:2, 10-1 Chron. 13:7, 13; 2 Sam. 23:13, 23-1 Chron. 11:15, 25; 1 Kings 10:7, 19-2 Chron. 9:16, 18; 2 Kings 22:8, 16, 20-2 Chron. 34: 15, 24, 28; etc. The matter is discussed, among other places, by Ibn Janach, *Sefer HaShorashim*, s.v. *'l*, and Radak, *Sefer HaShorashim*, s.v. *'l*. The existence of these parallel passages in the Bible seems to have escaped the editor of *Tehillim*, who notes in reference to Psalm 18 "This Psalm has the distinction of being the only chapter in Scriptures which is recorded twice" (211)!

Hebrew verbal system is one of the most complex aspects of the language, some data concerning it are certain and should not lead readers or interpreters astray. Imperfect verbs, for instance, can be used to describe both what will occur in the future (future tense) and what ought to occur in the future (jussive). In dozens of cases, therefore, it is impossible to tell from the context if a particular act is commanded, predicted, or described. In fact, a whole series of disagreements between Rabbi Ishmael and Rabbi Akiva centered around this exact problem; Rabbi Ishmael interpreted these regulations as optional (*reshut*), Rabbi Akiva saw them as obligatory (*hovah*).[27] In fact, the imperfect forms may also connote present and even past action.[28] Awareness of these linguistic usages should have eliminated some of the distortion imposed on certain verses.[29] At the very least it would have aided the reader to understand the underlying reasons for the different interpretations.

In addition to other grammatical difficulties, there are problems in vocalization. The word *ht'ym* may be vocalized two ways, each carrying a different meaning. The plural of *het'*, "sins," is vocalized with *hatef-patach* on the first letter; the plural of *hata'*, "sinners," is vocalized with a *patach*. Thus, Ps. 1:1 is translated correctly as "path of the sinful," though one would be better served by the comments of the Malbim and Hirsch who distinguished between *hote'*, "sinner," and *hata'*, "perpetual sinner," than that incorrectly attributed to Hirsch: a differentiation between *rasha'* in the previous phrase and the word *hote'* which is not actually used in the verse. Somewhat perplexing, though, is the observation on the same word "sinners" (vocalized with a *patach* and parallel to *reshayim*) cited from Ps. 104:35 in *Tehillim*, p. 115, and translated "Let sins cease from the earth." The Talmudic explanation notwithstanding, the Massoretic Text means "sinners" not "sins" and must be translated in this manner. This error has been repeated in *Tehillim*, p. 423.

Popular errors in language, both in pronunciation and word meaning have infiltrated at various points in the commentaries. One of the most important is the word *zw*. Hebrew has two words that are spelled *zw*. The first, vocalized *zo*, is equivalent to *z't* (*zot*) a femine form of the word *zh* (*ze*), and means "this." The second word, *zu*, for the most part limited in use to biblical texts, means "which," and is found in phrases like *'am zu ga' alta* (Ex. 15:13) and *'am zu qanita* (Ex. 15:16) meaning "the people which . . . ." Nonetheless, there is a list of places where *zu* is confused with *zo*: Ps. 9:16, 31:5, 32:8, etc. Some readers may be interested to note that the proper form of the wedding

---

27   For a list of sources and related discussion see J. N. Epstein, *Prolegomena ad Litteras Tannaiticas* (in Hebrew; Jerusalem, 1957), 534-35.

28   See Ibn Janach, *Sefer HaRiqmah*, ed. by M. Wilensky (Jerusalem, 1964), 322, lines 6ff.; also the statement of Samuel Bar Hofni in M. Zucker, *Al Targum Rasag LaTorah* (New York, 1959), 260.

29   E.g., Gen. 2:16, 2:25, 17:16, 18:12, 22:12, Ps. 38:14.

formula is "behold you are consecrated to me with this ring—*beṭabaʿat zo* . . . (not *zu*)."[30]

This ignorance of certain grammatical phenomena is accompanied by a rather inaccurate usage of many linguistic and exegetical terms. Thus we frequently find "homiletical" when "midrashic" is meant, e.g., *Tehillim*, pp. 199, 248-9; "paraphrase" is used for "translate," *Bereishis*, p. 463; *'et* is correctly a particle not a participle as in *Bereishis*, p. 434; "translate," which properly refers to the transfer of material from one language to another, is very frequently used to mean "explain" or "paraphrase," i.e., that which the Talmud or Rashi did when they proposed one Hebrew word to explain another; foreign words adopted into a language are correctly called "loan words" not "borrow words," *The Megillah*, p. x (an error that sounds like a mistranslation of the Hebrew term); the discussion of nouns and verbs in *Tehillim* 7:12 is meaningless because participial forms may be both nouns and verbs—the words should be analyzed syntactically as subjects, objects, etc.

It is evident that Artscroll possesses a certain sensitivity to comparative linguistics. Thus "firmament" is associated with the Latin *firmare* (*Bereishis*, p. 45). Occasionally words in rabbinic dicta are labeled as Greek: Radak's use of French *algae* is alleged (*Yonah*, p. 113);[31] Arabic is mentioned (e.g., *Bereishis*, p. 563, cited from Rabbi David Hoffman); etc. Nonetheless, we find no attempt to relate Hebrew to other *ancient* languages—Phoenician, Akkadian, Ugaritic, etc.—in spite of the many useful and edifying observations such comparisons allow. It is also very misleading to cite Rashi's use of Canaanite in connection with the comment that *Senir* (Deut. 3:9) is related to *Schnee* "snow" (*Shir haShirim*, p. 135-6). The accuracy of the claim aside, not all texts of Rashi note that it is both German and Canaanite, and the latter refers to Old Czech, not to the language of the ancient Canaanites in which the word for "snow" should be a cognate of *sheleg*.[32]

---

30 Note also Nahum Ish Gimzo (Gimzo is a place mentioned in 2 Chron. 28:18), who is associated with the statement *gam zo leṭovah*, *Taanit*, 21a.
    Other inaccuracies include reading the Aramaic negative particle *l'* as Hebrew *lo* rather than as *la*; and the homiletical claim that *tyqw* (*tequ*) should be taken as an acronym for a phrase meaning "Tishbi (Elijah) will answer or resolve all contradictions and questions" when it is a form of the word meaning "to stand" and means that the matter stands.

31 In point of fact, Radak's translations are to Provençal, not French; cf. Talmage, *David Kimhi*, 63-65.

32 The word is apparently not attested in Phoenician or Ugaritic, but close cognates appear in Arabic, Aramaic, and Akkadian.
    Vernacular glosses in Slavic, or more precisely Old Czech, are always labeled *leshon Knaan* ("Knaanic") in the biblical and Talmudic commentaries of Rashi and other medieval works, most notably the *Or Zarua* of Isaac b. Moses of Vienna and the *Arugat ha-Bosem* of Abraham b. Azriel. (Although some Slavic glosses in medieval Hebrew writings are assumed to be scribal interpolations originating much later, the integrity of this particular reference in Rashi is attested within a century and a half by Nachmanides.) For further discussion see I. Krinsky, *Mehoqeqei Yehudah*, Deuteronomy, vol. 5, p. 28. The sources of the glosses, as well as their

The early writers were well aware of the importance of comparative linguistics, and approved writers who used this approach include
Rabbi Levi (third century), Saadia, Ibn Janach, and Ibn Ezra. Usually
fluent in three Semitic languages (Arabic, Hebrew, and Aramaic) and
occasionally others as well, these men were keenly aware of the value of
interlinguistic study and very frequently used this approach to explain
difficult biblical passages or to clarify the precise connotations of words
whose range of meanings may not have been known. Modern Semitic
studies is the direct outgrowth of this field of interest and must be a
legitimate method of inquiry, even for the pious Artscroll series. (See
below, note 70.) Ignorance of Judeo-Arabic in eastern Europe and the
unavailability of and lack of interest in many of the primary works that
developed this comparative approach allowed this valuable discipline
to decline and to be revived by linguists and scholars outside the
Artscroll purview. This, coupled with the pious desire to deny any
possible interaction between the Bible and foreign languages and cultures, has built an almost impenetrable wall between Artscroll and this
field of research. We must conclude, though, that in this respect modern linguistic scholarship is closer to the approach of the *Rishonim* than
Artscroll itself.

The production of an accurate translation of any document is an
excellent exercise, and, if properly executed, the translation can provide a very satisfactory, if limited, opportunity to read and understand
the original text. Many translators strive to represent the translated
text in a manner as faithful as possible to its original form and meaning,
even though this is never completely possible. Others treat translation
as a highly subjective interpretive activity in which the text is rendered
in accordance with specific theories of translation or ideologies. Many
Bible translations of the first type already exist in English; the Artscroll
translations are an attempt to exemplify the second type. While this is
quite clearly stated in every book and is surely not inappropriate, the
simple meaning of the text was the starting point for many of the
writers whose comments are cited in the anthology-commentary, and
the avoidance of this starting point clouds the exegetical process. Given
their goals and assumptions—which stress the desire to understand the
text in the light of the traditional commentaries—the Artscroll translations must be evaluated in terms other than those normally used to

importance for the history of Old Czech in general and the language of the Jews in
Bohemia in particular, is surveyed, with documentation, in a preliminary mono-
graph by Roman Jakobson and Morris Halle, "The Term *Canaan* in Medieval Hebrew," in *For Max Weinreich on his Seventieth Birthday: Studies in Jewish Languages,
Literature, and Society* (The Hague: Mouton & Co., 1964), 147-72; cf. also Max
Weinreich, *History of the Yiddish Language*, vol. 1 (Chicago: University of Chicago
Press, 1979). The entire literature on the subject of Judeo-Slavic, including the
numerous discussions of Rashi's aforementioned reference to *leshon Kanaan*, will be
delineated in the annotated *Bibliographia Linguistica Judaeo-Slavica*, now in preparation by Brad S. Hill, graduate student at McGill, to whom I am indebted for these
references.

judge translations. The huge number of acceptable commentators from whom the editors could choose and their lack of desire to criticize any of them means that virtually any meaning is possible and available for use in the translations.

Although this method is adhered to throughout the series, it is most evident in the translation of The Song of Songs, which differs from the standard English translations more than those of the other books. Basically, the Hebrew is translated to reflect one or another rabbinic interpretation, but the confusion that surrounds this process is quite remarkable. Many of the accompanying comments attempt to explain the translation. Some stress the literal meaning of the Hebrew, others call it an allegory, and still others, a metaphor, but whatever is meant, all three cannot be the primary meaning. One instructive example involves a reference in The Song of Songs to the lover's breasts. According to Artscroll "when the commentators say that *shenei shadayikh*, *your bosom*, refers to Moses and Aaron, they are not departing from the simple literal meaning of the phrase in the least. . . . They, Israel's sources of spiritual nourishment, are not implied allegorically or derived esoterically from the verse; the verse literally means them" (*Shir haShirim*, p. lxiv). Nonetheless, we are also told: "For the English reader's convenience and so that he might better appreciate how the allegory is derived from the text, a literal translation of every phrase is included in brackets after each entry in the commentary" (p. xii), and in the commentary to 4:5 the phrase is indeed given literally as "your bosom is like two fawns," etc. According to the overview the meaning "Moses and Aaron" is *not* derived, and the verse literally means Moses and Aaron; in the commentary we are told that the allegory *is* derived and the verse literally refers to a bosom. Elsewhere in the commentary we find, "Although the other songs also contain sacred and esoteric allusions, they are open to simple and literal translation; whereas God-forbid that the Song of Songs should be interpreted in any way but as its most sacred metaphor" (p. 68). Clear definitions of "literal meaning," "metaphor," "allegory," and similar terms would certainly help clarify the editors' presentations.

Related to this example, one continually notes the care with which the translators avoid sexual matters. While modesty has always been a Jewish virtue, the tradition is not prudish, and those passages that have been misrepresented because of their sexual aspects should be corrected, even if certain parts of the anatomy must be mentioned. Such inaccuracies include *betulot*, translated alternately "girls" and "maidens" (*The Megillah*, pp. 61-62). *Shadayim*, translated "bosom" (*Shir haShirim*, pp. 131, 200, etc.), obviously should be rendered as "breasts," particularly when accompanied by a plural. *Beṭen* means "womb" not only "stomach" (e.g., *Kohelles* p. 186); perhaps using "surplusage" for "foreskin" fits this pattern also (*Bereishis*, p. 570).

Hebrew has a long history during which many words evolved in meaning and usage. While for midrashic purposes it is appropriate to read later meanings into earlier texts (e.g., rabbinic *maqom* "God" for Biblical *maqom* "place" or "shrine"), cases where this is done should be designated as "derash, a practice that has not always been followed. An excellent example of this type of misusage is the word *nefesh*, which has a wide range of meanings, including "person," "people," "appetite," "life force" and even "neck." While the Artscroll translations frequently demonstrate a sensitivity to the range of possibilities in translating the word, they often add a note that destroys one's confidence in their complete mastery of the term. Thus we find "those who seek my life [lit. soul]," Ps. 40:15; "to the wishes [lit. soul]," Ps. 27:12; "please take my life [lit. soul]," Jon. 4:3; etc. This problem also manifests itself in many places where the double translation has not been provided and only the connotation "soul" has been presented. One obvious error is in the presentation of the *midrash* cited in *Bereishis*, p. 795. Here Satan is described as disguising himself as a river and causing Abraham and Isaac to be covered to their necks (*ṣawa'reihem*). A few words later, Ps. 69:2 is cited as proof that the water has reached their necks, demonstrating an assumption on the part of the *midrash* that the word *nefesh* in this verse means "neck" as it does in Ps. 105:18, where Joseph is described as having chains around his *nefesh*.[33] In fact the concept "soul" is properly a post-biblical one and virtually every place where the word *nefesh* occurs in the Bible necessitates a translation somewhat different from that generally understood by this English term.

These last examples point to a general problem in the relationship between the translation and the commentary. While there are only occasional places where the two actually disagree,[34] the commentaries very frequently include "literal" renderings designed to clarify the idiomatic translations.[35] As noted above with respect to prepositions, the idiomatic translations are usually better. The literal ones reflect very primitive, almost ignorant attempts at presentations of the text. They tend to weaken our confidence in Artscroll's complete mastery of Hebrew, and create the feeling that the writers would have been happier with more mechanical, less accurate translations. Linguistic sensitivity was the hallmark of all rabbinic interpretation, and the *midrashim* are among the most sensitive exegetical texts available. Proper appreciation of language would only be in keeping with traditional forms and values, yet the Artscroll effort has not attained the high level set by its predecessors.

---

33 Ps. 69:2 reads *hoshi'eni eloqim ki ba'u mayim 'ad nafesh*—"Save me, O Lord, because the waters have reached my neck."

34 E.g., the commentary to Gen. 2:2 seems to suggest that the translation of the verse should be "And *by* the seventh day God completed . . . ," but the translation actually reads "On the seventh . . . ."

35 Some inaccurate "literal" translations include *wayyitten* "he gave," correctly "he paid" (*Yonah*, 85); *holekh weso'er*, "was going and storming," correctly "was growing stormier" (*ibid.*, 101); *zo't happa'am*, "this, the time," correctly "this time" (*Bereishis*, 109).

We will now examine the translation and presentation of the exegetical texts. Here, too, more awareness of the dynamics of language might have prevented many problems.

2. *Errors in the Presentation of Exegetical Texts*

The primary activity in which the Artscroll editors have engaged is the condensation and presentation of earlier sources. A mammoth effort has been exerted to achieve this goal and the quality of work is generally satisfactory; nonetheless we note many passages that appear to have missed the mark. Examples include texts from the Talmud, midrashic literature, *targumim*, and later commentaries.

(a) Talmud and Midrashic Literature

The Talmud (*Berachot* 5a) recommends that one always incite the good inclination against the evil inclination. In support of this idea it cites Ps. 4:5, *rigzu we'al teḥeṭa'u*. The Artscroll translation, following the Talmud, is "Be agitated and do not sin" (p. 86), but it is clear that the intent of the talmudic passage is "Agitate [the good inclination against the evil one] and do not sin."

Omission can encourage misunderstanding almost as much as mistranslation. Thus, in *Bereishis*, p. 109, we find the *midrash* about God's decision to create woman from the rib, which is modest, rather than from one of the other organs that might have proved a source of some negative characteristics. Of note, though, is the concluding passage of the *midrash*, which has been omitted. Perhaps intended humorously, perhaps seriously, the rest of the passage indicates that in spite of God's efforts to prevent all of the negative characteristics symbolized by the head, eyes, mouth, etc., woman has managed to possess all of them anyway. Omission of this last section appears to alter the intent of the statement and may conceal its true sentiment.

The sentence *biqshu ḥakhamim lignoz sefer qohellet mipnei shedebaraw sotrim ze et ze* (*Shabbat* 30b) means that the rabbis wanted to take Ecclesiastes out of circulation because its statements contradict each other. The Artscroll translation (*Koheles*, p. xli), later emphasized and italicized (*ibid.*, p. 50), reads "because its statements [apparently] contradict one another." This clouds the issue and may not correctly reflect the sentiment of the source. That the rabbis did not consign the work to *genizah* is not because its words are not contradictory, but rather because the beginning and end reflect a different, more positive attitude.[36]

---

36 Other sources (e.g., Leviticus Rabbah 28:1) reflect a different position. See the literature cited in Sid Z. Leiman *The Canonization of Hebrew Scripture: The Talmudic and Midrashic Evidence* (Hamden, Connecticut, 1975), 175, note 322.

Another example of misreading a rabbinic statement is found in *Koheles*, p. 202. Here, in a discussion of the statement in Eccl. 12:12 about there being no end to the making of books, we find the midrashic statement that anyone who brings more than twenty-four books into his house brings confusion into his house. It is generally agreed that this passage was originally intended to prevent acceptance of any non-canonical literature, but the Artscroll addition of "and the *Talmud* and commentaries which explain Torah," while perhaps a little more appropriate for today's religious reader, really misses the point of the passage and distorts it.

In order to understand *derashot*, it is often necessary to know how Hebrew and Aramaic were pronounced by those who composed them. Thus we may observe talmudic statements on the pronunciation of gutturals, on the tendency to elide consonants that we would find virtually impossible to elide, and on various linguistic phenomena, all of which demonstrate that rabbinic Hebrew was quite different from the biblical and modern dialects.[37] It might not alter the philosophical importance of the statements, but readers would be helped in appreciating the stimuli for the various *derashot* if they were told, for example, that *mwt* "death" and *m'd* "very" sounded almost identical in antiquity, and that the *derash* that saw death as good in a very real sense depended on this phonetic association to make it stick (*Bereishis*, p. 78).[38]

Another factor in many *derashot* was the similarity between certain Hebrew words and unrelated but similar sounding words in other languages. Would the reader not be better able to understand the basis of the *derash* on Gen. 22:8 (Abraham's response to Isaac's question about the availability of a *se* "sheep" for the offering) were he told that the word *se* in Greek means "you" and that the midrashic reading of the verse saying that God will provide "you" as the offering is based on this word play?[39] Similarly, a foreign word may underlie the midrashic motivation to understand *efratim*, Ruth 1:2, as "courtiers." Some writers have tried to associate it with *apirion* (*Ruth*, p. 64). Rabbi Baruch Halevi Epstein (in his *Torah Temimah*) associates it with *palatin*. Also possible and a little closer in sound is the Latin *praetorium*. Other examples abound, but are not presented by Artscroll.

A talmudic text that is routinely cited in any discussion of the allegorical interpretation of The Song of Songs is in Mishnah, *Yadaim* 3:5, and includes the observation that "all of the *ketubim* are holy and The Song

---

37 These are treated in varying degrees in the standard grammars of rabbinic Hebrew and Aramaic and in A. Sperber *A Historical Grammar of Biblical Hebrew* (Leiden, 1966).

38 See the data cited by E. Kutscher, *The Language and Linguistic Background of the Isaiah Scroll* (Hebrew) (Jerusalem, 1959), 408-09 and Sperber, *Historical Grammar*, 174.

39 This and other examples (but not all available) are discussed by James Barr, *Comparative Philology and The Text of The Old Testament* (Oxford, 1968), 50ff. This particular passage is discussed on p. 57, but the source should be corrected to *Pesikta Rabbati*, from *Pesikta de Rav Kahana*, as cited; see also M. Friedmann's edition, 170b.

of Songs is the holiest of the holy." In *Shir haShirim* (p. 68) we are told that the meaning of *ketubim* in this passage is "*Writings* [Hagiographa]," i.e., the third part of the Bible. While this is possible, as is the argument that the entire Bible is intended, it is important to note that there is a serious uncertainty in the textual tradition of this particular word. Some *midrash* and Mishnah manuscripts and printed editions, particularly those associated with the Palestinian tradition, read *kol hashirim qodesh* "all the poems are holy . . . ," and this appears to be the preferred understanding of the passage, if not the preferred text.[40] In discussing the symbolism of seeing individual biblical books in dreams, mention is made of *ketubim gedolim* and *ketubim qetanim* (*Berachot* 57b), from which we see that parts of the Bible other than the entire third unit may be called *ketubim*. More interesting is the fact that the *ketubim gedolim* include Psalms, Proverbs, and Job and omit one of the largest of the books, Chronicles; similarly, the *ketubim qetanim* include Lamentations, The Song of Songs, and Ecclesiastes, but omit the smallest of them, Ruth. We submit that the reason these six books are designated as *ketubim* is that they are poetic, and the omission of Ruth and Chronicles from consideration is because they are prose; or, to put it differently, the word *ketubim* may mean "poetry." Thus in the Mishnah one may accept either of the equivalent readings of *shirim* or *ketubim* (*ketubim* would appear to be preferable), but the meaning is the same: "all the poetry is holy but The Song of Songs is the holiest of the holy."[41]

One of Artscroll's favourite talmudic statements is: *hb' lthr ms'yyn 'wtw*, translated as "He who comes to purify himself receives divine assistance" and the like.[42] The verb *lthr* (vocalized by Artscroll as *letaher*) should be seen as a passive form of the verb and means "one who comes to be purified" or possibly as a reflexive "one who comes to purify himself." Though correctly understood, the word is improperly vocalized and should be read *litaher* as if had a *Yod* after the first letter, *lythr*. This spelling has important manuscript support and must reflect the proper vocalization.[43]

---

40   E.g., Codex Paris 328-29 of the Mishnah (Makor facsimile, vol. 3, 1207). For additional data see S. Lieberman "*Mishnat Shir HaShirim*" in G. G. Scholem, *Jewish Gnosticism, Merkabah Mysticism, and Talmudic Tradition* (New York, 1965).

41   If it is true that *ketubim* means "poetry," then, contrary to Leiman's statement, *Canonization*, 71, para. 45, the passage may be very significant for understanding the history of the third part of the canon, as some of the parallels collected from apocryphal and Christian sources clearly point to a division of poetry (see Leiman, *Canonization*, chap. 1). Thus far no other passages where *ktb* refers exclusively to poetry have come to our attention. The opposite is possibly attested, however, as *shira* (Deut. 31:19) is interpreted by the works that list and discuss the 613 *mitzvot* to refer to the entire Torah (not to the poem that follows immediately in chap. 32) and to include the commandment to write a Torah. This is usually claimed to include the entire Torah, because the Torah should not be written in small units, thus precluding the possibility that the verse refers to Deut. 32.

42   Cited from *Yoma* 38b (but also found in *Avodah Zarah* 55a, *Menachot* 29b, and *Shabbat* 104a) in *Tehillim*, 194, 310, *Bereishis*, 726, etc.

43   This is the spelling attested in the Vilna edition of Shabbat 104a and in the important *Avodah Zarah* manuscript of the Jewish Theological Seminary 44830, published in

(b) Targumim

In *Tehillim* 35:8 we find citations from the *targumim* of Ezekiel and
Zephaniah for the word *šw'h*. The texts, we are told, read *'trgwšt'* and
'trlwšt' from *rgš*. The word *šw'h* and its inflected forms appear thirteen
times in the Bible and, using the best editions of the available *targumim*
for all of these verses, we have found no text with a reading like the
second listed above. We have not made an exhaustive check of all the
printed editions, and it is highly possible that one has *'trlwšt'* by mistake, but even if it exists alongside the obviously correct form, why use
both, and why say that *'trlwšt'* also has as its root *rgš*? But, even better,
why not use the critical texts of the *targum* and avoid the entire problem?

In *Tehillim* 38:11 we are told that the *targum* of *sbyb* is *shwr*, this to
explain the Hebrew word *shrhr* in the verse. The translation of Hebrew
sbyb is usually *shr shr* with a doubled form (or *hzwr hzwr* in the Hagiographa) and surely this is closer to the desired form than that cited.[44]
The entire passage is based on the comment of Radak, *a.l.* While there
may be some texts that omitted the double form of the word thinking it
to be a dittography, correct editions of Radak read *shr shr* just as we
should have expected.

Again, in *Tehillim* 50:14 we are told that according to the *targum*
the verse means *"Offer sacrifice* by placing your Evil Inclination before
God and this will be reckoned as if you had brought an actual *thanksgiv-
ing offering."* Why anyone should place his evil inclination before God
escapes us. Actually, the *targum* suggests something quite different:
"Overcome the evil inclination and it will be considered before God like
the offering . . . ."

Bereishis 12:11 contains the phrase *hinei na' yada'ti*, translated "See
now, I have known." The editor then notes that Onkelos always translates *na'* as "now." This is sometimes true, but not always, as is evident
from Onkelos' translation of Numbers 12:13.

In *Bereishis* 2:14 we are told in the name of *Nesinah LaGer* and
Lechem VeSimlah that, though Onkelos did not translate the names of
the other three rivers in the Garden of Eden, he did translate that of the
Tigris, rendered *dyglt*. The forms of these names appear as described,
but with the exception of the Samaritan Targum (which gives different
names for the second and third rivers), all of the available Aramaic
translations (including the Syriac Peshitta and the Syro-Palestinian
version, both of which are available in Hebrew script) use these names
as in Onkelos. One might therefore suspect that these were accepted
names in Aramaic (names are frequently not translated in the *tar-*

---

facsimile (New York, 1957) (*lytm'* has been corrected by the insertion of the *Yod*).
Vatican MS 108 (Makor, 1972) reads *lthr* but *lytm'*. R. Rabbinovicz, *Diqduqei Soferim*,
Yoma, 104, note 6, also cites a reading of *lhthr*. For the use of *lw* in place of *'wtw*, see
Diqduqei Soferim, Menachot, 73, note 90, and *Shabbat*, 234, note 80.

44   See E. Levita, *Meturgeman-Lexicon Chaldaicum* (n.p., 1591), *s.v. shr*.

gumim). The Aramaic form of *ḥideqel, dyglt*, of course, is not a translation but simply the Aramaic equivalent of the Hebrew, which is exactly the point of *Nesinah LaGer*. Tigris is not a translation either, but the equivalent, consonant for consonant.

The *targum* to Ps. 27:6 translates *b'hlw* "his tent" as *mashkenei*. The verse refers to sacrifices that will be offered in this tent and "tabernacle" or "temple" are appropriate associations, but it is in Hebrew that *mškn* means "tabernacle." In Aramaic it is primarily the word "tent," the literal translation of the Hebrew *'ohel*, and carries the notion of "tabernacle" only secondarily. The Artscroll explanation, which stresses the meaning "temple," should be modified accordingly.

Similarly we are told (*The Megillah*, p. 55) that the *derash* that finds Mordechai's name in the Torah refers to Onkelos' rendering of "flowing myrrh" in Ex. 30:27 as *myr' dky'*, "which both in spelling and sound resemble *Mordechai*." The reference is actually to Ex. 30:23, and the preferred spelling is probably *mwr' dky'* vocalized *mura' dakhya* or *mora'* though many texts of Onkelos have *meira'* (not *mira*). The form with the *Waw* is obviously closer to the name Mordechai and is more appropriate for clarification of the *derash*.[45]

(c) Other Commentators

The word *ḥrbwt* in Ps. 9:7 is problematic, as there is some doubt as to whether the first letter should be vocalized with a *ḥatef-kamets* and mean "ruins" or with a *petach* and mean "swords." There is some discussion of this subject in the medieval writers, and it is summarized in *Tehillim*, p. 136. Artscroll's printed Hebrew text has a *ḥatef-kamets* and should be rendered "ruins." Rashi's interpretation was preferred for the Artscroll translation, which reads "because of the eternal sword" (singular). It should be clear that Rashi's text differed from that printed, and that the printed text and translation are not compatible.

Ps. 19:14 contains the rare word *'ytm*, often taken to mean "I will be perfect" or the like. According to Artscroll's explanation (*Tehillim*, p. 250), Rashi suggested the word to be "a contraction of two words *'hyh tmym*." Actually Rashi says nothing about a contraction. He just says *'z 'ytm: 'hyh tmym*, i.e., the word *'ytm* is a future form meaning "I will be perfect." This is a grammatical observation, not a claim for *Notarikon*.

---

45 This matter is really more complex than it may seem. (1) It is not certain that "and we translate" must refer to Onkelos, though that is frequently correct in other places. (2) According to Rabinowitz (*Diqduqei Soferim, Megilla*, 37, note 20), there is important support for spelling the Aramaic translation referred to in this passage as *mry dky, myr' dky', mwr' dky'*, etc. (3) The *mwr'* spelling is also supported by Syriac and Mandaic, two eastern dialects of Aramaic that share much with the language of the Babylonian Talmud. The English myrrh from Latin *myrrha* may appear to support the *myr'* spelling in Aramaic; cf. the Greek spelling *myrra*. The Babylonian form is closer to that suggested above, though the Greek is obviously related to both. Note also that similar connections are alleged for the name Moriah and the word *myrrh*. Cf. Akkadian *murru*.

Gen. 12:3 contains the phrase *wenibrekhu bekha kol mishpeḥot ha'adamah*. Artscroll translates "and all the families of the earth shall bless themselves by you," claiming that "this translation which understands the *niphal* form of the word *wnbrkw* as a reflexive follows Rashi." Rashi never calls this word a reflexive form, and nothing in his comment in any way indicates that he was reacting to the verb, much less its conjugation. It seems, rather, that he was concerned with the use of the preposition *b*- in *bekha* and wanted to clarify if it meant "through you," "by you," or whatever. In any case, the *form* of *wnbrkw* cannot be reflexive (only perhaps the meaning), but it is very doubtful if that was Rashi's intention.

The Artscroll statement about the double meaning of *weyirdu* (Gen. 1:26), attributed to Radak, is found neither in Radak's commentary *a.l* nor in his dictionary *s.v.* *yrd* or *rdh*, but a comparison of these sources indicates that he undoubtedly favoured *rdh* as the stem. In fact the type of midrashic explanation offered in his name is inappropriate for his style, and the paragraph is almost a verbatim translation of Rashi's comments.

The phrase *'iwrym na'u* (Lam. 4:14) means either "the blind wandered" as understood by Rashi or "they wandered as blind men" according to Ibn Ezra. Contrary to the Artscroll statement, the latter did not suggest that *'iwrym* is an adverb; he suggested that the preposition is lacking but understood, an observation he made in hundreds of other passages as well.

Eccl. 10:16 contains a clause that ends with the phrase *shemalkekh na'ar*, rendered by Artscroll as "Whose king acts as an adolescent [lit. 'that your king is a youth']." This, we are told, follows Rashi and Metzudas David "and is in harmony with other commentators who all agree that the reference is not simply to a 'youthful' king [or else he would have used the word *yeled* 'boy']." While the latter part of this observation correctly reflects the statement of Arama, the former has missed the point of Rashi and Altschuler, whose observations stress that *na'ar* is a verb meaning "acts as an adolescent" not a noun in pausal form meaning "is a youth." The literal translation is therefore inappropriate.

In Est. 1:16 the name Memuchan is spelled *mwmkn* not *mmwkn* as it is elsewhere. A comment of Rabbi David Tevele Posner, cited *a.l.*, reacts to the fact that *mwmkn* can be broken into two words and read as "a blemish is here." Though we have not been able to check the original work, there seems to be no reason to challenge the presentation. The Artscroll vocalization of *kn* as *ken* is problematic, though, as the word should read *kan*, "here." Interestingly, the spelling of *kn*, "here," is attested in one inscription from Beth Shearim: *kn hn mnḥt*, "here lie . . . ."[46] Other errors are present but must be omitted in the interest of space.

---

46   Inscription 15 from Catacomb 20, N. Avigad, *Beth She'arim*, vol. 3 (New Brunswick, 1966), 241-42. See also Z. M. Rabinovitz, *Ginze Midrash* (Tel-Aviv, 1976), *passim*.

Some readers may disagree with a few of our comments and corrections, but the impression that there are many striking inaccuracies remains. It is puzzling that these have not come to the attention of the many authorities and scholars who are thanked for their approbations, assistance, corrections, and proofreading in every volume. Rabbi Moses Feinstein's comments (after the volume on Esther) are admittedly based on his son's reading. Have the others who commented also not read the books? Why have they not noticed these errors? Of course it is possible that rabbinic authorities are more concerned with piety than with accuracy in enterprises such as this. But the fault may also lie with the editors who have published letters of greeting as "approbations" and created the impression of nationwide input and involvement by rabbis and scholars by profusely thanking many people for what were really minimal contributions.

This may all sound very harsh, but note the following data: Of the ten volumes considered, all but those on Psalms have a "Haskamah" from Rabbi Moses Feinstein, in six of which (*Bereishis II* has none) he says that his son, Rabbi David Feinstein, "saw the book and praised it a lot." Each of the volumes so introduced also has a *mikhtab berakhah* from Rabbi Aron Zlotowitz, father of Rabbi Meir Zlotowitz, the main editor. In addition, *Bereishis I, Shir haShirim*, and *Yonah* each has a *mikhtab berakhah* from Rabbi Mordechai Gifter; *Bereishis I* has one from Rabbi Gedaliah Schorr; and *Yonah* has one from Rabbi Shneur Kotler. *Tehillim* has no *haskamah*, but Vol. 1 begins with a *mikhtab berakhah* from Rabbi Gifter, the father-in-law of the editor. From the letters themselves, it is clear that most of the correspondents saw their contribution as a *mikhtab berakhah*, not a *haskamah*. Though clear in Hebrew, this distinction is completely blurred in the English tables of contents present in all volumes except *Tehillim*. In the *megillot* the letters of Rabbi Feinstein are called "Haskamah" in English, while the other letters are called "Approbations." Since "approbation" is the customary translation of *haskamah*, this distinction is hardly meaningful (but some distinction must be intended). In *Bereishis I* the table of contents lists "Haskamah/Approbations," the significance of which is not clear, but in *Yonah* (written after the Five Scrolls), all four letters are called "Approbations/Haskamot" confirming our suspicion that no real difference is intended. Even parts of Rabbi Feinstein's letters sound more like *mikhtevei berakhah* than actual *haskamot*. Thus, when we get right down to it, there is really much less *haskamah* than meets the eye. Rabbi Moses Feinstein saw *The Megillah*, and Rabbi Gifter checked a few of the galleys of *Bereishis I*. On the other hand, the acknowledgments in every book offer profuse thanks to the many people who assisted, checked, offered advice, etc. Since responsibility for the work can hardly rest with those who offered their services to assist in some way, it would be most unfair for us to blame those who are listed in these acknowledgments and who are claimed to have read and corrected the various books or their respective sections for the many, many shortcomings. But this also means that the impression of approval, support, and agreement that these lists provide should also not be taken too seriously. The work is that of the editors, and accuracy must be measured in these terms, not with reference to the many names mentioned in the approbations and acknowledgments. Of course, we have not explained the reason for the errors. Perhaps the technical skills and erudition required to attain eminence in Talmudic and halachic studies differ from those required to produce outstanding works on the Bible. Perhaps the *yeshivot* should devote more time to Bible study. Perhaps qualified Orthodox university scholars, many of whom live in the home towns of the Artscroll editors, should have been invited to participate in the project. Perhaps more attention to detail will help alleviate these problems in future volumes.

D. The "Torah-Version of History"

A passage in *The Megillah* (p. xx), states: "Most of us have become indoctrinated with a non-Jewish, anti-Torah version of history." It is hardly worth debating how the writer knows this, but one might justifiably ask exactly what a Torah-version of history is and how it is to be presented. Judging from Artscroll, it seems to include an Israel-centred, perhaps God-centred approach, but no formal definition of the term is available, and we are forced to deduce for ourselves exactly what is meant.[47]

Presumably, all calculations should be based on Torah-chronology, thus all dates in the Artscroll volumes are *anno creatio mundi* and do not follow the Christian dating to which we have become accustomed. The accompanying charts and tables also follow this pattern. When dealing with the early part of Genesis, such a procedure enhances one's appreciation of the dates, for it enables the reader to see in graphic form exactly what is expressed in the various geneological tables and scattered chronological statements. This may become a little cumbersome in the later books, though, and we can only hope for an occasional correlation with the calendar generally in use. Of course it would be of infinitely greater value for these chronologies to add all equivalent dates in the Christian calendar, but one can understand the principle that is being upheld.[48] One can also understand the resulting ease with which many of the real problems of working out a defensible chronology of Biblical events can be ignored. It is in developing the

---

47 Orthodox writers frequently prefix "Torah-" to various words, e.g., Torah-scholar, Torah-true, Torah-chronology. In such cases "Torah-" refers not to "The Torah," i.e., The Pentateuch, but to the vast resources of rabbinic teachings. "Torah-true" is true to the accepted rabbinic teachings and unrelated in many cases to the contents of the Pentateuch; the Torah-version of history is, therefore, not the history of the Pentateuchal period.

48 With all of the effort exerted to avoid using Christian dates, it is interesting that the admittedly Christian chapter divisions have been retained, even though there are other Jewish divisions for the text. See *Shir haShirim*, 144.

comparative chronology and in associating biblical events with confirmed datable events of world history where the real challenge lies.

Another dimension to the recovery of Torah-history seems to be the assumption that all narratives in Torah-sources report events that actually occurred. This is not the place to enter into the debate on allegorical interpretation of the Bible or the difference of opinion between Maimonides and Nachmanides on the historicity of many of the narratives in the Torah, but one must note that the approved literature does allow for the possibility that some of these stories are not historical events.[49] This also seems to be the principle underlying the following famous passage from the Zohar:

Rabbi Simeon said, "Woe to the person who says that the Torah's purpose is simply to teach stories and the words of commoners. For if that were the case, even today we could produce a Torah from the words of commoners, even better than the others.... Rather all the words of the Torah are ethereal matters and lofty secrets. . . ." (Vol. 3, 152a).

Such a position exists with respect to the Torah itself; it must be accepted as a given for many of the stories found in rabbinic sources. Our point is not to attack the Orthodox belief in an authoritative tradition or the claim that *halachah* derives from a revelation to Moses. We suggest that Artscroll take seriously the idea expressed by a host of earlier authorities (but which appears unfashionable among many later ones) that the purpose of rabbinic *midrashim* need not be the presentation of an accurate description of past events. If the purposes of these writings were not historical, then it is foolish to treat them as such on the assumption that it would be unfaithful to do otherwise. It may not be easy, but somehow a traditional commentator must be prepared to work with midrashic literature as a form of Biblical exegesis that demonstrates great sensitivity to the text, preserves essential aspects of ancient law and lore, and contains important principles of religious truth, without running amuck in the assumption that all of it is historical. The implications of such an approach are extremely pervasive and would require evaluation of popularly accepted views of such matters as: patriarchal observance of the *mitzvot*, including rabbinic legislation; the doctrine that the Torah existed before the creation of the world; the accuracy of the rabbinic images of biblical figures; the claim that the entire Torah (the Pentateuchal text) was given to Moses on Mt. Sinai; the letter-perfect accuracy of the biblical text, including the Torah; the assumption that all biblical (or even talmudic and post-talmudic) books reflect one unified approach on any and all subjects; etc. Lest one suspect that these are new, critical, or scientific corruptions that have no place in authentic religious literature, we hasten to add that lengthy

---

49   See, for example, Nachamides on Gen. 18:1 and Maimonides' opinion, cited there and analyzed. Also of note are various sections of Joseph Sarachek, *Faith and Reason: The Conflict over the Rationalism of Maimonides* (New York, 1935).

lists of discussions of these and many other similar problems may be culled from the same approved writers whose teachings fill the Artscroll pages. Selective disregard of these problems by Orthodox institutions has placed many people in the position of not recognizing what is a valid issue and what is not. When the problems finally surface, they are met with disbelief, denial, or even by a hostile rejection of Judaism as a religion of totally irrational and nonsensical folklore. Serious treatment of these issues as an ongoing part of Orthodox intellectual interests can only serve to strengthen the commitment of the uncommitted, one of the avowed purposes of the Artscroll effort.

To a large extent the problems of reconstructing biblical history depend on the careful reading of many narrative passages, and these are the texts that have been subjected to the most midrashic manipulation. Thus, if one is to probe biblical history, he must first peel off the layers of midrashic analysis and get down to the bare text.[50] Artscroll need not reject all *midrashim*, but it should focus on their purposes. Some *midrashim* were composed to teach moral lessons, others for halachic reasons; some represent important theological and philosophical statements, others were intended as jokes. Determining which is which is sure to meet with less than unanimous support, but the attempt should be made. Of course the real conflict arises when a midrash appears to have been written with historical intentions but really is not accurate. Nonetheless, the general attitude of the early writers was flexible, and one need only turn to the statements of Hai Gaon, Ibn Ezra, Maimonides, Nachmanides, Joshua Boas, and many others to see that acceptance or rejection was very subjective. Note, for example, the words of Samuel HaNaggid:

You should know that everything the sages of blessed memory established as *halachah* in a matter of a *mitzvah*, which is from Moses our Teacher, peace unto him, which he received from God, one should not add to it or detract from it. But what they explained with regard to Biblical verses, each did according to what occurred to him and what he thought. We learn those of these explanations that make sense, but we don't rely on the rest . . . .[51]

---

50   Of course we do not assume that the reconstructed history will be identical to the simple meaning of the biblical text, but that must be the point of departure.

51   Samuel HaNaggid, *Mavo' HaTalmud*. Other sources expressing a similar attitude include the statements of Hai Gaon and Sherira Gaon cited in Lewin, *Otzar HaGeonim, Hagigah*, Commentaries, 59-60; Maimonides, *Guide* 3. 43; the essay attributed to Abraham ben HaRambam printed in the beginning of *Ein Ya' aqov*; Joshua Boas-*Shiltei HaGibborim* (printed with Alfasi) *Avodah Zara*, 6a; Disputation of Nachmanides with Pablo Christiani (in Chavel's Hebrew edition of Nachmanides' collected writings, vol. 1, 308); *Ohel Yosef* (Commentary of Yosef HaSefaradi on Ibn Ezra on the Torah), Ex., 42b, as well as his *Ṣophnath Paneaḥ* (ed. D. Herzog) Ex., 192. Some of these as well as other important parallel statements are cited by S. Lieberman in *Shki'in* (Jerusalem, 1970), 81-83. To be sure, many of the medieval commentators were very sensitive to the differences between *peshat* and *derash*: Rashbam, Bechor Shor, Ibn Ezra, Nachmanides, Bachya, and many more were very careful to distinguish between midrashic and non-midrashic elements of their comments. An interesting but ambivalent attitude is typified by the Artscroll presentation of

This feeling is not limited to medieval authorities, as may be seen, for example, from the writings of the nineteenth-century figure Rabbi Zvi Hirsch Chajes.[52] In contrast, a non-judgmental attitude toward *midrash* is reflected in various contemporary writers. *Hazon Ish*: "And I return to the simple belief in the Oral Torah and I don't engage in arguing 'why'; my only desire is to be like a simple Jew who relates 'what' he received.[53] Rabbi Ahron Kotler: "No part of Torah [*halachah*, *aggadah*, *dinim* and stories, (his words)] can be properly assessed by man using only his limited faculties."[54]

This shift in attitude towards *midrash* (between the earlier readiness for subjective response and the later preference for total acceptance) reflects the fluctuations in intellectual movements that have come and gone over the centuries. The early midrashic approach was replaced, suppressed, and/or manipulated by medieval writers so that they could use the midrashic material they wanted and bypass the rest. With the rise of the mystical influence, particularly strong in the sixteenth to eighteenth centuries, rationalism was replaced by another midrashic approach that frequently absorbed and strengthened the early attitudes that had been circumvented previously.[55] Following this period, the Jewish community lost its more unified attitude on this matter, and different groups favoured approaches that could be called mystical, talmudic, scientific, midrashic, and rational, as well as various mixtures of them. Each group, in turn, claimed authoritative sources for its approach, and because of vacillations that had occurred over the centuries, each really could justify itself within the overall traditional Jewish world. Further external stimuli such as the Enlightenment, the development of Reform Judaism, and the advance of scientific discovery also helped shape the various Orthodox hermeneutics, all deriving from a common pool of writers, but each one contributing its own elements and producing a literature different from the others.

Nachmanides' view on the subject. In some places he appears prepared to divest himself of the need to follow the *midrashim*, while in others he seems to describe their divine origin in ways that would preclude any policy other than complete acceptance. Whatever the rationale behind this type of ambivalence, and there are several ways to explain it, it would seem that he and almost everyone else readily acknowledged the right, if not the necessity, to be somewhat subjective in dealing with this material. (See *Bereishis*, 128, 264, 349, etc.) *Midrash* is fine for one level of analysis, but it is not the *peshat*, which is also important, and in seeking to uncover the *peshat*, traditional commentators need not be bound by the limits of material whose purpose is to analyze the text on another level.

52   Chajes' attitudes pervade many of his writings, but a most important text is his *Mavo' HaTalmud*, available in English under the title *The Student's Guide Through The Talmud* (New York, 1960). The second part of this work, chaps. 17-32, represents one of the most important breakthroughs of any recent writer on the religious position regarding the development, methods, and authority of *midrash* and *aggadah*.

53   S. Greenemann, ed., *Collected Letters of the Hazon Ish* (Hebrew), vol. 1, no. 15, p. 42.

54   *How to Teach Torah* (Lakewood, N.J., 1972), 3-4.

55   Cf. the analysis of G. Scholem, *On the Kabbalah and its Symbolism*, chap. 3, "Kabbalah and Myth."

Whether motivated by the rejection of Reform, acceptance of certain mystical teachings (particularly when supported by earlier rabbinic doctrine), the generally perplexed nature of belief in today's world, or some combination of these and other factors, Artscroll has followed a model of interpretation that accepts *midrash* as historical. While it is theoretically possible for many midrashic passages to be discussed as part of the traditional, multi-layered exegesis, and occasionally they actually are, frequently we are given the impression that the primary level of interpretation is, in fact, the midrashic one.[56] Like Ibn Ezra in his time, we observe today that the men of our generation have also made the *derash* the basis of their hermeneutics. They explain the Bible according to *derash* and think that it is according to *peshat*, but in fact this represents only one part in a thousand.[57]

Traditional Jewish hermeneutics offer a commentator the choice to accept or not to accept *midrash* as history. Since the Artscroll approach sees *midrash* as primarily historical, and since it presents this view as Torah, i.e., correct and binding, a serious conflict is generated with other sources of historical information that contradict certain midrashic statements. If the *midrashim* must be taken as presented, then the faithful must believe: that David knew of Homer (*Tehillim*, p. 251); that the King of Nineveh at the time of Jonah was the Pharaoh of the exodus (*Yonah*, p. 124); that, because no wars were mentioned before Genesis 14, there were, in fact, none (*Bereishis*, p. 473); that Abraham, Joshua, David, and Mordechai were the only men whose coinage was accepted throughout the world (*ibid.*, p. 429); that Ishmael married women named Adisha and Fatima (*ibid.*, pp. 767-68); etc.[58] What makes these statements mistakes is the assumption that they are historical; otherwise they might be evaluated on other grounds.

Being committed to the divinely revealed status of the Bible and to the idea that the revealer could and in fact did hint at future events, much post-biblical exegesis has consisted of the association of contemporary events with verses in the Bible that appeared to foreshadow them. This was the assumption of the *pesher* texts from Qumran, Christian typological exegesis, the biblical support cited for movements like the Sabbatians, and, in fact, is quite basic to the hermeneutic of any

---

56 Theoretically the difference in the size of the print indicates a difference between *peshat* and *derash*, at least in *Bereishis*, but we are hard pressed to discover any real differences in the material so printed.

57 Cf. Ibn Ezra, *Sepha berura*, ed. by Gabriel Lippmann (Furth, 1839), 4b-5a.

58 The lack of historicity in some of these examples is self-explanatory. As for the coins of Abraham, etc., it is generally agreed that minting coins was begun in the seventh century B.C.E. and that references to monetary payments prior to that time refer to weights of precious metal. Adisha and Fatima were the wife and daughter of Mohammed and were associated with Ishmael. This was known to various writers and is discussed by Radal (*Pirkei deRabbi Eliezer*, chap. 30, note 48) who rejected the idea, and Chajes (*Iggeret Biqqoret, Collected Writings*, vol. 2, 514), who accepted it. Both writers seem to be reacting to the observation of an earlier scholar (Zunz?). See, in reference to Chajes, a letter addressed to him by N. Krochmal in S. Rawidowicz, ed., *The Writings of Nachman Krochmal* (London, 1961), 449.

believing group. Wolfson has used the term "prophetic predictive interpretation" for this approach, further dividing it into historical (present or past) and eschatological (future) categories.[59] Whatever it is called, it is a common element in the traditional interpretive literature and plays a role in shaping the Artscroll translation and interpretation of many passages, and presumably the claims of ancient historical statements. While this has always been an accepted mode of interpretation to all but those whose interest has been limited to the reconstruction of the Bible's ancient context, its only real value for historical study is the presentation of ancient observations relating biblical texts and subsequent (biblical or post-biblical) history. With the exception of a few apocalyptic passages that are intentionally vague (but not necessarily intended as projections into the far distant future), Bible texts presented according to this method are probably best understood according to their simple meaning, with the "prophetic predictive interpretation" reserved as a form of *derash*. Objection to its being a primary form of historical analysis rests not in God's inability to hint at yet undetermined future events nor even on the assumption that the original authors could not possibly have intended these future references, though both arguments merit serious consideration. Rather, it is the unlimited number of events allowed by an unfolding human history and the totally subjective manner of associating them with the text which, though interesting and edifying, precludes any primary role for this form of analysis.

Reflecting the attitude of the passage in the Zohar quoted above, the Artscroll commentary tells us about the arrival of Lot's visitors in the evening (Gen. 19:1): "It must be re-emphasized that the Torah is not merely a 'history book' and would not tell us that they arrived *in the evening* unless a message was to be derived from the fact." It thus seems that not only are historically impossible *midrashim* accepted as historical, but also that ostensibly factual information is ignored or homileticized. It remains to be proved that most readers have an anti-Torah view of history; it should be clear that Artscroll has an anti-historical view of Torah.

E. The Artscroll Polemic

The prefaces of the various volumes (particularly the earlier ones) and occasional comments scattered throughout the work leave no doubt that one of the major interests of the Artscroll effort is the replacement of certain unacceptable Jewish commentaries.

Though never mentioned by name, the apparent objects of attack are the commentary on the Torah edited by Chief Rabbi J. H. Hertz and the similar commentaries on the rest of the Bible edited under the

---

59   Harry A. Wolfson, *The Philosophy of the Church Fathers*, vol. 1 (Cambridge, 1970), 24ff.

direction of Rev. Dr. A. Cohen and published by the Soncino Press.[60]
The foremost English contribution to Jewish Bible study of the earlier
part of this century, Hertz's work began to appear in 1929, has been
reissued in various one-volume formats, and may be found by the
dozens and hundreds in virtually all North American synagogues. Its
popularity is best attested by the number of copies published, but its
impact has, to the best of our knowledge, never been evaluated. As he
pointed out in his preface, Hertz used the work of four other writers,
which he freely edited and moulded. A thorough comparison of their
individual contributions might prove interesting, but it is the finished
product in Hertz's name that commands our attention. Using the
British and Foreign Bible Society's Hebrew text and the Jewish Publication Society's 1917 translation as a base, Hertz produced a highly
eclectic commentary on the Torah including the observations of the
Jewish and non-Jewish ancient, medieval, and modern writers listed on
pp. 976-79. Hertz's policy of "Accept the truth from whatever source it
comes" (Maimonides, introduction to *Shemonah Peraqim*, see below
II.G) is stated at the outset and is attempted throughout the work. One
might criticize his penchant for excising and including the favourable
comments of writers hostile to his religious outlook, for this creates a
false sense of scholarly and critical approval. Nevertheless, Hertz succeeded in presenting a commentary, that, for several generations, has
served as a popular model of the mixture of religious tradition and
modern scholarship.

Since there is no other work worthy of the attention that also fits
the criticisms of the Artscroll editors, we must conclude that the
Artscroll series, in a very real sense, has as one of its *raisons d'être* the
refutation of almost every aspect of the Hertz and Cohen efforts. Hertz
and Cohen used the Jewish Publication Society's translation; Artscroll
produces its own. Hertz and Cohen used both Jewish and non-Jewish
writers; Artscroll uses only approved Jewish ones (except for occasional lapses into the likes of Josephus and Yefes). Hertz and Cohen
identified their sources; Artscroll provides biographical sketches as
well. Hertz and Cohen covered the entire Bible; Artscroll is doing
likewise and, like Hertz, has extended its interests to liturgical texts, but
is working on the Mishnah as well. Hertz and Cohen used only English
in the commentary; Artscroll translates almost everything, but also
includes much Hebrew material. Hertz and Cohen initially produced
eighteen rather small volumes (the Torah was later republished in

---

60 The Soncino Chumash, now sold together with the above set, is of a different cloth.
    It is a one-volume anthology of comments culled exclusively from traditional
    sources. It is out of character with the remaining Soncino Bible Commentaries and,
    as far as this writer has observed, is used much less extensively in home, synagogue,
    and school than the more broadly based work by Hertz. Perhaps its later date of
    publication left it handicapped against the massive number of Hertz's volumes
    available. Perhaps its lack of popularity can be attributed to its narrower frame of
    reference. M. Waxman has a description and analysis of Hertz' work, *A History of
    Jewish Literature*, vol. 4, 647-50.

different formats); the Artscroll project is likely to fill fifty to seventy-five volumes. Hertz and Cohen tried to be true to the tradition and sensitive to modern scholarly issues; Artscroll has disavowed any involvement in the latter. Hertz and Cohen addressed the English-speaking Jewish world at large; Artscroll is concerned with a smaller, but more committed, reading public.

The vast differences in both physical and ideological makeup, as well as the number of copies in print and their relative costs, mean that the replacement of the Hertz-Cohen volumes will be slow and incomplete. Barring a change in format, Artscroll will not attain the popularity of Hertz as a companion to the weekly Torah reading. As a text for study, though, particularly for the hundreds of less known and untranslated traditional works, it is a useful source of material. It is of lasting value and may very well help to stimulate a renewed interest in the entire field of traditional biblical interpretation. But as we have clearly demonstrated, the effort has been marred by serious shortcomings, and the intelligent reader must appreciate them together with the contributions.

F. On Modernity in Bible Study

The past few centuries have witnessed many varied trends in the study of the Bible, but "modern" Bible study is distinguished by several factors. Starting with Spinoza and those with him who form the beginnings of biblical criticism, we see a growing challenge to the divine authority of the Bible, a serious doubt about God's role in the Bible's formation, and distrust of the Bible's claim to relate what really happened in antiquity. While this sceptical attitude has become the basis of much that passes for modern biblical scholarship, it is not the primary characteristic of being "modern." Beginning with the discovery of the ancient Near East by Napoleon, learned readers of the Bible have reoriented their approach to the holy text in a conscious effort to see the biblical characters in the light of their authentic ancient environments rather than as reconstructed in the clothes, habits, and ideologies of the ages of the readers themselves.[61] To be sure, no amount of archaeological data from cognate civilizations will enable the absolutely certain recovery of the ancient past, and even the availability of original documents directly related to the events in the Bible will not answer all of the possible questions.[62] But this type of approach, stress-

---

61 To some extent this principle has been developed by Maimonides (see below, note 70), but his sources were late. Perhaps he assumed the antiquity of medieval pagan practices which might then be compared to similarly ancient Jewish ones. The principle enunciated in the Guide (3, 50) is most important, however: "Just as . . . the doctrines of the Sabians are remote from us today, the chronicles of those times are likewise hidden from us today. Hence if we knew them and were cognizant of the events that happened in those days, we would know in detail the reasons of many things mentioned in the *Torah*" (trans. by Pines, 615).

62. An interesting example is the story of Sennacherib's seige of Jerusalem in the eighth century B.C.E., related in Isaiah, Kings, and Chronicles. The availability of Sen-

ing the ancient, original context of the Bible rather than its current
potential, is what distinguishes modern biblical study from that of
centuries and millenia ago.[63] Approaches that dispute Spinoza's
philosophical scepticism would be called religious, as would those that
insist on the relevance of the Bible for modern life. Those that totally
ignore the study of antiquities are simply not modern. Traditional Jews
may feel somewhat threatened by this notion, because rabbinic tradition has based its claims on a vertical pattern of authentic transmission
from antiquity to the present, and some pious readers may feel uncom-
fortable with a horizontal approach that stresses only ancient sources and
preferably those close in time and space to the text under discussion.
But surely there can be no serious threat to religious belief from the
ancient artifacts, texts, and buildings that were used by the very people
about whom they so strongly desire to study. To be sure, there is a wide
gap between the attitudes of many of the modern scholars who make
these materials available to the general public and the religious leaders
who ignore them; but it would seem crucial that this material not be
ignored and that it be subjected instead to the same rigorous analysis to
which the traditional commentators submitted the sources available to
them. Only in this way can the useful aspects of the data be made
available to strengthen the commitment of the faithful on scientifically
verifiable grounds wherever possible.[64]

We must hasten to add that the comparison of these ancient
materials (usually documents) with the related parts of the Bible will
not necessarily confirm all aspects of the traditional interpretations of
the Bible. While their challenges to the authority and accuracy of the
Bible are as much a function of the nature of the authority and accuracy assumed to exist as the testimony of the Bible itself, they do offer
possible solutions to exegetical questions that have been answered
differently by the commentators over the centuries. Thus, the challenge is primarily directed at the commentaries, the *midrashim*, and the
philosophers, and, accordingly, the only intelligent approach is to

nacherib's own annals should theoretically have answered many questions and has,
but whether he beseiged the city once or twice still remains a scholarly problem (for
details see John Bright, *A History of Israel* [2nd ed.; Philadelphia, 1972], 296-308).
What seems to have gone unnoticed is that the one invasion-two invasion problem
was anticipated by Radak and Abarbanel, and no one has really improved on their
observations very much, though new facts, theories, and conjectures have clarified
other aspects of the subject.

63   The history of archaeological discovery and the deciphering of ancient literature
have been described in John A. Wilson, *Signs and Wonders Upon Pharaoh* (Chicago,
1964), and more recently by Maurice Pope, *The Story of Archaeological Decipherment
from Egyptian Hieroglyphs to Linear B* (New York, 1975).

64   This should not be taken as a claim that archaeology or modern scholarship offers
no challenge to the accuracy of any biblical text; far from it. While the availability of
new materials often confirms what was not accepted previously, it often poses new
problems as well. But in which period of Jewish intellectual history was there no
challenge from new modes of thought or sources of information? The challenges of
modern discovery may be more solid than earlier philosophical ones, but the latter
were probably taken more seriously by Jewish religious writers.

rethink one's devoted attachment to the approved writers of previous generations, a process that was routine over the centuries but that has gone out of style in certain latter-day Orthodox circles. Religious readers need not reject all that has gone before; a serious reading of these materials more than justifies a careful study of many of the treasured commentators right along with the best of the modern writers (and some contemporary writers have finally come around to this way of thinking).[65] But it is crucial that readers see the process of biblical interpretation as an ongoing (perhaps never-ending) open search. They should rely on the classical, medieval, and modern traditionalists for contributions in the areas of their strengths, but, together with these, they must seek out, examine and assimilate the relevant elements of the scientific contribution of modern times. The very worst that can come of it is that one of the seventy "faces" traditionally assigned to the study of the Torah will be designated (perhaps as an adjunct of *peshat*) as the recovery of the original contexts of the biblical texts. Needless to say this procedure has not been followed by Artscroll.

Another aspect of modern study centres around what one might call historical perspective. All writers are products of the ages in which they lived. This means that one can understand them better by relating their work to the ages and areas in which they lived, an attitude accepted by Artscroll. Thus, in *Eichah* (p. xxxv) we are asked "Can someone pretend to understand today's Sephardic Jews without understanding nineteenth-century Yemen and Morocco? Or understand Ashkenazi Jews without knowing the Pale of Settlement and Austro-Hungarian Empire?" While the subjects are obviously more complex than these questions might suggest, any intelligent analysis must include these concerns. In the same breath, though, we feel compelled to ask two similar questions. Can someone pretend to understand the Jews of the Bible without understanding ancient Canaan and Mesopotamia? Or can one understand the Israelites who wandered in the desert without understanding the world of ancient Egypt and the Pharaohs? The unfortunate fact is that virtually all historical perspectives on the ancient, medieval, and modern books cited and discussed in the volumes are lacking. The reader is never given any serious historical information that can be used to evaluate the contributions of anyone cited by Artscroll. What point is served by these grand questions? The Artscroll effort has fallen short of its own standards.

Another point of interest in modern biblical studies, especially important because of the development of literary criticisms of various

---

65 Modern Jewish scholars who have used the classical writers to great advantage include B. Ehrlich, *Mikra Ki-Pheshuto*; Umberto Cassuto, commentaries to Genesis, Exodus; Moshe Held in a series of articles; Moshe Greenberg, *Understanding Exodus*; and others who have consciously endeavoured to build a modern Jewish approach on the contributions of earlier writers. Non-Jewish recognition of this area is less frequent, but see B. Childs, *Exodus* (an excellent example); M. Pope, *Song of Songs* (Anchor Bible), etc.

types, centres in the names of God that appear in the Bible, particularly in the Torah. Frequently modern scholars lose sight of the fact that areas which concern them have bothered other intelligent readers of the Bible over the centuries, and that there have been alternate solutions proposed; in this case the Artscroll selections should go far to dispel this misconception. Throughout the volumes covered, we frequently find careful attention given to the various divine names, including an ongoing attempt to understand exactly what may be deduced from certain unexpected or apparently inconsistent usages. It is difficult to determine if the editors' interest in this subject comes from the desire to collect random earlier comments or to refute one of the essential elements of modern criticism. We suspect that it is a combination of the two, but there is no hint either at the challenge or at any of the solutions that modern scholars have offered. In any case, the authorities excerpted in the commentaries, particularly the medieval ones, were definitely sensitive to the problem, and in the Artscroll volumes we find a good but disorganized sample of the older responses that have been proposed.[66]

There are other aspects to modern Bible study, but these typify Bible study only as part of the general field of modern inquiry. Thus, for instance, no one would consider studying any ancient or medieval text from a popular edition, if a critical one were available. It's not that popular editions are valueless, they are simply inadequate. The thousands of variant readings and citations from published manuscripts and early writers are invaluable in reconstructing the best possible versions of the Mishnah, *targumim*, *talmudim*, *midrashim*, and medieval writers. That we have virtually no such editions for the last of these groups does not in any way reduce the value of the many volumes of *targumim*, *midrashim*, Tosefta, and even certain tractates of Mishnah and Gemarah, which have been so edited. By ignoring such efforts, the Artscroll editors have not only repudiated one of the most useful sources of precise information on dozens of important texts, they have also popularized, perhaps even sanctified, vulgar editions, inaccurate readings, and errors, all in the desire to be uncritical and unscientific.[67]

---

66   There is an important attack on the Documentary Hypothesis that has been completely ignored: David Hoffman's *Die wichtigsten Instanzen gegen die Graf-Wellhausensche Hypothese*, originally published in 1904 and translated into Hebrew under the title *Ra'ayot Makhriyot Neged Wellhausen*. Hoffman's other works are cited frequently. Had Artscroll been prepared to admit being engaged by contemporary problems, it might have referred to this work also.

67   We appreciate the fears of those contemporary writers who oppose the use of "critical" editions and new texts that have not been part of the traditional *yeshiva* education, but this is not justifiable. After all, Hebrew manuscripts have values other than providing aesthetically pleasing dustjackets.

    These attractive illuminations are not without their own message, though. The bucolic scene of David playing his lyre while surrounded by animals (on the dustjackets of *Tehillim*) is a case in point. This was a very popular manner in which this king was portrayed by artists over the centuries, but many art historians have interpreted such pictures as a transfer to the biblical David of the characteristics of

Among the important features of all literatures are their reactions to contemporary events. They aid in the dating of many ancient works and are most interesting for readers who appreciate the contexts in which the works were produced. On the assumption that the same should apply to these volumes, we watched for comments or references to the two major Jewish events of the twentieth century, the holocaust and the founding of the State of Israel. Very little is said about either. In *The Megillah* (p. xxviii) we are informed that to have killed Hitler before his destruction of Europe would have been an unparalleled act of mercy. In *Eichah* (p. xxiii) various modern tragedies are associated with the Ninth of Av, and on pp. 67-68 we learn that "the atrocities of the Nazis are also foreshadowed in the lament of Jeremiah." In *Kohelles* (p. xi) the editor quotes the statement of the Hazon Ish that one cannot understand the implications of the holocaust now, but at the end of days it will be possible. This, of course, frees one of all serious confrontations with the problems that the holocaust poses for modern religious thought. The question of the righteous sufferer, so basic to many analyses of the event, has had no impact at all on the naïve selection of midrashic passages that have been presented to explain the suffering and problems of various Biblical characters.

As unsatisfying as any reaction to the holocaust may be, the event lies outside the purview of biblical studies. Much closer to the point is the importance of Israel. Throughout the Artscroll volumes there are many references to the Land of Israel, its importance in the classical literature, its sanctity, etc., all very much in keeping with the values of the tradition. What is almost unbelievable is that no mention has been made of the fact that the land is now under Jewish control. In fact, the only reference to modern Jerusalem that we recall is the report of the monthly walk around the walls of the city by some of the rabbis who lived there (*Tehillim*, p. 607). References like the inclusion of the British as the last in the line of conquerors of the Holy Land (*Bereishis*, p. 413) really add little of a modern dimension and only serve to emphasize the lack of attention to the modern Jewish state. The religio-political ideology of the Artscroll volumes regarding Israel is clear; nonetheless, pro-Israel readers may smile at the association of the Land of Israel, the people of Israel, and the Torah in *Bereishis*, p. 408. Other contemporary developments mentioned in the Artscroll series include the domination of world politics and finance by Arab oil and the conquest of space by modern technology (*Koheles*, p. xlviii). If concern with modern events were the only evidence, one might question if some of the Artscroll volumes were actually a product of this century. Modern events are occasionally mentioned, they are not of great concern.

Orpheus, son of Apollo, who charmed the wild beasts by playing on his lyre! It is indeed strange for Artscroll to have chosen this portrayal of David for the covers of several of its volumes.

G. Torah and *Scientia*

Throughout this presentation we have alluded to the tension existing between interpretation that is limited to "approved" sources and that which is not.[68] Had the editors simply ignored all unapproved materials, our reaction might differ, for surely there is value in anthologizing the many traditional commentaries, but Artscroll's open hostility to all that it does not accept as "Torah" theoretically means that this other material has been considered and rejected (though we suspect that there has been much more rejection than consideration in the preparation of these volumes).

Occasional references to non-Torah sources point to a strange inconsistency that must be pressed, but the implications of this criticism of general knowledge lead to an important observation. While most of the time the Artscroll series accurately presents the words of the authorities and sources that it cites, in its failure to utilize materials beyond those canonized by these sources it has admitted that it cannot effectively cope with the intellectual challenges or even the factual information being made available to the modern reader.[69] The Artscroll response to the huge number of linguistic, historical, and archaeological discoveries of the past century is to declare them scientific distortions, or, more frequently, to omit them entirely and to accuse others who do not similarly bury their heads in the sand of being apostates of a sort.

Criticism of this narrowness may be derived from a careful study of the same religious writers on whom the Artscroll editors drew and not from some external, heretical ideology. Briefly, from the writers cited we would note that Maimonides routinely analyzed the pagan

---

68   What is perhaps most interesting, and also most problematic, is the fact that nowhere do we find a clear statement informing us who or what is an approved source. Obviously Rashi is approved and Hivi HaBalkhi is not, but what about the less obvious cases? Who decided to cite Josephus, Yefes ben Ali, and, given the Vilna Gaon's hostile attitude, Hasidic literature? Omissions are possibly accidental, but aside from the Italians (who have been discussed above, II.B) we note the absence of many minor *midrashim* as well as Immanuel of Rome, Rabbi Kook, Rabbi J. B. Soloveitchik, Benno Jacob, Nehama Leibowitz, Martin Buber, Abraham Heschel, Arnold Ehrlich, Yechezkel Kaufmann, Yehuda Ibn Hayyuj, Yehuda Ibn Kuraish, etc., etc. Regardless of one's religious position, all of these writers cannot be lumped together as simple heretics. And what about the leaders of the Lubovitch and Satmar Hasidim? Where did Artscroll draw the line? And, even more important, what were the criteria for inclusion or exclusion? Need one be both a supporter of Zionism and a university professor to be ignored, or is one qualification enough? Do suspected heterodox tendencies disqualify an otherwise respectable writer, or does employment by a particular institution suffice? Does citation by an approved source render an otherwise unacceptable writer approved? What made Berosus acceptable (above, note 22) but rendered Cassuto unacceptable?

69   Fairness necessitates our repeating the debt owed the editors for their inclusion of many dozens of little known but important works in their anthologies. They have in fact, expanded the list of known, acceptable works, but they have not gone far enough. We wonder, though, if their final lists will some day represent a semi-official canon of Kosher Bible commentaries and related books.

literature for its bearing on understanding the Torah and even made it the basis of the rationale for the *mitzvot*; Nachmanides cited the Apocrypha and an archaeological discovery of his time; Abarbanel constantly made use of the interpretations and observations of non-Jewish writers; most of the medieval philosophers produced works that are syntheses of traditional Jewish sources and various combinations of Aristotelian and neo-Platonic philosophies—Menasseh ben Israel's *Conciliator* (cited in *Bereishis*, p. 528) is an excellent example of this type of blend of Jewish and non-Jewish sources in a commentary; Rabbi Z. H. Chajes cited and explained the importance of many ancient texts from the Apocrypha and elsewhere; Rabbi David Hoffman also utilized these materials constantly in his exegetical writings.[70] The list could be longer, but the point is clear. Facts were used from all sources. To be sure, there are authoritative writers among the Artscroll sources who did not employ and even objected to this method, but if the method of those who use outside sources is not to be accepted, should not their observations be omitted also? If the method is proper then let it be utilized. It is as important to follow the procedures and methods of authoritative writers as it is to examine their conclusions. It is also important to be consistent. To be fair, it should be noted that a small amount of scientific information is found in Artscroll, but it is rarely quoted firsthand. Thus, the author of *Kesses HaSofer* was able to utilize any archaeological data that *he* found relevant, and Artscroll may quote it even if it does not correspond with information made available from other traditional sources, but no contemporary archaeologists or their works are ever mentioned. Certain geographical information is

---

70   Maimonides: *Guide* 3. 29, 37, etc., *Sefer HaMitzvot*, Negative Commandments 42; Nachmanides: Introduction to Commentary on the Torah, end of Commentary on the Torah; Abarbanel: see the sources cited in M. S. Segal's collected studies entitled *Massoret uBiqqoret* (Jerusalem, n.d.), 255-57; Chajes: *Mavo' HaTalmud*, end of chap. 18 (English translation, 152-53), etc. Interesting for comparison is Maimonides, *ibid.*, 10.

While spokesmen for more open approaches were not lacking, frequently their works had to be defended from attacks (real or anticipated) from innocent, ignorant, or foolish critics. One less known apologia of this type is found in the conclusion of Ibn Aknin's commentary on The Song of Songs (490ff.), a work cited and approved by Artscroll. After admitting that his reputation might deter otherwise zealous antagonists from accusing him of heresy, Ibn Aknin outlined how some of his methods really derived from Hazal. Comparative philology derives from the rabbis' use of Greek and various Semitic and non-Semitic languages to explain many biblical words. (Cf. the introduction to Ibn Janach's *Sefer HaRiqma* for an earlier text arguing the same point.) Rav Hai, it is noted, used not only Arabic words but also love poetry, the *Koran*, and the *Ḥadith* for comparative purposes. Saadiah did likewise even earlier, in fulfillment of the rabbinic teaching "Anyone who states something wise, even if he be non-Jewish, is called a wise man and one is obligated to transmit it" (Megilla 16a). Rav Hai, it was reported, even wanted to consult the local Catholicos on the meaning of a verse in Psalms. When his messenger to the churchman hesitated, he reprimanded him, noting that the earlier authorities consulted members of other religions for linguistic information. It is not clear from this version of the story if the messenger or Hai himself then met the Christian leader, but the desired information was obtained and recorded.

provided to complement the statements of the approved writers, and astronomy is referred to on occasion, but there is really very little pure science included in the books and virtually nothing of the other scholarly disciplines that have been developed and that might have made important contributions.

The problem of the admission of scientific data into the system of Torah has been dealt with at some length in an article by Russell Jay Hendel.[71] He begins by citing passages from the *Talmud*, Maimonides, and elsewhere that openly state that knowledge, including what one might call the physical sciences, is Torah. He then "intuitively" rejects this idea in favour of a definition of Torah that relates to the source of a statement, not its content. This logic, when applied to Bible study, yields the observation:

> Rabbis are often confronted with anti-traditional statements coming from Biblical criticism. Intuitively, one would like to classify these statements as heretical. Yet, this seems inconsistent with acceptance or recognition of apparently similar statements among some *Rishonim*, who made statements differing from the accepted Talmudic opinion.
>
> This dilemma vanishes as soon as we realize that, like *Talmud Torah*, *epikorsus* (heresy) is defined by its *source*,—not just by its *content*. The Rishon's antitraditional statement, [sic] emanates from an ideologically committed person who is attempting to study our tradition by logically analyzing Biblical texts. The *epikorus'* antitraditional statement [sic] emanates from an antiideologically committed person analyzing Biblical texts. Thus, the *Rishon*, on both a personal and textual level, *relates* to a *source* of *kedusha*—hence, his act is one of *Talmud Torah*. The *epikorus* however, relates on a personal level to a *source* of *Toomah* (uncleanness) and *epikorsus*—hence his act is classified differently.[72]

Nothing could be clearer. Only the author of a particular idea is important; the content of the idea is all but irrelevant. It is very difficult to correlate this notion with the attitudes of the medieval writers under discussion, but Hendel's statement undoubtedly reflects the thinking of many contemporary Orthodox Jews and, in the absence of any more-articulate presentation, appears to be a close approximation of the Artscroll position.

All else aside, the system breaks down when it comes to dealing with errors in the scientific data, an aspect of the problem that Hendel has ignored. As man's knowledge of the world has advanced, many of the scientific claims of earlier epochs have been refuted or replaced by later ones. Thus some of the science that was incorporated into the authoritative religious literature of earlier centuries needs to be brought in line with certain modern perceptions, but their being in these works makes the ideas Torah, and one is therefore faced with the need to change Torah because of science. This is perceived as desecration of sacred texts.

---

71   Russel J. Hendel, "Towards a Definition of Torah," *Proceedings of the Associations of Orthodox Jewish Scientists* 3-4 (1976).
72   *Ibid.*, 183.

The presence of this outside material in the writings of approved authors must mean that its admission was not prohibited. Presumably it is also desirable, and some writers insist that it is even necessary. A significant statement, referred to by Hertz (above, II.E), and a worthy model for enterprises like Artscroll, is the methodological note of Maimonides in the introduction to his commentary on *Pirkei Avot* (*Shemonah Peraqim*), which he saw as a collection of other writers' observations:

Know that the ideas that I will present in these chapters and in the subsequent commentary are not of my own invention, nor are they explanations that I discovered, but rather I have gleaned them from the words of the sages in the *Midrashim*, in the Talmud, and in others of their works, also from the words of the philosophers, both ancient and recent and also from the works of many [other] people—Accept the truth from whoever said it.

Priority was given to the words of the sages, but the teachings of ancient and (for Maimonides) modern philosophers were also included, as were the relevant and correct ideas of many other people. Truth was not the monopoly of philosophy, or of antiquity, or even of rabbinic authority. It should be accepted from wherever it comes; its source neither precludes nor guarantees its being truth, and the directive to accept it (Arabic: *'sm'*, imperative) is unmistakable.[73]

Artscroll's procedure has failed to carry out what we have described. The reader is blocked from using the most advanced knowledge available, but he is told in the name of Torah: that he cannot deal with the halachic problems of *megillah* readings on Purim that relate to questions of walled cities (*The Megillah*, pp. 125-26); that a woman who resigns herself to widowhood for ten years to the day loses the ability to bear children (*Ruth*, p. 75); that the purpose of leaves on plants is to protect the fruit (*Tehillim*, p. 62); that chiromancy (palm reading) is meaningful (*ibid.*, p. 225); that an increase of light would enable people to see very small objects (*Bereishis*, p. 40); that the gestation period for a snake is seven years (*ibid.*, p. 128); that man was originally created a *duparsophon* (double body, male and female) (*ibid.*, p. 167); that the stars can *influence* human destiny (*ibid.*, pp. 510-11);[74] etc., etc. These statements cannot be considered reliable for various reasons that include ignoring the potential contribution of scientific exploration (e.g., dating walled cities) and the inclusion of folklore in place of scientific fact (e.g., the gestation period of snakes).

One of the most interesting examples of the misapplication of ancient sciences centres on the kidneys. In several places Artscroll notes that the kidneys are the seat of the intellect (*Bereishis*, p. 409;

---

73 We have followed the text of J. I. Gorfinkle's edition, *The Eight Chapters of Maimonides on Ethics* (New York, 1912), but the translation of this passage has been modified.

74 Cf. the description of the stars as God's "emissaries to preside over the natural functioning of the universe" (*Bereishis*, 600).

Tehillim, p. 622; etc., based on *Rosh HaShanah* 26a, etc.). This notion is then utilized to explain how Abraham managed to observe the Torah before it was given to Moses—his "spiritual kidneys" filtered out the waste of the world and left him with Torah purity. To be sure the basis of this comment is rabbinic (Gen. Rab. 61:1), and Rabbi Gifter, who apparently is the source of the spiritual-kidney theory, may have intended it metaphorically. But how can a modern reader be expected to accept either the rabbi's claim about kidneys or the assumption underlying the application of the claim to Abraham's observance of the *mitzvot*?

All of these observations are quoted from Torah-authorities; they are Torah. The editors have anticipated to some degree that the Orthodox reader may not accept all of these unscientific statements, for in some places where the literal meanings of rabbinic statements contradict what science has proved to be true, the texts are explained metaphorically. Thus, because earlier writers tried to explain the Bible in the light of the science of their days, contemporary readers are bound, if not literally, then in some metaphoric way, by their errors, and they must accept ideas that were not at all what the original writers intended. It would be valuable if future Artscroll volumes consider more carefully the words of The *Taz* (*Divrei David*, Gen. 2:23): "We should not divest the words of our rabbis of their simple meanings."

The value of scientific determination in religious matters has been clearly supported by Rabbi M. D. Tendler in his reply to Rabbi A. Soloveitchik's criticism of his position on the halachic status of brain death. While we are not voting in the dispute, it is important to observe Rabbi Tendler's argument:

The interface of ethics or religion and medical practice is a treacherous area because it demands dual expertise to traverse it safely. In the issue at hand, a mastery of the fundamentals of physiology is necessary for the proper elucidation of the talmudic references.[75]

Clearly, Rabbi Tendler believes that the correct understanding of the passage, in this case based on the ability to differentiate between the two possible meanings of a text, may be had only with the benefit of scientific training. A similar dual expertise must be demanded in biblical interpretation and in the reading of secondary sources that would explain the Bible, but under most circumstances textual interpretation is part of the humanities, not the sciences, and this is a much more touchy business.

Torah and science, originally thought to be incompatible, have become united by limiting science to technology and leaving speculation, interpretation, or value judgments to Torah.[76] This united front

---

75 The matter is discussed in *The Journal of The American Medical Association* 238: 15, 16. The quotation is from 240/2: 100.
76 Cf. the various essays in A. Carmell and C. Domb, eds., *Challenge: Torah Views on Science and Its Problems* (London, 1976).

of the two supposedly invincible disciplines, Torah and science, now confronts the humanities as subjective, ephemeral, human distortion. Anyone who attempts a response to a particular problem using the methods or values of the humanities is, by definition, operating outside the Orthodox camp; he is in Artscroll's words "a secular humanist." What is so seriously missed in this position is the realization that Torah, as it developed over the centuries, also included what we would now designate as aspects of the humanities, though the fields seem to have parted company. The conflict of Torah and science against the humanities is thus the result of science's generally acknowledged resistance to this sphere of thought and Torah's facile rejection of it for being anti-Torah and not even scientific. Actually, Torah and the humanities have much in common (perhaps a source of the tension between them) and much to learn from each other. They would profit greatly from a closer relationship, even if science were to become a little jealous.

We described above an Orthodox attitude toward science that values but limits scientific elucidation. Such an attitude is typical of the publications of the Association of Orthodox Jewish Scientists, where one sees highly educated, even decorated, scientists blending what appear to be sophisticated scientific arguments with Torah. Totally lacking in many of their presentations is a comparative level of sophistication in treating the Judaic elements of their work. The blend is extremely incongruous, but it obviously works for many educated people. Orthodox thinkers might consider adding to the proposed treatment of a given problem the perspectives available from other intellectual disciplines. The opportunity to employ the humanities would afford the insights of history, linguistics, geography, comparative literature, philosophy, etc., all of which have counterparts in extant Torah-literature. The challenges presented by these and other academic disciplines may also prove valuable and stimulate new attempts at Orthodox interpretation of the Bible.[77] Should this happen, the advantage of hindsight would be present, in that previous attempts at religious appropriations of the academic disciplines would be available for scrutiny. The penalty for intellectual failure would be greater, though, as would be the criticism of "borrowing," which is almost inevitable in some areas.

It hardly needs to be stated that neither of the positions just outlined has been followed by Artscroll. The humanities are shunned and science is basically ignored, leaving Torah to be studied by itself, as if that were really possible. The doctrine that the only *proper* sources to be used in the elucidation of the Torah are Torah-sources is clearly

---

77 Modern analyses of the creation and flood narratives by geologists and by historians of religion differ greatly. What scholars of science may declare impossible or errors, scholars of the humanities actually perceive as important religious advancements. Is there no way for Orthodox thought to accommodate itself to these different approaches?

enunciated in Rabbi Gifter's Hebrew forward to *Bereishis I*. This brief document deserves to be translated into English for those readers who are unable to read the Hebrew, but for now we must excerpt several statements. Most interesting is the principle that "God's Torah may be explained only in the light of Torah." This idea dovetails with the Rabbi's statements that the Oral Torah is the only proper manner to explain the Written Torah, that no non-Jewish efforts to understand the Torah are acceptable, and that any deviation from the Oral Torah in the explanation of the Written Torah is heresy, even in the narrative portions that contain no obvious references to halachic practice. This elimination of all options in the analysis of biblical narrative and poetry (even non-halachic passages) is very radical, particularly when compared with the many traditional commentators who did not accept this position; but what is most striking is its similarity to the teachings of a seventeenth-century philosopher who, in his desire to free biblical interpretation from the clutches of subjective rabbinic distortion, stated, "Our knowledge of scripture must then be looked for in scripture only."[78]

The difference between the attitudes of Rabbi Gifter and Spinoza is at the time very great and very slight. Spinoza limited scripture to scripture, while for Rabbi Gifter scripture is "Torah" in general, but both men limit the terms of reference to the closed corpus under discussion. Spinoza, of course, added certain claims for the inability to use reason as a tool of exegesis; Rabbi Gifter has not addressed this particular question. It is difficult to know the extent to which he is prepared to trust human reason, presumably not at all when it comes into conflict with anything considered Torah. The fact that he has declared any deviation from the Oral Torah to be heresy may not be surprising, but some attempt should have been made to correlate this belief with those of the earlier, more-flexible rabbinic authorities.

Returning to the observations made above that the two most prominent attitudes of modern biblical study are scepticism and the search for the Bible's ancient context, we would like to advance a further comparison of the ideas of Spinoza and Rabbi Gifter, who has provided the only document that might be called a statement of the Artscroll hermeneutic. Spinoza did not emphasize the value of archaeology, probably because he lived before the advent of archaeological discovery, and did not fathom the role that modern discovery might take in elucidating the Bible.[79] Rabbi Gifter, while he would appropriately reject Spinoza's religious scepticism, also has no use for discoveries. His approach therefore lacks both of the characteristics of modernity, and we must conclude that while Spinoza's position is partly modern, Rabbi Gifter's is premodern! Given the sanctity attributed to Jewish tradition and the general hostility of the modern world to religion, it should be

---

78   Benedict de Spinoza, *A Theologico-Political Treatise*, chap. 7.
79   But see the beginning of chap. 8, *ibid*.

obvious that nothing insulting is intended by this observation. But, if this attitude really reflects a premodern unawareness of recent discoveries and the ability of these discoveries to advance the cause of true, accurate, Torah (or Bible) study, can it really serve to convince, much less to guide, twentieth-century people? One who accepts his approach is fenced in from both sides. One the one hand, he is unable to deviate from *anything* handed down in the tradition; on the other hand, he is barred from taking seriously anything else which may seem of value in treating a problem. If ever there was a doctrine that justified Toynbee's claim that Judaism is a fossil, this is it.

H. On Anthologizing

Up to now we have discussed and evaluated, for the most part, what the Artscroll editors have done. We must still examine what appear to be errors of omission as well. In such an endeavour it is important to realize that all anthologies are selective and by definition incomplete. Nevertheless, in the following pages, we refer to global issues, not the interpretation of words, verses, or details.

1. Problems and Solutions or "Torah"?

The production of any anthology necessitates a clear working plan on such matters as quantity, selection of sources, manner of presentation, organization, etc. In addition, an anthology of materials on the interpretation of the Bible must reflect a clear and articulate posture on the principles of biblical interpretation. While the Artscroll volumes have defined their priorities in a general way, allowing for consultation of the traditional authorities in some sort of chronological order and including a wide sampling of different types of material, there is a much more important priority for selection that has been utilized only occasionally. Like precious pearls that have been stimulated by some irritant in the oyster, so are many of the *midrashim* and exegetical comments stimulated by real or apparent ambiguities, questions, grammatical difficulties, or contradictions. It is these problems or questions that have engaged all who would explain the text and have, to a large extent, shaped their understanding of it. Of course there are other factors, and all writers did not address themselves to all of the problems, nor did they necessarily agree on what the problems were, but it is the *problems*, the irritants, if you will, that lie behind the interpretive literature, and these problems must be presented, defined, and solved in the course of any discussion that would call itself a commentary.

The definition of the problem prior to its solution has not always been part of the classical commentaries, indeed one of the main concerns in the study of Rashi has always been defining the problems that gave rise to his comments. However, there are models like the commentaries of Abarbanel and Rabbi Isaac Caro where the problems are clearly defined, and this must be the pattern of any anthology that would compare the comments of various writers on the same phrase or word. This procedure would give definition to the verse and would clearly focus on the issues in the Bible text while allowing free expression of general matters developed by individual writers. Such an open system, focussing on the questions and the suggested answers, would also convey the impression that other possible answers may exist and would stimulate new thought as much as it taught the content and appreciation of the old. It would make the give and take, the arguments, and the analysis the main concern. Focussing on the answers without the problems turns discussion and analysis into fiat and a system that encourages thoughtful creativity into dogmatic antiquarianism.[80] To be sure, our suggested manner of exposition has been adopted on occasion, and it is not totally suitable for the analysis of every biblical verse where it has not been adopted. But it could have been followed much more often, and the lack of this type of Bible-centred organization frequently gives the impression that the words of the sages are of primary importance, not the scriptural passages that they all laboured so valiantly to analyze.

In all likelihood this situation results from an editorial attitude that prefers to collect and explain but not stand in judgment of the words of the revered sages who wrote the books cited. We have no quarrel with reverence to deserving sages, and the Jewish people has been blessed with many, but virtually all Bible commentaries and *midrashim* have been produced for one reason, stimulated by one stimulus—the Bible text—and a collection of comments from these works that fails to make this the primary focus may not actually be a commentary. Appropriate descriptions of the volumes that may have been sensitive to this question are those of Rabbi Moses Feinstein, who sees the Artscroll production as anthologies of precious things collated from the words of the sages for the religious purposes outlined above (II.A). Nowhere in his many approbations does he state that these volumes are commentaries or explain the Bible!

2. Authorship

One of the issues in the traditional literature is the authorship of the biblical books. Notwithstanding the statements of the *baraita* cited in *Baba Bathra* 14b, beginning with the discussion of the Gemarah, *a.l.*, there has never been complete agreement on the authorship of all parts of all of the books assigned in the *baraita*. Thus we may note that according to Ibn Ezra twelve (not eight) verses at the end of Deuteronomy were added to the Torah; Abarbanel disagreed with the

---

80 The interested reader may consult the many volumes of material collected and analyzed by Nehama Leibowitz and available in both Hebrew and English. This type of model would be appropriate for Artscroll, too, with the obvious adaptation to a commentary format.

dating and authorship of several books in the introduction to his commentary on Former Prophets; the attribution of Proverbs, particularly the last two chapters, to Solomon, has received less than unanimous support; various sources have added Ezra to the talmudic list of contributors to Psalms; the question of the authorship of Job was never settled; the beginning and end of Ecclesiastes have been attributed to the editor, not the author; etc. Some of these books have not yet been commented on by Artscroll, but the problem is a pervasive one. However one views the give and take of the question, it must be conceded that there is much more discussion than one might deduce from the meagre attention given to the issue in the Artscroll volumes and the simplistic manner in which it is discussed when included.

3. The Bible's Literary Qualities

A concern for the literary qualities of the Bible may not be the hallmark of most contemporary religious approaches to the holy writ, but it was an integral part of the analysis of the earlier writers. Concern for repetitions in wording or content received a great amount of attention as did the occurences of *leitwoerter* and visible patterns of literary expression (for example as developed in the various cycles of events in the story of the plagues in Exodus). Nachmanides in particular was very interested in the literary qualities of the Torah, and many of his comments have found their way into the Artscroll volumes.

Modern literary analysis of biblical narratives is a natural development of this field, is far from the hostile criticism it is assumed to be, and adds an important dimension to one's understanding of the text. Literary sensitivity necessitates careful study of every text as a unit and stresses the dynamics of the whole as well as the significance of individual parts. The integration of such an approach would offer an important balance to many of Artscroll's observations that tend to remove individual units from their literary contexts and, in the process, allow them to assume meanings of only secondary and tertiary importance, without ever explaining their primary significance.

Another literary concern that is only minimally reflected in Artscroll is an awareness of the qualities of biblical poetry. Approximately one-third of the Bible is poetry, including all or parts of about half of the Artscroll volumes currently available. After the observation that biblical poetry is composed in Hebrew, the next most obvious observation is that it is composed of balanced lines, a phenomenon usually referred to as parallelism. The existence of parallelism is not a modern discovery, as may be seen from the discussion of this phenomenon in the writings of Menachem Ibn Saruq, Rashi, Rashbam, Ibn Ezra, Radak, etc.,[81] and the Artscroll translations have taken note

---

81   The classical understanding of biblical poetry has frequently been discussed, but no definitive studies are available. The standard work on biblical poetry, G. B. Gray's *The Forms of Hebrew Poetry* (n.p., 1915), has been reissued by KTAV (1972) with a

of this structural pattern by printing the translation of poetic passages in poetic form. A corollary of the parallel nature of biblical poetry is that it is repetitive, or, to be more precise, in expressing any given idea, it is stylistically appropriate to repeat the idea in parallel lines. This, too, was known by the medieval authors, although they did not always agree on the exact nature of this double expression—when it represented two versions of the same thought and when it was to be taken as different innuendos, not exactly identical. Both positions were espoused on various occasions and often discussed. Though obviously familiar with some of these passages, the Malbim rejected as out-of-hand the possibility that there could be any sort of repetition in the Bible and that one may properly assume, like the earlier masters, that any two lines actually say the same thing.[82] This approach necessitated a careful analysis of the Hebrew lexicon and has enriched our understanding of Hebrew synonyms. But, it must be tempered with the observation of the earlier writers that there is such a phenomenon as "repetition of the same idea in different words" calling into question the linguistic and literary validity of any exegetical effort that totally disregards this possibility.

---

lengthy prolegomenon by David Noel Freedman that updates much of Gray's work. Unfortunately no attempt has been made to correct the errors in Gray's original presentation of the attempts by Jewish writers to describe and evaluate the phenomenon of parallelism. The subject is far removed from the other areas in which Gray and Freedman could claim unquestioned expertise, but a new presentation is still necessary. Note, for example, Gray's ignorance of the observation of parallelism prior to Ibn Ezra (twelfth century). This phenomenon is clearly noted in the *Mahberet* of Menachem Ibn Saruk (*s.v. 'b*) and in other early writings, but even the general thesis that the rabbis were ignorant of the phenomenon is also incorrect. As Segal correctly observes (*Massoret uBiqqoret*, 271-81), the composition of parallelistic poetry in the Talmudic period more than substantiates the claim that the phenomenon was known; and various midrashic passages seem to make sense only on the assumption that the subject was discussed. In fact, one might conclude that educated readers of the Bible always knew about parallelism, even though it may not have been a major topic of conversation until the medieval period.

82   This attitude pervades his introductions and commentaries on poetic passages and books.

The obvious similarities between the parts of poetic lines led to disagreements over the use of synonyms and the extent of difference between them. Midrashists were motivated by the assumption that any changes in the details of an expression must, of necessity, point to differences in meaning. This notion was challenged, however, by another powerful argument. The Bible, indeed, the Torah, contains many passages (e.g., the two versions of the Ten Commandments and recapitulations of instructions and narratives) where changes in phraseology were not always perceived as indications of changes in meaning. Thus it need not necessarily be assumed that all slight variations in language point to significant differences in meaning, even in legal texts. Ibn Ezra strongly supported this idea in his commentary on the Ten Commandments (Ex. 20:1). Lest this be perceived as another of Ibn Ezra's alleged indiscretions, compare the following statement by the Rashba: ". . . because Scripture (*hktwbym*) does not preserve the [same] words [in similar contexts], only the meanings. And this occurs even in matters of Torah (*gwpy twrh*). This also happened in the Ten Commandments, and the Torah concerned itself with preserving only the ideas. This occurs with people's names also. . . ." Responsa of The Rashba, vol. 1, 12. There is no reason why similar arguments should not be applied to poetic passages as well.

While the Artscroll volumes occasionally discuss the problem as it relates to individual passages, this issue, important as it once was and still is, does not receive the attention it deserves. This gives the impression that the only valid approach to biblical poetry is that of the Malbim, who categorically denied the possibility of such a literary form. Interestingly, the lack of complete commentaries by the Malbim and Hirsch (who also engaged in such linguistic endeavours) on Lamentations has visibly altered this aspect of the Artscroll presentation of that book.[83]

4. The Lack of Challenge to Traditional Writers

One of the most important but frequently ignored aspects of the motivation for most of the traditional commentaries on the Bible was dissatisfaction with the commentaries of previous generations. While to some extent this type of bold discontent was voiced more for recent

---

83 It has been impossible to treat each biblical book separately, but there are other aspects of interpretation that vary from book to book. In terms of wealth of exegetical material, the Torah is by far the richest biblical text, a situation that is reflected in the length and variety of materials cited in Artscroll. The *megillot* are less endowed, but also possess a rich literature. Because Psalms is poetic, not narrative, and is important for its contribution to the liturgy, many of the commentaries focus on pious themes. While *peshat*-oriented works are not lacking, the former approach has dominated the Artscroll commentaries. The commentary on Jonah has its *raison d'être* in the book's use as the *haftarah* for *Yom Kippur* and focusses to a large extent on repentance. Its white cover (for purity) also points to this theme. Indeed several of the commentaries have their *sitz im leben* in a modern liturgical context rather than in literary, historical or text-analytical ones.

The fact that the Torah, Psalms, and the *megillot* have been chosen to inaugurate the project is also interesting. Unlike the Israeli, scholarly-traditional series of commentaries *Daat Miqra'*, which has yet to publish a volume on the Torah, Artscroll has accepted this challenge almost from the outset. Strong precedents for interpreting the Torah are of great help in this endeavour, but perhaps another dimension of exegetical and ideological influence is being expressed. In describing mystical interpretation of the Bible, Scholem observes: "A large part of the enormous Kabbalistic literature consists of commentaries on Books of the Bible, especially the Pentateuch, the Five Scrolls, the Psalms, the Song of Songs, the Book of Ruth, and Ecclesiastes " (*On the Kabbalah and its Symbolism* [New York, 1965], 33). Scholem's list is redundant, but with the exception of Jonah, which was published for use on *Yom Kippur*, all of the Artscroll volumes in print correspond to those in Scholem's list. One might see this similarity as coincidence—liturgical interest being the factor that motivated the Kabbalistic writers also—but another possibility presents itself, namely, that Artscroll shares this same interest in mystical matters or at least receives a significant stimulus from the twentieth-century residue of this earlier mystical activity. The choice of Daniel and Ezekiel (also of mystical importance) to follow in the series bears this out, as do Artscroll's Zoharic attitude on biblical history and frequent references to Hasidic ethics and philosophy. The ready acceptance of the Artscroll enterprise by the contemporary Orthodox world may be seen as evidence for the fact that such mystical values or notions have survived and/or been revived in this American Jewish community. Whether this is true for other aspects of Jewish life is worthy of study; a positive response is very possible. We believe this influence is unquestionably a factor in the way this group of Jews studies, teaches, and preaches about the Bible.

writers or contemporaries than for those of the more distant past, in many cases centuries separated them, not decades. Thus, for example, Ibn Ezra in the introduction to his commentary on the Torah managed to indict virtually everyone who preceded him, including the *geonim*, Karaites, Christians, midrashists, etc.; elsewhere Rashi felt the brunt of his wrath, as did a host of lesser figures. Also of note is Abarbanel's comment in the introduction to his commentary on the Former Prophets where he passed judgment, sometimes harshly, on his predecessors. The Maimonidean Controversy focussed on many issues, and disagreement over matters of biblical interpretation was one of them. More modern examples include the openly critical attitude of S. D. Luzzatto to Ibn Ezra, compared with his strong sympathy for the commentaries of Rashi. Rabbi Baruch HaLevi Epstein expressed dissatisfaction with Rashi's commentary, though in this case it is for his omission of many important *midrashim* rather than for their inclusion, which stimulated most of the earlier criticisms. The existence of these strong reactions to earlier exegetical efforts is to be expected, for if the writers did not feel that the Bible said something to them that had not yet been said by everyone else, there would be no justification for the composition of yet another commentary on the holy text.

Whereas the earlier traditionalists felt a deep reverence for the efforts of their teachers and predecessors, they also felt able to improve upon them and to offer differing opinions within certain limits (though these limits varied with the different writers). The dissatisfaction expressed by the Artscroll editors is not for adherents of the rabbinic tradition, but only for those outside it. Thus, secular humanists, irreligious Jews, Christians, scientists, and others may be wrong in their statements or approaches or attitudes; the rabbis are never wrong. Dissatisfaction with their statements is never voiced, and the freedom of expression felt and exercised by the earlier writers is totally lacking.[84] The problem this causes is not that so much is accepted with never a doubting comment as much as the resultant impression of the impropriety of trying to improve on the words of the sages. In closing off the doors to innovation and sealing them in the face of all external ideas and information, we see the expression of the most revolutionary concept in the entire history of traditional Jewish biblical interpretation.

Given the many statements on the acquisition of secular knowledge and the exegetical methods apparently preferred by the Artscroll

---

84   A recent study that includes much valuable and readable discussion of the intellectual conflicts within the past 1500 years of rabbinic Judaism is Moshe Carmilly-Weinberger's *Censorship and Freedom of Expression in Jewish History* (New York, 1977). This volume is an eloquent testimony to the fact that the greatest rabbis have been subjected to very harsh criticisms, and that positions which may seem heretical or questionable have often been espoused by unimpeachable authorities. One must conclude that the often-presented, monolithic image of Torah is false, and that any attempt to portray the intellectual history of religious Jews in this manner is fraudulent.

editors,[85] we can only wonder if the inclusion of Caspi, Rabbi Z. H. Chajes, Rabbi David Hoffman, Mennaseh ben Israel, Ibn Janach, and even, to some extent, Ibn Ezra, Rashbam, and Maimonides, has not been a source of embarrassment. Some of the interpretive methodologies of these writers are so far from what Artscroll really sees as proper that, but for their reputations, these men could find almost no place in the work. Conversely, Mendelssohn's *Biur* enjoys a very hostile reputation in the Orthodox world[86] and is never cited, but it is, in many ways, more conservative than some of the ideas in these other books.

The response to this problem is seen in the very essence of the anthology format. Since an anthology by definition omits a great deal, certain problematic areas may easily be avoided or, if treated, approached in a manner more acceptable to the anthologizers' own position. This is perfectly natural and appropriate, but since there is such a wide range of authoritative and approved religious approaches to the study of the Bible, great care is necessary to prevent distortion. Correlative to this, we must state that the Artscroll effort is by no means *just* an anthology of traditional materials. The process by which it came into being and the organization, selection, and omission of specific materials make it an original, innovative project. It may fancy itself the voice of the past, the presentation of "a Chazal's-eye view" of the Bible, but only the sources are old. The attitudes imposed on them are late-twentieth-century, east-Euromerican, *Yeshiva* World. One might question how such a revolutionary development has been promoted by writers whose entire effort is allegedly designed to be so conservative, but such are the virtues of Artscroll's unhistorical approach. The editors can be radical innovators without even being aware of it!

Many of the Artscroll attitudes that we have described are probably accepted by most contemporary Orthodox Jews. The interplay of European, Israeli, American, scientific, Zionist, religious, secularist, reformist, and nationalist elements in today's Jewish world is fascinating to observe but potentially dangerous to certain religious interests, and the Artscroll position on this interplay is clear and strong, although we expect that not all equally committed readers will be able to identify with the fears it seems to express. There are some very positive modern contributions to the understanding of the Bible, and the acknowledg-

---

85   This attitude is carried so far that Psalm 19 "proves in six ways that the comprehension of God gained through Torah scholarship surpasses the perception gained through scientific research" (*Tehillim*, 239). Also "Time should not be devoted to literature outside of Torah" (*Koheles*, 203).

86   For a discussion of Rabbi Ezekiel Landau's attitude(s) toward Mendelssohn's enterprise, see Alexander Altmann, *Moses Mendelssohn: A Biographical Study* (Philadelphia, 1973), index, *s.v.* Landau, Ezekiel. Cf. the clearly positive statement by Rabbi Zvi Hirsch Lewin (Levin) on pages 379-80. Much of the negative feeling towards Mendelssohn's work was directed toward his German translation which is now of little use—or danger—to the American religious community. The commentary published with it is of more lasting value.

ment of these contributions can only enhance several millenia of serious biblical interpretation and simultaneously add to the credibility of one's rejection of those other elements of modernity that really are hostile or useless.

CONCLUSION

Over the centuries the Torah has taken on many symbolic images including a well, a tree, a nut, salt, and light. Each of these was chosen to portray a specific aspect of the Torah's character, but, in order to clarify our evaluation of the Artscroll commentaries, it is perhaps most appropriate if we compare the Torah to clay. Clay has some permanent properties that impose limitations, but the maleability of clay enables it to be moulded into an infinite number of shapes. The nature of these shapes is determined by the canons of style of the artisans who mould them as well as the available tools, functions of, among other things, the time and place in which the clay is worked. One of the properties of clay is that, if continually worked, it remains soft and pliable, but, if left by itself, in a short time it hardens and loses its most basic characteristic. Hardened clay becomes brittle, is easily broken, and may lose its value, or, if nicely shaped, assume greater value, be admired, venerated, and ultimately be turned into an idol that is worshipped.

While we have pointed to many errors in the Artscroll presentation, there is little doubt that it represents a legitimate attempt to mould the clay (except where it is simply and carelessly inaccurate). It has not done all it could to explain the tools and methods of its artistic expression, but virtually all that it contains is authentic and part of the system it tries to present. We hasten to add, though, that all of the criticisms discussed above are equally part of that system and offer a different but no less authentic approach to the Bible and its normative Jewish interpretation. It is not the errors in presentation or even the differences in attitude that are so problematic, but rather the impression conveyed to, and most likely accepted by, the average reader that the Artscroll project is not just one possible way to mould the clay but the only proper way. This may be appropriate for a small percentage of the intended readership, but it is not an acceptable attitude for the many categories of educated readers to whom the volumes are addressed. This reaction, partly encouraged by the editors themselves and partly the assumption of the innocent readers, must be prevented. The Artscroll Bible commentaries are simply one additional attempt to shape the Bible, and they must be seen as such. Any other reaction to these volumes or their hermeneutical assumptions can only result in allowing the Bible to harden and to become broken by the less accepting readers and worshipped in a particular shape by the more accepting ones. Our hope, with the Artscroll editors, is that their work will serve to stimulate additional study and commitment to the value of that which has been done heretofore to mould the clay.[87] But, unlike these men, we would suggest that not only the results, but also the methods and attitudes of their most enlightened traditional predecessors, as well as the contributions of modern discovery, be utilized to help shape the Orthodox hermeneutics that will be used to continue the process in the coming generations.[88]

---

87 To date there is no adequate history of Jewish biblical interpretation, though we hope to rectify this situation. The most comprehensive treatment of the subject is found in selected chapters of M. Waxman's five volume *A History of Jewish Literature* and I. Zinberg's massive work of the same title, available in Hebrew, Yiddish, and English. Also useful are chaps. 28-30 of Baron's history; Sarna's study (cf. above, note 24); various works in Hebrew including Segal's brief *Parashanut HaMiqra'* and the fourth part of his *Mavo HaMiqra'*; M. Soloveitchik and S. Rubasheff, *Toldot Biqqoret HaMiqra'*; etc. E. Melamed's recent two-volume work on Bible Interpreters in the Talmudic and Medieval periods (*Mefarshei HaMiqra'*) is also useful. It is more an anthology than a critical study, though his organization of the sources enables some clear perceptions of various exegetical principles and approaches. Some readers may find chap. 8 of L. Jacob's *Principles of the Jewish Faith* valuable, also.

88 While I was proofreading this essay, an interesting, new book reached my desk: James Barr, *Fundamentalism* (London, 1977), a work that describes the problems of biblical hermeneutics among certain groups of believing Christians. Many of the problems are similar for believing Jews; the reader may judge for himself the extent to which the ideologies and their solutions to problems are parallel. (Completed in May, 1979.)

Some Jewish Theological Reflections on the Holocaust*

HOWARD JOSEPH

To speak of post-Holocaust theology is to underscore a consistent phenomenon in Jewish history by recognizing the fact that Jewish theology has received its most serious inspirations as well as challenges from events in the life of the Jews. The Exodus, Sinai, the destruction of two Jerusalem Temples and Exile, the Inquisition and expulsion from Spain, the emancipation in Europe, and, in our time, the Holocaust and the birth of the State of Israel—all these enter into theological discussion as revelatory events for they are seen to reveal—often forced to reveal—some knowledge about the nature of God, his relation to nature and the history of the world, as well as some speculation on the life and destiny of the people of Israel. Thus, together with the demands and categories of reason, experience has great input into the theological discussion. Hence, the usually elusive nature of the issues.

Given the fact that the Holocaust was not the first catastrophe in Jewish history, it is no surprise that conceptual alternatives long available in Jewish thought have been re-examined and revised. Indeed, many major thinkers, such as Buber, Kaplan, and Heschel, who lived through the events, saw nothing new in Holocaust evil that was not apparent before. They claimed that their philosophic systems survived intact, and interpreted the event within them.

---

* I am indebted to Jerome Eckstein, my friend and teacher, for his insights into many of the issues discussed here.

Furthermore, one prominent theologian, Emil Fackenheim, claims that a radical restructuring of theology would be a way of giving Hitler a posthumous victory in his attempt to destroy Jews and Judaism. Fackenheim is not against theological innovation, but he specifically attempts to counter the thought of Richard Rubenstein, the radical theologian, in his questioning of certain classical Jewish beliefs based on the Holocaust experience as a radical, new phenomenon.

Three issues arise in the Holocaust theological literature. First, the age-old question of theodicy, understanding and justifying God's ways with the world. How can evil exist in a universe managed by a good and omnipotent God? What is God's relationship to the universe if evil and suffering are continuing presences? Traditionally many thinkers have qualified the attribute of omnipotence in some respect because of their wish to retain the category of divine, perfect goodness.

The second issue that receives attention is the place of Israel, the Jewish people, in the world. In what way, if any, is Israel an instrument of divine purpose?

Third is the Christian role in the Holocaust. The Holocaust took place in the heartland of Christianity. The camps were run by Christians, and Hitler and friends were never denounced by their own churches and excommunicated. Apparently the Catholic Church as an institution did little or nothing to stop the slaughter, while the rest of the Christian, civilized world watched; not a few may have applauded. All this occurred after two thousand years of Christian teaching that includes considerable material on the Jews.

This third issue has inspired a painful and honest discussion among many recent Christian writers—Flannery,[1] Eckhardt,[2] Reuther,[3] Davies,[4] Littel,[5] and Baum,[6] among others—have tried to evaluate what changes are necessary to eliminate the teaching of contempt for Jews and Judaism from Christian doctrine, taking their lead from the late Pope John XXIII.

Obviously this topic deserves its own independent treatment at a different time. However, briefly, the mood of these writers is reflected in the prayer attributed to John called "Act of Reparation":

---

1   E. H. Flannery, *The Anguish of the Jews* (New York: Macmillan, 1965).
2   A. Roy Eckhardt, *Your People, My People* (New York: Quadrangle, 1974); also his earlier works, especially *Elder and Younger Brothers* (New York: Schocken Books, 1973).
3   Rosemary Reuther, *Faith and Fratricide* (New York: Seabury, 1974).
4   Alan T. Davies, *Anti-Semitism and the Christian Mind* (New York: Herder and Herder, 1969).
5   Franklin Littel, *The Crucifixion of the Jews* (New York: Harper & Row, 1975).
6   Gregory Baum. See his introduction to Reuther, *Faith and Fratricide*.

We are conscious today that many centuries of blindness have cloaked our eyes so that we can no longer see the beauty of Thy chosen people, nor recognize in their faces the features of our privileged brethren. We realize that the mark of Cain stands on our foreheads. Across the centuries our Brother Abel has lain in blood which we drew, or shed tears we caused, forgetting Thy love. Forgive us for the curse we falsely attached to their name as Jews. Forgive us for crucifying Thee a second time in their flesh. For we knew not what we did.[7]

John had hoped that this prayer would become part of the liturgy but he died before he could accomplish this goal.

II

Richard Rubenstein is illustrative of these issues, and because he was the first to formulate the challenge so clearly and honestly, I will describe his approach in detail.

Rubenstein's first book is entitled *After Auschwitz*,[8] as Auschwitz has become the major code word for the Holocaust. It conveys the image of Jews being rounded up by Germans like cattle, packed into trains, being brought to slave and death camps, being gassed in so-called "shower rooms" and cremated in huge ovens while the world stood by and the Allies refused even to bomb the rail links to the camps, or the camps themselves, in this "War Against the Jews" that was not stopped until six million Jews had been destroyed.

For Rubenstein this is a radically new evil which requires a new theology, and he relentlessly pursues a process of demythologizing and revaluation of the major concepts of the Jewish religion, as well as an assessment of the Christian role. Despite his revision of the concept of God, and the elimination of the chosenness of Israel, he somehow manages to salvage traditional Jewish values and observances on the basis of an existential and psychoanalytical approach to the human condition, for he believes that "Jewish theology must be a theological anthropology," i.e., rooted in an understanding of man. That understanding begins with Auschwitz.[9]

Rubenstein would solve the problem of theodicy by eliminating the concept of an omnipotent and beneficient God, for this claim is usually associated with the view that God is the "Ultimate Omnipotent actor in the historical drama."[10]

Although Hamilton and other death-of-God theologians consider Rubenstein one of their number, Rubenstein does not accept the

---

7   Eliezer Berkovits, *Faith After the Holocaust* (New York: KTAV, 1973), 26. Berkovits quotes this prayer from an article by John Cogley in the *New York Times*, June 13, 1965.

8   Richard L. Rubenstein, *After Auschwitz* (Indianapolis: Bobbs-Merrill, 1966).

9   *Ibid.*, x, 133, 246.

10   *Ibid.*, 153, 223.

designation for numerous reasons. He prefers to say that "we live in the time of the death of God, I mean, that the thread uniting God and man, heaven and earth, has been broken. We stand in a cold, silent, unfeeling cosmos, unaided by any purposeful power beyond our own resources. After Auschwitz, what else can a Jew say about God?"[11]

Rubenstein is not happy about this situation—a situation primarily cultural rather than metaphysical. He does not accept the theory that God is the enemy of man's moral autonomy, and this distinguishes him from Christian "Death of God" theologians. But, he says, the Holocaust experience prevents us from experiencing the presence of God in our lives, in our culture. The ancestral notion of the omnipotent, beneficient, comforting God must be replaced by another concept, namely, "the Holy Nothingness known to mystics throughout the ages, out of which we have come and to which we must ultimately return . . . omnipotent nothingness is the Lord of all creation."

To embellish this concept Rubenstein relies on concepts such as Tillich's ground of being (he was a student of Tillich's at Harvard) and especially the cosmology of Lurianic Kabbalah.

In the latter, "Nothing" is the primordial Godhead itself which gives birth by contraction—Tzimtzum—to the universe of created beings who yearn to return to their source, and ultimately do so.

The Holy Nothingness is not a void but an indivisible plenum, so rich that all existence derives from it.[12] This God, an impersonal, unfolding, and developing God of nature, must replace the omnipotent Lord of History.

He expects Jews—especially in Israel—having returned to the land and its cultivation, to return to this ancient mother-earth type of concept through their experience on the land as a full nation.

Rubenstein now turns to the issue of chosenness.[13] After Auschwitz, this doctrine, too, cannot be maintained in its traditional form. Rubenstein offers various reasons for re-evaluation such as the fact that if there is no personal God, then no personal choice is possible. In addition, election is a dangerous doctrine since it arouses resentment, highlights Jews as targets, and its main effect has been to support Christian claims. Judaism can live very well without it.

Election also prevents Christians from viewing Jews as real people but always presents them in theological or magical categories. Rubenstein's objection is not due to any resemblance to modern racial doctrines of superiority, for, on the contrary, Jews always felt unworthy because of chosenness. He suggests that there is a case for a doctrine of religious uniqueness. We must assert our peoplehood, gain the power to live as a full community and protect ourselves, for we have learned from the Holocaust that powerlessness is death. Reli-

---

11 *Ibid.*, 152.
12 *Ibid.*, 219-20, 230-31; also R. Rubenstein, *Morality and Eros* (New York: McGraw Hill, 1970), 185.
13 Rubenstein, *After Auschwitz*, chap. 2, "The Dean and the Chosen People," 47-58.

gious uniqueness is fine—but there should be no claim to being at the center of the divine drama of salvation and redemption on earth. Rubenstein is a religious relativist.

Rubenstein maintains that we must remain loyal to the Torah and its commandments, for they give us our order and structure as a community and join us together to share in the critical events of life, the rites of passage, as well as in facing the drama of sin, guilt, and atonement that we all experience.[14] For Rubenstein, social and psychological utility now validate that which was validated by the revelation of God's will.

The reactions to Rubenstein's theological programme have ranged from critical sympathy to outrage and, even as we have seen, the implication of his betrayal by giving Hitler new victories. However the case may be, let us now look for their context and effect, as well as for questions that may yet disturb us.

First, his God concept appears to be a pagan monotheism, an impersonal God beyond good and evil, rooted in the cycles of nature. How adequate is this for a post-Holocaust theology? As Bellow's Mr. Sammler says, "the sense of God persists." Rubenstein in no way accounts for the experience of religion. In fact, he denies the possibility of this persistence today. True, there is social and psychological utility, but religion is considerably more than that. Religion claims that we can have some relation with God—even if we must conceive of this God as *Urgrund*, or Nothingness, contracted. Rubenstein has not yet developed the concept, but he has not done so for ten years, and he has regrettably shifted to other issues in his writing. The Lurianic mystics claimed a personal relationship, and Buber has explained how we can so conceive the absolute or Godhead that it can enter as person into relations. On this issue there is a much more sophisticated variation of Rubenstein's approach offered by Hans Jonas. I will return to this later.

On the question of Israel's chosenness, Rubenstein is not the first to suggest a revision, although the reasons are his own. However, which concept of chosenness does he find inadequate? The doctrine he rejects is one possible understanding of chosenness, a very popular one within nineteenth-century liberal Judaism, heavily influenced by Christian notions, rather than a more traditional Jewish view. The latter regards the source of chosenness as the acceptance of the Torah, God's revelation at Sinai. Choosing to accept the Torah and obeying God's commandments is the uniqueness of the Jews. This doctrine is formulated by Maimonides and reflects the consciousness of the Jew in his daily prayers. Clearly, Rubenstein's doctrine of religious uniqueness rests upon a different foundation but structurally resembles the above. The history of the Jews as the stage of the total historical drama of salvation is not a view that is at all necessary or

---

14 *Ibid.*, 145-46.

prominent in traditional Judaism. One need not be a Jew to participate in salvation. All people struggle in this drama.

For the Jews, grace is available through prayer and worship and
through the Torah—its study and observance. However, history is too
elusive—you cannot see my face, Moses is told, and you cannot acquire a formula for understanding the process of history. From time
to time God may descend and reveal himself to man in the events of
history, but it might require a prophet to confirm that moment. It was
only at Sinai that the Jews said they "saw God"; after the Exodus they
only said they had seen his mighty hand.

III

Eliezer Berkovits in *Faith After the Holocaust* makes a passionate and
valiant effort to refute Rubenstein's position. He does so without even
mentioning Rubenstein, but it is obvious against whom his remarks
are pointed. Probably his most successful point is in his refutation of
Rubenstein's contention that the traditional religious view was that all
suffering can be attributed to sin.[15] He calls this a simplistic and
obscene doctrine. This kind of calculus is an escape from the issue, for
it in effect justifies the evil doer. There may be suffering resultant
upon sin but that may not be the only cause. Certainly, with regard to
the Holocaust, we must view it as an absolute injustice totally unde-
served by the six million. That is our beginning.[16]

How then does a Holocaust occur? Berkovits' approach follows
what has usually been called the "free will defense." God's hiding of
his face, his silence before evil, his non-interference in the suffering
of the innocent is necessary and not a result of indifference—if man is
to be man. Man has the freedom to choose his own course of action;
God waits patiently for man to choose the good—meanwhile the innocent suffer because of God's patience with the evil doer. If he were to
intervene, this would destroy man's freedom to choose and, in effect,
destroy man.

For Berkovits, the question is not "Why is there suffering?" but
"Why is there man?" Given man, suffering and evil can only be eliminated by the elimination of man. Man has the possibility of good or
evil, and God takes his chance with us; he has decided for this world.
Such is Berkovits' explanation of suffering and injustice, duly supported by numerous biblical, Talmudic, and Midrashic references.[17]

---

15 Strangely, Rubenstein's main source for this view is Dean Gruber. When a Christian
    claims that the Jews are being punished for their sins they have specific sins in
    mind. For an example of a contemporary Orthodox Jewish view accusing Euro-
    pean Jewry of sins, see I. Jakobovits, *Journal of a Rabbi* (New York: Living Books,
    1966), 435-36.
16 Berkovits, *Faith*, 89-91.
17 *Ibid.*, 93-96, 101-13.

There are, however, serious difficulties with this position, certainly a view much more traditional than the one Rubenstein sets up to destroy.

First, Berkovits covers only moral evil, evil caused by man, completely ignoring the random suffering, disease, and catastrophe which is nonhumanly caused. Thus, Berkovits does not offer a total defense. The more serious difficulty is that if God can intervene on occasion as he did in Egypt, why not in Auschwitz? Constant intervention might destroy our freedom, but apparently the rare exception would not. What conditions would bring about God's intervention? We cannot conceive of any greater necessity than the Holocaust! Must we discard this notion of even occasional intervention, or reinterpret it anew? Or do we answer, "I don't know; it is beyond our comprehension"? If so, then we have not advanced very far. Free will doesn't explain very much.

We can understand Berkovits' reluctance to enter into the reinterpretation of biblical instances of God's intervention. Throughout his writings he has been avoiding medieval philosophic rationalism or Buber's modern suggestions as being "less Jewish" than his approach.[18] Although he seems to pick his positions for the critical task before him, he often irks one by beginning to move in those directions he has hitherto avoided.

This ambiguity is clearly manifest on the issue of divine intervention. Can Berkovits' God intervene in the world? He seems to subscribe to this possibility but in the heat of polemics he offers another suggestion. Berkovits' God emerges as inactive. He says God does not do good (or evil)—he does not strive for value; he is Value. Man is a being who strives for and creates value.[19] Does this mean that God can and does not do so, or that he cannot intervene in our affairs?

If the former is Berkovits' view, then he owes us a scenario in which we can expect the mighty redemptive hand. The Holocaust is certainly an instance in which that mighty hand would have been welcome. If the latter view is Berkovits', then we must deal with other issues. Aside from the problem of divine attributes one wonders what Berkovits would mean by *Imitateo Dei*? Also, if God is inactive by necessity, then we are moving into philosophical and theological areas that require great delicacy rather than tantalizing polemics.

Berkovits also suggests that suffering does find its redemption beyond history in a different dimension. This, too, is of little help, for if God can create a dimension without suffering in which man could be man, then why not here—why is suffering necessary for us?

Berkovits leaves these and other questions unresolved, and, therefore, we must find his explanation far from adequate, if not a

---

18 See Berkovits, *God, Man and History* (New York: Jonathan David, 1959); also his *A Jewish Critique of the Philosophy of Martin Buber* (New York: Yeshiva University Press, 1962).

19 Berkovits, *Faith*, 105.

total failure. We are left, however, with a few promising leads:
(1) Man's freedom and God's risk: If we can make this freedom absolute with God unable to intervene, we would then have real and significant freedom for man and a real risk, so to speak, on God's part. We could then understand how humanly caused evil occurs and why God is powerless to interfere. We have here sacrificed the concept of God's omnipotence in its simple sense, which may be a dubious loss since it caused the problem in the first place. It is of questionable Jewish origin as well, and because of the problem this concept, derived from classic Greek thought, has always given to thinkers in the biblical tradition (Jewish and Christian), it has often been re-interpreted to preserve other divine attributes.[20] (2) This would leave the problem of non-moral evil, natural evil. Here we turn back again to the Kabbalists, specifically the Lurianic doctrines used by Rubenstein and more elegantly by Hans Jonas.

IV

Jonas' views are found in his article "The Concept of God After Auschwitz."[21] Generally following the Lurianic method, one must conclude that imperfection is necessary in all creation. There cannot be creation, existence, being, without it. Only God is perfect. But God is No Thing. Thinghood, existence of things, could only come about by a contraction in God's perfection, a reduction of his fullness. Imperfection is at the heart of existence. This concept of God's hiding of the face enables us to understand that not only must there be a hiding of the face for man to exist, but also for the world to exist as well. Jonas weaves a new cosmological myth, the warp and woof composed of Lurianic mysticism and evolutionary theory. The myth is strengthened by a logical analysis of the concept of omnipotence, which produces a sophisticated understanding of its role in traditional theologies. The total result is one in which God's goodness and man's freedom and responsibility are maintained.

It is an interesting historical phenomenon that these kinds of concepts have been highly attractive following times of catastrophe. The appeal of Gnosticism in the Roman Empire after the destruction of the second temple, and the growth of an almost universal adherence to Lurianic notions among the Spanish exiles as well as their contemporary European Jews seem to indicate that these notions ring true to sorely distressed souls. They are not comforting notions unless you really believe that misery loves company, because they claim that our suffering is part of a universal phenomenon, the human condi-

---

20   See Jerome Eckstein, "The Holocaust and Jewish Theology', in *Midstream* 34/4 (April, 1977).
21   Available in A. H. Friedlander, ed., *Out of the Whirlwind* (Garden City: Doubleday, 1968) 465-76. See also Jonas, *The Phenomenon of Life* (New York: Delta, 1966), chap. 11.

tion, and yet are hopeful because they attribute significance to human choice and deed. We can try to repair some of the damage done in the act of creation by returning the scattered holy sparks to their source.

V

There is more to report in Holocaust theology. After almost two decades the discussions began in earnest, and the literature blossomed. Some prefer silence, and others agree with Mr. Sammler, Bellow's unforgettable creation:

During the war I had no belief, and I had always disliked the ways of the Orthodox. I saw that God was not impressed by death. Hell was His indifference. But inability to explain is no ground for disbelief. Not as long as the sense of God persists. I could wish that it not persist. The contradictions are so painful. No concern for justice? Nothing of pity? Is God only the gossip of the living?

Or one may lament with the tailor when the rabbi complained to him that it took God only six days to create the world while the tailor took six weeks to make the pair of pants. The tailor said, "Look what you get with such a rush job—a mess; on the other hand, look at these fine pants—you will be proud to wear them!"

נדודים המתוארות בחומש, נמנע ההגיון הוא להתעלם מן
האבחנה בין התגלות מסטית ובין שימושית.

משה רבנו שהיה נתון במועקה רבה וקשה נמצא במצב אוביקטיבי
וסובייקטיבי אידאלי שבו יכול היה לרתום את סוסי-הרוח-
האלוהית המתגלה לעגלת-השלטון התקועה ולחלץ אותה ואת עצמו
מן החול המדברי. הרי לא היה איש שסבל יותר ממשה מן
ההשלכות החברתיות-שלטוניות של ה"בשר". אך בתשובתו למי
שיהיה כובש ארץ כנען מבהיר משה הבהר היטב שאפילו בעיצומו
של טקס הקדשה והתגלות דתי (מסטי, נומינוזי, וכו') שבו ה'
בכבודו יורד בענן אין להגביל את משמעות האירוע למקום
המוגבל, שבו הוא נראה קורה, אלא להתיר לאוידנטיות של
ההתגלות, לעוצמתה, לחירותה, להתפשטותה – לדבר בעד עצמה.

משה מצליח להבחין בהבדל המהותי הקיים בין עצם התגלות הרוח,
התגלות או "האצלה" שמשמעותה הדתית היא עמוקה ומהותית
כשלעצמה; ובין תיפקודה של האצלת-רוח כזו במערכת השלטון
שנוסדה בגלל הבשר (תרתי-משמע!) וכדי להקל על השליטה בעם
התאו בשר. גדולתו של משה בולטת דוקא ברגע שבו האבחנה בין
שני היסודות האלה הצפונים בהאצלה עשויה להטשטש והיסודות
ימוגו זה בזה עד לבלי הכר, כפי שמקובל, למשל, בתקופות
מודרניות יותר.

משה המתלונן והקובל על בשר באופן "בשרי" הופך למשה העונה
ליהושע באופן אירוני, מעודן ועמוק כאשר תפס שהמדובר
(פס' 17: "ודיברתי עמך שם") ברוח.

האבחנה המודרנית בין דת ובין מדינה היא, כידוע, אחד מפרותיה
של המהפכה הצרפתית. בישראל דימינו אבחנה זו מוכרת, כמובן,
היטב, אלא שהיא מופרת ביודעין ולעתים אף בזדון. מן הסתם
אין לגזור גזרה שווה בין הלאומיות היהודית-עברית-ישראלית
החדשה מצד אחד ובין הדתיות היהודית לזרמיה המתרבים מצד שני;
בין המיזוג שהיה הרמוני בין שני היבטים בל-ייפרדו אלה עד
לעת החדשה ובין ההפרדה הקלה יותר בין הכנסיה הנוצרית
(קתולית ובודאי גם פרוטסטנטית) ובין לאומיות אמריקנית,
הולנדית או אירית. אפשר גם לקרוא בפרק י"א ולהגיע למסקנה
(הנובעת מתוך הטקסט, במקום כזו הכפויה עליו) ש"הבשר"
ו"הרוח" חפוסים ואחוזים זה בזה וכך נועדו להיות עד קץ-
הימים. אפשר גם לטעון שדוקא ב"בשר" - המצוות מתגלה ומתממשת
"רוח" אלוהים, אפילו - או דוקא - כאשר מדובר בהלכות (או
מה שיהפוך בעתיד הפרשני - משנאי, תלמודי, רמבמ"י ושולחן-
ערוכי) להלכות מלכים, מדינה ושלטון. אך נראה גם שעל פי
הטקסט של פרק י"א, ואיתו גם מה שמשתמע מתוך ארבעים שנות

ללכת* ולדווח. מובן שעובדה פשוטה זו – לכאורה טעונה
מטח לרוב. האם אלדד ומידד הם מרדנים? במשה? באלוהים?
האם הם סוטים דתיים? פוליטיים? המתח עולה כאשר יהושע,
ולא משה שאליו הופנה הדיווח ("ויגד למשה") עונה, ולא
לפני השהיה מחוכמת האמורה להעלות את ערכו של האיש לפני
שנמסרים דבריו: "ויען יהושע <u>בן נון</u>, <u>משרת משה</u>, מבחוריו
ויאמר", ואפילו דבריו עצמם נמסרים כמי שאין ספק שהוא
הנאמן למשה – (משרתו, מבחוריו) "<u>אדוני משה</u>" ולבסוף הניסוח
הלאקוני, הפשטני, הישיר, ה"ביצועיסטי" – "כלאם". בלי לומר
דבר על אלדד ומידד מתחבר מה חשב יהושע – ואיתו הקורא
ה"תמים" על התנבאותם. אלא שמשה מיטיב לדעת: "המקנא אתה
לי? ומי יתן כל עם ה' נביאים, מי יתן ה' רוחו עליהם!"
לבד מן הדברים שכבר נאמרו על תשובה זו של משה מבחינת
מקומו כדמות בסיפור, חשוב כאן בעיקר העניין הבא: משה מפנה,
תחילה, את מוקד העניין מעצמו אל ה': "המקנא אתה לי?" ובכך
מרמז על כך שמדובר ברוחו של ה' ששרתה עליו <u>וממנה</u> האציל
משהו גם לזקנים וגם לאלדד ומידד. וממנו עצמו לא נגזל
דבר; אדרבא, ובניגוד לבשר, שסוג ה"קיצוב" שלו שונה לגמרי,
משה עונה בכך על שתי שאלות אפשריות: האם אסור <u>להתנבא?</u>
או שמא אסור להתנבא <u>במחנה?</u>

יתרה מזאת. בדבריו משה אינו טוען רק במובלע שאין לכפות
על הרוח את חוקי הבשר, וכביכול לחשוב שהרוח כבולה לתחום
החלל של האוהל. משתמע מדבריו בבירור שאין לרתום את
ההתגלות וההאצלה הרוחנית של אלוהים למסגרת השלטון החילוני–
בעיקרו אפילו מסגרת זו נמצאת ממש ברגע זה בתהליך הווצרותה.

_____

* ראה שמ"א ג' – שמואל <u>הולך</u> בפעם השניה שקורא לו אלוהים
ואינו רץ עוד ...

"לא יום אחד"... וכן תאור איסוף השלו בפס' 32) הרי הרוח
(ואפילו תאור המן) מדגישה <u>איכות</u> ולא כמות. היא מתוארת
כדבר שיש לקצוב אותו, להתקדש בעבורו, לאסוף קבוצה נבחרת
מתוך קבוצה גדולה יותר וכן הלאה. לפיכך גם במובן זה
תשובתו של משה איננה אלא אישור לכך שהבין את הנרמז בפס'
18 – "התקדשו למחר ואכלתם בשר". ראשית, הוא מבין מהו
באמת אותו <u>בשר</u> שנרמז בתוכנית – אלוהים, הרוח היא היא
"בשר" האלוהים, ולא רק השלו שאכן ירד. ושנית, הוא מאחל
לעצמו, לעם – שה' יתן מרוחו על כולם – במקום שהכל ירצו
בשר.

חוקי הרוח שונים מחוקי הבשר – ועניין זה מודגש בסיפור אלדד
ומידד. קיימת הבעיה הפרשנית הידועה בדבר ו"המה בכתובים".
האם למרות שהיו בכתובים (ואזי משמע בין ה–70) "לא יצאו",
או שמא <u>מאחר</u> שלא היו בכתובים (ואזי "כחובים" משמע הרשימה
שמתוכה <u>נבחרו</u> ה–70) לא יצאו האוהלה? ניתן להעלות השערות
לכאן ולכאן, אך מתקבל על הדעת שהיו <u>70</u> זקנים שאכן ירדה
עליהם הרוח ב"סביבות האוהל" ועם אלדד ומידד היו, איפוא 72.
(מספר שבטי ישראל – האם יוצגו ע"י 6 אנשים כ"א)? יותר מן
הספקולציה הסטטיסטית חשוב לבדוק את עניין ההתנבאות –
התוצאה הישירה וההוכחה לכך שרוח אחן ירדה על הזקנים – ואת
היותה של ההתנבאות הזאת בלתי מוגבלת לתחום פיזי <u>מסויים.</u>

המשך הפרק מסביר אפיזודה כביכול – צדדית זו ושוזרה לתוך
הסיפור כולו באופן משכנע ביותר. נער (שליח כלשהו? מעין
מרגל-בית? סתם מישהו?) רץ ומדווח למשה שאלדד ומידד
"מתנבאים במחנה". הטקסט פשוט מציין את העובדה אך טורח
להאיר את דחיפותה, לפחות בעיני הנער <u>שרץ</u> במקום, נאמר,

אם נבדוק את כל המשתתפים בעלילה ביתר קירוב נמצא שקיימת

היררכיה ברורה בדירוגם:

אלוהים

משה

יהושע (מן הבחורים

כתובים

אלדד

שוטרים, זקני העם

ומידד

העם

אספסוף

ניתן לערוך כמה אבחנות בסידור חברתי זה.   גם האספסוף –

היינו השכבה החברתית הנמוכה ביותר וגם המנהיג משה בעצמו

נמצאים בקרב העם.   (פס' 4, 21) כפי שיסתבר להלן, למרות

הריבוד החברתי הקיים ממילא, ולמרות הצורך בחלוקת המשא

ובהאצלת סמכויות-שלטון למיעוט נבחר,   ברור שהפער העיקרי

והעקרוני קיים בין כל האנשים שמהם מורכב העם ובין אלוהים.

משה הוא אמנם המנהיג הגדול אבל אפילו הוא יושב בקרב עמו,

ועמדת התיווך שהוטלה עליו אינה מעמידה אותו מבחינת מעמדו

והכרתו בחצי-הדרך שבין אלוהים ובין עמו.

עמדתו של משה בפרק זה ראויה להערה נוספת: משה, עצמו מטיל

ספק ביכלתו של ה' להאכיל שש מאות אלף איש – ובכך הוא

נתפס, אם כי באופן מתון ומעודן יותר מן העם, לחטא "בשרי".

על כך, ולו מנקודת-המבט שבה נבחן משה כאדם וכדמות בסיפור,

הוא מכפר במשפט המפתח "מי יתן ה' רוחו" וכו'.   משה הבין,

כנראה, שהתשובה האלוהית הנאותה דומה מבחינת המנגנון

המפעיל אותה – היינו ההמאסה (אף!) – לחטא, אך שונה מהותית

בתוכנה – היינו רוח במקום בשר.   משה מבין, כנראה, ענין

נוסף.   בעוד שכל הקשור בבשר מתואר בעזרת אמצעי רטורי של

הכברה – (פס' 5, החזרה על המילה בשר, הפירוט בפס' 19:

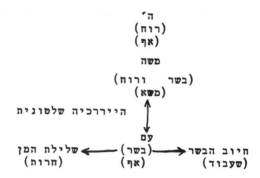

הטבלה מתארת את המשתתפים הפעילים ביותר בפרק בתוך   שהיא

נעזרת בתאור הגראפי גם במילות-מפתח התדירות בו.

ה' מתואר, כמובן, במונחים של רוח וכן אף. (עם המשמעויות

השונות שיש למילה אַף בהקשרים שונים במקרא) משה עובר

מהפך זוטא. יש בו גם מן ה"בשריות" וגם מן ה"רוחניות" כפי

שמסתבר מן האופן שבו הוא קובל על בשריות העם – ונגרף בה

בעצמו, והן מן האופן שבו נאמר במפורש שנחה עליו רוח ה'.

נראה שממשא שעליו הוא שהסיט את תשומת ליבו מעיקר לטפל

ואח"כ נפנה לחזור אל העיקר. (עם זאת, אפילו לאחר שהוסר

מעליו משהו מכובד המשא הוא נאסף אל המחנה – פס' 30 – ואינו

הופך "רוחני" מדי ...) על העם עצמו הרוח אינה שורה – למרות

משאלתו של משה שאיננה רק מוצדקת כשלעצמה, לפחות מבחינתו,

אלא גם מעוגנת היטב-היטב ומוסברת בטקסט. אך מעשה אלדד

ומידד בא להוכיח שלא מדובר כאן ביסוד אֶלִיטִיזְם רוחני אלא

אולי במעין "דמוקרטיה" אפילו בתחום הרוח שאינו כבול לחוקי

הכימות של ה"בשר". הרוח נועדה אפילו למי שאינם מאורגנים

ב"מסגרת" כלשהי. השאלה, כמובן, עדיין עומדת: מיהם, בדיוק,

אותם אלדד ומידד, שאמנם היו בכתובים אבל "לא יצאו האוהלה"?

העם נע בין שלילת המן ותאוות הבשר – אל הרוח (עדין) לא

הגיע.

(פס׳ 26) משה מחזיר, כביכול, את ה"רוח" למקורה (פס׳29) –
"מי יתן ה׳ את רוחו עליהם". בפעם האחרונה שהמילה מוזכרת
בפרק מדובר על "רוח נסע מאת ה׳" וכאן, כמובן, המשמעות
ה"רוחנית" של רוח מתלכדת היטב עם המשמעות של רוח כתנועה
של אויר.

(מרטין בובר הבין יפה ענין זה בתרגומו לגרמנית!).

הן הבשר והן הרוח יוצאים מן <u>האף</u>. אף ה׳ חרה בעם ארבע
פעמים (פס׳ 1, 10, 20, 33) ולכן בעונש, יצא הבשר מאפם של
בני-ישראל. המאיסה ברוח ה׳* ("יען כי מאסתם את ה׳ אשר
בקרבכם") נעשת במאיסת הבשר ובו בזמן מאציל ה׳ <u>עוד מרוחו</u>
על אנשים נוספים בעם. הקישור בין הבשר ובין הרוח כקשר
בין החטא ובין העונש הוא גם קישור בין החרות הלאומית
והרוחנית מצד אחד ובין השעבוד למצרים ולסיר הבשר מצד שני.
הבשר יצא איפוא מאפו של העם, אולי כדי שיפונה מקום ליתר
"רוח" ...

מלים רבות משורש "נשא" מופיעות בפרק: לשום, משא, שאהו,
ישא, לשאת, שמתי (שורש קרוב), נשאו, חשא וכו׳. שורש
זה מציין את מועקתו של משה "התקוע" בין קובלנתו של העם
ובין יראת-ה׳. על תלונת המשא הכבד מנשוא, בגלל הקובלנה
על הבשר, נענש משה בעקיפין שדוקא הרוח היא שתקל מעליו את
המשא, ולא שהוא עצמו יקבל עוד "רוח", אלא דוקא יאציל
מרוחו <u>ויתן</u>.

מלות המפתח שצויינו לעיל (וכן המילה "עם" המופיעה 20 פעם!)
ניתנות לארגון סכמטי:

---

* השווה, למשל בראשית ב׳ ד – "וייצר ה׳ אלוהים את האדם...
ויפח באפיו נשמת-חיים ויהיה האדם לנפש חיה".

קישואים, אבטיחים, חציר, (!) בצלים, שומים ויותר מאוחר בפרק

גם צאן, בקר ודגי-הים. בפעם השניה (פס׳13) המילה מופיעה

פעמים באותו פסוק: "מאין לי בשר ... חנה לנו בשר ונאכלה".

בפעם השלישית המילה מופיעה שלוש פעמים באותו פסוק: "ואכלתם

בשר... ונתן לכם ה׳ בשר". העם בוכה ומבקש פעם אחת, משה

חוזר על המילה פעמיים, ה׳ חוזר עליה שלוש פעמים, וברור

שעקרון ההכברה מדגיש בחריפות את החטא שבעצם הבקשה לבשר.

(בדומה לפירוט היתר של סוגי המזונות!) בפעם הרביעית המילה

מופיעה בהקשר היציאה ממצרים (פס׳ 22) ואח"כ (פס׳ 33) "הבשר

עודנו בין שיניהם טרם יכרת ואף ה׳ חרה בעם"... פיזורה של

המילה בשר בפרק מראה ש"בשר" הוא יסוד מארגן בעל חשיבות

מרכזית. מוטיב הבשר קשור בפרק עם תאווה, הוא סמל לטוב

שנעזב במצרים, הוא מנוגד לתאור הפיוטי של המן, הוא מה שאין

למשה לתת לעם, הוא הנלוז, המאוס. הבשר איפוא גם בשר ממש,

וגם מטפורה לכבילות לעבדותו של עם-ישראל שזה לא כבר יצא

ממצרים ועתה הוא קובל, ומואס ברוח. מעניין להוווכח שעד

שה"בשר" מגיע לאלוהים משמעותו השלילית מועצמת ולו על פי

החזרה המשולשת על המילה. חומרת החטא גוברת לפי זוית-הראיה

של המתבוננים בחטא.

המלה רוח מוזכרת שש פעמים. אלוהים מבטיח להאציל מרוחו של

משה על זקני העם (פס׳ 17) וכך המילה רוח מתייחסת לרוחו של

משה, בעצם, גם בפעם השניה שהיא מוזכרת (פס׳ 25). באותו

פסוק מדובר על הרוח, זו גם הרוח הנחה על אלדד ומידד.

"כדרך יום כה... אֶפְתַיִם,... כל היום... כל הלילה... וכל
יום המחרת... חומרים" וכו'.

אף ה' חרה במי שרוחו יצאה מאפס, ולכן גם הבשר, ולפיכך המכה
המעונישה באה ברגע הדרמאטי ובעיתוי מדוייק – ה"בשר עודנו בין
שיניהם, טרם יכרת". הקטע הזה עומד, כמובן, בניגוד לקטע
הקודם (של האצלת הרוח) אך גם משלים אותו. אלוהים נענה הן
לתביעה להקלת המשא והן לצורך להעניש את העם. מהפסוק הקודם
מסתבר שאילו היו כולם "נביאים" לא היה צורך בשלטון
אדמיניסטראטיבי – "חילוני" ולא בעונש על התאוה לבשר ועל
אכילתו. ושוב – נקל להווכח במהותו של הקישור בין שני
הצירים.

בסיכום, בפס' 34–35, מקבל מָקום – האירוע שם: "קברות התאווה"
והמסע לחירות נמשך. האם אמנם נקברה התאווה עצמה בקברות –
התאווה או רק העם המתאוים – על כך אין תשובה בפרק. קיים,
עם זאת, קישור שודאי איננו מקרי בין "בקרבו התאוו" ובין
"קברות התאווה", בחינת קרבת הקרב והקבר. מה שנמצא בתוך,
בקרב, הוא שיקבע אם יהפוך הקרב לקבר.

הסיפור בפרק בנוי במתכונתה של הפתיחה. חלקו הראשון דן
בעיקר בבשר, חלקו השני – ברוח ובתוך כדי כך נפרשים בפנינו
הקשרים המסועפים שבין שני הצירים התמטיים ומשמעות העמדתם
זה בצד זה.

בדיקה של מלים החוזרות בפרק מראה עד מהרה מהן מילות–המפתח:
בשר (8 פעמים) רוח (6), אף (4), תאוה (5), משא (7), ה' (17)
משה (14) ועם (20). המילה בשר מופיעה, כאמור, שמונה פעמים
בפרק. בפעם הראשונה (בפס' 4) "מי יאכילנו בשר" ואח"כ מעין
פירוט של "בשר", עכ"פ האופן שבו הוא נראה בעיני העם: דגה,

24-25: משה עושה כמצוות ה' ואוסף את שבעים הזקנים. ה'
יורד בענן ומאציל מרוחו (של משה, כפי שמסתבר מפס' 17, אך
העמימות המכוונת המצויה במלים "מן הרוח אשר עליו" – על
מי?! מאפשרת להסיק שזוהי רוחו של אלוהים עצמו. משה מחזק
ראיה זו בהמשך) היורדת על הזקנים שנבחרו. ראוי לשים לב
לביטוי "מן הרוח" המדגיש שרק משהו מן הרוח מספיק להתנבאות.
בעניני רוח חל, איפוא, מעין חוק-חסכון בניגוד לשפע המוגזם
של הבשר. (משל לנר שאינו מאבד מאורו גם בחלקו ממנו לנרות
אחרים!) פרשת אלדד ומידד (פס' 26-29) היא מרכזית. שנים
אלה זכו שתנוח עליהם הרוח במחנה ולא בסביבות האוהל. הנער
שראה אותם מתנבאים במחנה רץ לספר למשה. יהושע רואה
בהתנבאות חוץ – "תקנית" זו מרד, שכן זוהי התנבאות מחוץ
למקומה המיועד מבחינת ריכוז השלטון וביקורת המנהיגות על
התגלויות אלוהים. משה מתקן את אשר קלקל קודם – לכן ומאחל
"מי יתן כל עם ה' נביאים, מי יתן את רוחו עליהם" ובכך אומר
במובלע משהו שבנוסח מודרני היה נקרא כ"אין להצר את המשמעות
הדתית של התגלות רוח ה' למסגרת השלטון האדמיניסטרטיבי".
בענין זה אפרט בהמשך.

בפס' 30-33 חוזרים ומקושרים עניני "הרוח" עם עניני "הבשר".
רוח ה' מביאה את הבשר – המעופף והוא נערם בשפע (מגעיל) על
האדמה – ובשונה מן המן היורד כטל. האכילה התַאֲוָה של המן
ממיתה רבים מן העם ואפילו מבחינה פדגוגית אנו נוכחים כיצד
העונש עולה בקנה-אחד עם החטא. עצם הגשמתו של חטא התאווה
ע"י האכילה היא היא העונש עצמו. מי שתאַוּ לבשר יעֻנש בבשר.
מי שמאסו ברוח ה' והעלו את אף ה' יעָנשו בבשר שיצא מאפם.
מאיסת הרוח תעָנש במאיסת-הבשר המאוס.
בקטע זה חוזר הטקסט ומשתמש גם בתחבולת ההכברה החושנית –

בדיעבד שמשה לא ידע מראש על אלדד ומידד. צפונה אירוניה
מסוימת גם בצירוף "התקדשו למחר ואכלתם בשר" כאילו ההתקדשות
אינה באה למען האצלת הרוח. גם אלוהים נוקט בטכניקה של
הכברה שכבר נראתה קודם לכן באמרו "לא יום אחד, ולא יומיים
ולא חמישה ימים" וכו' ומשיג בכך אפקט של איום מפורש וזועם.
הוא אף משתמש שימוש דו-משמעי במונח "יצא מאפכם" שבו כלול
גם משה.

אחרי נאום הקובלנה של משה ונאום התשובה של ה' השניים
מחליפים ביניהם עוד "רפליקה". בפס' 21–22 משה מטיל ספק
ביכולתו של ה' להאכיל את העם בשר ובכך חוטא בקוצר אמונה
ממש. ה' עונה לו (פס' 23) בקיצור ומתוך הסתמכות לא על
הדיבור אלא על המעשה שיבוא ויוכיח. שני נאומיו של משה
ארוכים מאלה של ה': הדו-שיח כולו מתקצר לקראת הסיום ובכך
מחדד את העמדות המנוגדות. למשה, מצידו, אין מוצא אחר
לתסכולו, אלא לדבר, אך דבריו הם דיבורים גרידא. דברי
אלוהים, לעומת זאת, הם גם דבר וגם דיבור, כלומר, מעשיו
ודיבוריו של אלוהים חד – המה, במובן מסוים.

משה, בדומה לעם שדחה את המן, מפרט בדבריו גם הוא, אם כי
פחות מן העם, ומזכיר צאן ובקר ודגי-ים, כמי שחוטא בהכברה,
בבשריות ונסחף עם חטאם של מי שאותם הוא מוקיע. וכך, הואיל
ומשה נמצא, לדבריו, בקרבו של העם. הוא קרוב לעמו יותר מכפי
שנוח לו עצמו לחשוב, כמי שקודם לכן טען שהוא "הורה",
"אומן". דבריו האחרונים של משה מפחיתים, כביכול, מערכה
"הנומינאלי" של מטפורת ההורה.

בפס' 24–33 אנו עוברים לחלקו העיקרי השני של הפרק, העוסק
בהגשמת תוכניתו של אלוהים.

בהיותה מטפורה "שלילית", כזו הנדחית: "האנוכי הריתי ...
אם אנוכי ילידתיהו".   משה נמצא **מקורב** אל עמו דווקא בדהותו
את דימוי האב, האם והאומן; **ומרוחק** ממנו דווקא בהזכירו
"אבות" בהקשר דקדוקי חיובי – אשר נשבעת **לאבותיו**", שכן הוא
אומר "אבותיו" ולא, למשל, "אבותינו".   הדחיה והקירוב
המהופכים מבחינת משמעותם אינם אלא ממזג ריטורי נוסף המעיד
על הקונפליקט שמשה שרוי בו.   זהו ממזג המזכיר, בהקשרו
התמטי, את דחיית המן והתאווה לבשר של העם.   משה רואה עצמו
נתבע לספק תאווה לבשר – נתבע ואינו מסוגל.   עד מהרה יסתבר
שלמשה היה מה לתת – רוח זו שנאצלה עליו, אך ה' עצמו חייב
לומר לו זאת.   נאומו של משה נפתח ב"רע":   "למה הרעות" –
ומסתיים ב"רע": "אל אראה ברעתי".   תוכנו הוא הרצאת הקושי
לשאת במשא (הבשר) של כל העם.   בולטת בנאום הסתירה שבין
תפקיד   המנהיגות של משה ובין הנימה האישית מאוד הקשורה
בהרגשת אותה המנהיגות.

בפס' 16–20 אלוהים עונה למשה ומתווה תוכנית שתענה על הבעיה
המוחשית של העדר הבשר וכן גם על הבעיה הכללית יותר של
הנהגת העם הכרוכה בה.   בשני הפסוקים הראשונים בקטע נועדה
בעית המנהיגות לפתרון ובשניים הפסוקים הבאים – בעית הבשר.
בפס' 20 אלוהים מסכם ומפרש – כאילו קרא את הנימים ההבויות
(או ה"תת- טקסט"!) שבדברי העם ובדברי משה כאחת.   הוא מסביר –
"יען כי מאסתם" – וכולל, לפחות בפניה בגוף שני רבים, גם
את משה עצמו בפרשת ה**מאיסה**.   אלוהים הוא הקושר בין מוטיב
הבשר ובין מוטיב ההנהגה ה"מדינית" (ובקטבים ההפוכים מצויים,
כמובן "רוח" או התגלות "דתית") בקשר **סיבתי** וענייני.   כאן
מובלעים בדברי אלוהים כמה רמזים שיתפרשו בהמשך.   ה"אשר
ידעת", בהקשר עם פרשת אלדד מידד מקבל ממד נוסף.   יסתבר

הטענה "נפשנו יבשה" ולהראות שהבוכים בכו שלא בצדק ועוולו כפליים - בדחיית מאכל החירות ובתאווה למזון עבדות, במשיכה לרע ובאי-קבלה של הטוב. אמנם אלוהים הוא המפרש זאת כך, אך בינתיים משה הוא המתואר כמי ששומע את הקובלנות. עצם הבכיה, החזרה עליה אחרי תיאור הקישואים והבצלים והחזירה את הקורא ממושא התלוכה (בשר, מן) לתלונה עצמה.

בפס' 15-10 המתלונן הוא משה, תלונתו היא תוצאה מבכייתו הסוררדנית של העם ומן המרדנות הכמוסה בה והקושי לשאת במשא. מובן שה' שמע את הבכיות אך הטקסט מציין "וישמע משה" קודם ל"ויחר אף ה'" כדי להכין אותנו לפנייתו של משה לה', מאחר שהדבר רע בעיניו. בפתיחה של הפרק העונש על ה"כמתאוננים" הגיע מיד ואילו כאן העונש המצופה נדחה והמתח, לפיכך, גובר. הפעם התלונה מודגשת יותר, כללית יותר ("למשפחותיו", "איש לפתח אהלו"), מפורטת יותר והחטא - חטא התאווה וההדחיה הוא מפורש. לא רק ה' אלא גם משה כועס.

מעניינת כאן ההדגשה הנפרדת על "וישמע" לעומת "בעיני". כביכול כל חושיו של משה נפגעו. הפרק כולו הוא "חושני" מאד. זהו אמצעי ספרותי המחזק את מוטיב ה"בשריות" של הבשר ושל העם המתאווה אליו לעומת ה"רוחניות", החשובה הנאותה, והציר העלילתי המקביל האמור להחליף את הבשר. הרוחניות מתבטאת בתכנון, בהתקדשות ואפילו בדרך שבה מתואר המן. בקובלנתו של משה לה' מנסה המנהיג להקדים רפואה למכה (הוא למד מהנסיון הקודם!), אך במועקתו תחת המשא הוא עצמו נתפס למעין "בשריות". הוא רואה בקובלנות העם ביטוי לעול שהניח עליו אלוהים ומבקש לפרוק מעליו עול זה (כי כבד ממני"...) המטפורה המרכזית בדברי משה היא זו של הורים ההורים ונושאים ילדם בחיקם, מטפורה המצביעה על הקשר האורגני והעמוק דווקא

הבשר, המוזכר כאן לראשונה אינו רק מאכל-מן-החי אלא, ובהקשר
זה, גם מטונימיה וסמל לשפע המזון שהיה במצרים וניתן כביכול
חינם.   בנקודה זו הפרק מפרט מיני מאכלים: דגה, קישואים,
אבטיחים, חציר, בצלים ושומים. פירוט יתר בפרטים זוטרים
מתפקד כאירוני ונועד להפוך את עצם המשאלה למגוחכת,
באמצעות התחבולה הריטורית של הכברה.   הטענה שהבשר (והמזון
בכלל) במצרים ניתן חינם, מתעלמת, כמובן, מהעבדות ומעבודת-
הפרך שתמורתן ניתן ומרמזת, בו-בזמן, על כך שמחירו של המן
הוא מחיר-חירות.   שניהם נדחים ע"י העם.   רמז זה מתחזק
בהמשך.

המן צוין לגנאי בפס' 5 ועתה טורח הטקסט לאזן את הרושם
השלילי שנוצר כלפי המן, בעיקר אחרי הדחיה הבוטה   "ועתה
נפשנו יבשה, אין כל בלתי אל המן עינינו". בפסוקים 9-6
הסיפור סוטה ממהלך העלילה סטיה המיועדת להגביר את המתח
ע"י תחבולת ההשהיה, וכן כדי לטהור את דברי העם על המן
ולהאיר מזון-משמים זה באור הנכון.   תאוות העם לבשר ודחית
המן יסתברו, אחרי תאור המן באופן "אובייקטיבי" מצד המספר,
המתארב במהלך העלילה ו"מתקן" את דברי אחד מגיבוריה, כתאווה
וכדחיה שהן זדוניות בה במידה   שהן מטופשות. בעוד   שהמאכלים
במצרים מוזכרים ברשימה סתמית הרי המן מתואר ע"פ יופיו,
דרך ליקוטו, מיגוון אפשרויות הכנתו, טעמו ונסיבות ירידתו.
זהו תאור פיוטי הנעזר במטפורות ("זרע גד", "כבדולח")
ובאליטרציה רכה על הצליל ל': "... הטל ... על ... לילה...
עליו"המדגיש את רכותו ושלוותו של המן.   אמנם הטקסט אינו
מצהיר במפורש על עדיפות המן על הבשר לסוגיו, אבל דרך
התיאור מצביעה בעדינות אך בבירור על יתרונו המובהק של המן.
זוהי העדפה של __איכות__ על __כמות__.   הטקסט ניעור לסחור את

ישירות על העם.   כדי להסיר את הרעה צועק העם אל   משה.
קיימת בפתיחה חלוקה לחמישה חלקים:

1. **החטא** –   "ויהיו העם כמתאוננים רע באזני ה'"

2. **העונש** –   "וישמע ה' ויחר אפו, ותבער בם אש ה' ותאכל
בקצה המחנה"

3. **התירוץ** –   "ויצעק העם אל משה, ויתפלל משה אל ה'"

4. **הסרת העונש** – "ותשקע האש"

5. **סיכום** –   "ויקרא שם המקום ההוא תבערה כי שם בערה בם
אש ה'".

הן הסיפור בפתיחה והן דרך עיצובו מבחינת הדמויות והמבנה
מטרימים את מוקדי העניין בפרק כולו ויוצרים צפיות, כגון
עונש שיבוא אחר החטא, פתרון-מתח לאחר העונש וכן הלאה. אלה
צפיות הקשורות לתוכן ולדרך הטיפול הצורני בו.
הסיפור עצמו מתחיל בפס' 4. חלקו העיקרי הראשון נמשך עד
פס' 23 והוא עוסק, כצפוי, ובאופף מפורט במה שהוטרם קודם
לכן. בחלק זה מובאות קובלנותיהם של העם ושל משה וכן
תוכניתו של אלוהים לפתור את הבעיות שנתעוררו.
פס' 4-5: בחלק משנה זה האספסוף אשר בקרב העם מתאווה-תאווה
ובוכה על העדר בשר ועל מציאותו של המן. בשונה מה"כמתאוננים"
בפתיחה – ביטוי שאפיין את העם כולו, ביטוי המרמז על כך
שאולי התלונה אינה מפורשת, כאן העם מצטרף לאספסוף. ומתקיים
כאן הכלל של קל וחומר. אם על רמז-תלונה נענש העם באש
ועדיין לא למד לקח הרי על הצטרפותו לאספסוף ועל תלונה
מפורשת ודאי שיענש. לא נאמר למה נתאווה האספסוף אבל מידע
זה מסופק ע"י תאור בכית העם לבשר. נראה שזוהי התאווה –
חטא התאווה, וסימן להתדרדרות מוסרית וחברתית כאחת.

אלוהים ו"רוחו" מתפקדים בפרק כאותו מוקד-שבאינסוף שבו
נפגשים הצירים המקבילים. משמעותו של הפרק אולי איננה
מתמצית עם תום בדברי משה "מי יתן כל עם ה' נביאים"   אך
יודגש כאן שמאחר שעם ה' אינו כולו נביאים הרי שאסור גם
לרתום את רוח-ה' לעגלת שלטון ה"בשר" ה"חילוני" אלא להרשות
לה לפעול על-פי חוקיה שלה ואף לקבל את האוידנטיות שבעצם
ההתגלות האלוהית כתופעה נשגבת המאשרת את עצמה.

משה, המוצג בעיקר בפרק זה כמנהיג וכמתווך בין העם ובין
אלוהים, "תקוע" בין העם החוטא ומתלונן, הנענש וצועק ובין
אלוהים המעניש. במשה יש איזון שתחילה הוא מופר ואח"כ
מושג מחדש בין "בשר" ובין "רוח", אחרי תהליך של לימוד.
עם-ישראל, עם-ה', מוצג כעם קובלני וקולני, מרדן ונרגן. יש
לשלוט בו והפרק מראה כיצד, בתוך שהוא מדגיש את ההבדל
הברור הקיים בין הרצוי ובין המצוי.

נבדוק תחילה את מבנה הפרק והסיפור השזור בו. פרק י"א מתחלק
לכמה חלקים עיקריים וכן לחלקי-משנה; יש בו פתיחה וסיכום
מוגדרים וברורים.

<u>הפתיחה</u> (פס' 1-3): בפתיחה נמצאים יסודות של מבנה, עלילה
ודמויות המפותחים אח"כ בפרק כולו, בסיפור העיקרי. הפתיחה
היא אקספוזיציה והצגה בזעיר-אנפין של מה שעומד לקרות.
הפתיחה מתארת אירוע אחד בתולדות היחסים בין העם, מנהיגיו
ואלוהיו במסע המידברי מעבדות-מצרים לחירות בארץ המובטחת.
בפתיחה מופיעות שלוש הדמויות העיקריות. העם, כדמות קיבוצית
אחידה (בינתיים), אלוהים ומשה המנהיג והמתווך. עלילת
הפתיחה היא חטא ההתאוננות ועונש האש. בשלושה הפסוקים האלה
מותווים היחסים שבין הדמויות. התלונה מופנית ישירות לאלוהים
(עכ"פ אלוהים מבין את ה"כמתאוננים" כתלונה); העונש יורד

בשר ורוח, דת ומדינה

עיון בבמדבר י"א

שמעון לוי

אוניב' מקגיל.

פרק י"א בספר במדבר הוא סיפור מרתק בפרשת היחסים בין עם-ישראל, אלוהיו ומנהיגו; המתווך בין השניים. היחסים בין הדמויות העיקריות - דמותו הקיבוצית של העם (והריבוד הפנימי שבתוכו), דמותו של אלוהים ודמותו של משה, המנהיג המוציא את עמו מעבדות לחירות, מעוצבים ומאורגנים בפרק י"א בשני מוטיבים או צירי-עלילה. ציר אחד הוא ציר המתוח בין קוטב ה"בשר" ובין קוטב ה"רוח". הציר השני מתוח בין קוטב (במינוח <u>מודרני</u>) הדת ובין קוטב ה"מדינה" - ובכך הכוונה לשלטון אדמיניסטרטיבי, חילוני, חברתי וכדומה. לשני הצירים יש מוקד משותף שאינו אלא אלוהים; בחינת שני קווים מקבילים הנפגשים באינסוף.

הפרק עצמו, אם נתייחס אליו כאל יחידה (ספרותי, לפחות) העומדת ברשות עצמה, מעלה תמיהה מסויימת באשר לצירוף ענייני השלטון עם ענייני הבשר והרוח. במאמר זה יעשה נסיון להאיר את הקשר שבין שני ה"צירים" הללו ולבדוק את האופן שבו הטקסט עצמו (סגנונו, מבנהו, הדמויות שבו וכן הלאה) מוסר בידי הקורא כלים חשובים להבנת המשמעות הצפונה בו. אצביע, אם כי ברמז בלבד, על כך שפרק י"א עשוי לשמש פרק-מפתח בהבנת היחסים המורכבים שבין עם-ישראל, מנהיגיו ואלוהיו, לא רק בתקופה שבה ולמענה נכתב, אלא, אולי, עד עצם היום הזה.